D1607399

"Taken by the author's son, Blake Auchincloss, in the Temple of the Warriors, Chichen Itza, on a vacation in Yucatan in 1975."

Louis Auchincloss and His Critics: A Bibliographical Record

Jackson R. Bryer

With a Preface by

Louis Auchincloss

G. K. HALL & CO., 70 LINCOLN STREET., BOSTON, MASS.

Bryer, Jackson R
  Louis Auchincloss and his critics.

  Includes indexes.
  1. Auchincloss, Louis--Bibliography. I. Title.
Z8047.53.B79 (PS3501.U25)   016.813'5'4   76-25421
ISBN 0-8161-7965-4

This publication is printed on permanent/durable acid-free paper
MANUFACTURED IN THE UNITED STATES OF AMERICA

For Louis Auchincloss

and for my

father--two lawyer-gentlemen

Contents

CONTENTS

Preface

A bibliography is like the Day of Judgment. At the sound of
the trump all of one's sins and good acts, large or small, even shame-
fully small, awaken from their long slumber and take their position in
line before the avenging or rewarding deity. Bits of juvenilia, long
forgotten reviews of long forgotten books, shrill letters to newspapers, stories of a by-gone fashion or dealing with quaint social problems, here they all are. There is no evading the ultimate critic.
One's mind and heart are stripped. It is a question if the oblivion
so universally feared by writers be not a preferable state.

As I glance over the items in this little volume, I am appalled
at the quantity of them. It seems to me that they cover not only a
large gap of time but a wide number of subjects and interests. And
yet I realize that I may be giving myself the benefit of a doubt which
does not exist to others. A vein of criticism that persistently appears is that my fiction covers only a small geography and a tiny percentage of the world's inhabitants. According to such critics, the
size of the list serves only to emphasize my insularity.

Whether they be justified is a question, I suppose, for the
future. There is a tendency to overlook or even to applaud, in authors of an earlier time, restrictions of social vision which were
highly irritating to their own contemporaries. Few today, for example, would blush with Theodore Roosevelt that Henry James' "snobbish
little tales" of Americans abroad had been written by a fellow citizen, and most modern critics find that the limitations which Jane
Austen placed upon her art were as peculiarly fitted to the intensity
of her composition as were the dramatic unities to Racine's. What,
anyway, is abundantly clear to me from a review of this bibliography
is that an author is always writing and rewriting his own name. For
better or worse he is essentially limited, in subject matter, to himself. If he has the ability to make *that* interesting and significant,
he is a successful writer. If not...well, he is among the millions
who have tried. Jackson Bryer has written the record for my appeal.

Louis Auchincloss

Introduction

The curious position which Louis Auchincloss occupies in modern American literary history was graphically illustrated in the February 29, 1976, issue of the *New York Times Book Review*, when his newest book of fiction, *The Winthrop Covenant*, scheduled for March 1976 publication, was not deemed worthy of mention in a quite lengthy list of the "highlights" of the spring season. This omission is even more remarkable when one considers the admitted criteria for inclusion on the list: "the emphasis...is on 'name' writers or books arousing high commercial expectations because of their authors' previous track record." Among the novelists whose works were chosen over Auchincloss' on these bases were Lisa Alther, Ira Levin, Sidney Sheldon, Richard Condon, Anne Rice, Harold Robbins, Cynthia Propper-Seton, and William Kotzwinkle. All this despite the fact that *The Winthrop Covenant* is its author's eighteenth book of fiction in a career which has spanned twenty-nine years and has also included five books of literary criticism, a biographical study of Cardinal Richelieu, and an autobiography.

But quantity alone is never a criterion of quality. One of the major intentions of the second part of this bibliography is to demonstrate that Louis Auchincloss' writings have been highly praised by critics and scholars and to dispel some of the myths surrounding his reputation. One, that his fiction is local in subject matter and consequently in appeal and relevance, is belied by the praise lavished on it by newspaper reviewers from all areas of this country and by the high opinion of Auchincloss expressed by reviewers in Great Britain. In point of fact, local book editors--such as Alvin Beam of the Cleveland *Plain Dealer*, Minnie Hite Moody of the Columbus (Ohio) *Dispatch*, Stanton Peckham of the Denver *Post*, Fanny Butcher of the Chicago *Tribune*, Marjorie Holt of the Burlington (Vermont) *Free Press*, Theodore M. O'Leary of the Kansas City *Star*, and Richard Sullivan of the Chicago *Sun-Times*--have been his most consistent and enthusiastic supporters. But, as this bibliography demonstrates, Auchincloss' work has been praised by a wide range of commentators. Fellow-writers such as Elizabeth Bowen, John P. Marquand, Anthony Burgess, Kingsley Amis, John Betjeman, Mary Ellen Chase, and Peter Shaffer have rendered positive judgments, as have such leading critics on both sides of the Atlantic as Leon Edel, Peter Quennell, Arthur Mizener, Pamela Hansford

Johnson, Benjamin DeMott, Malcolm Bradbury, Maxwell Geismar, Cyril Connolly, R. W. B. Lewis, Walter Allen, Angus Wilson, and John Mason Brown.

Another misconception is that Auchincloss is a "one-book writer." Undeniably, *The Rector of Justin* has received the most attention and praise of any of his works. But each of his books before *Rector* was hailed by several reviewers as being his finest achievement to date; and, since *Rector*, each successive work of fiction has elicited similar expressions regarding his developing fictional skills. Further, his critical volumes on American writers have been praised by Perry Miller, Granville Hicks, Walter Allen, R. W. B. Lewis, Blair Rouse, and Viola Hopkins Winner; his book on Shakespeare was reviewed favorably by Ivor Brown in *Drama* and by Calvin D. Linton in *Shakespeare Quarterly;* and his study of Richelieu earned the approval of Howard Mumford Jones. These last-mentioned facts also answer the charge that Auchincloss' excursions into non-fiction represent the dabblings of a dilettantish amateur.

To be sure, the bibliography is not devoid of negative comments; but these are more widely recognized by the literary establishment: Auchincloss' writings are devoid of emotional impact; they deal with a too narrowly limited segment of society; they are written in a style which is outdated at best and irrelevant at worst. Further, too many of the critics whose comments are digested below use the same words--"deft," "urbane," "witty," "precision"--to describe Auchincloss' fiction. There is an alarming scarcity of essays and reviews which go beyond the surface, yet these same commentators often praise Auchincloss' achievements in words usually reserved for the leading writers of our day. Clearly, one of the reasons for this curious paradox is the fact that Auchincloss writes a type of fiction which is an anachronism in the second half of the twentieth century. Reviewers who are not accustomed to reading novels of manners usually react in one of two very predictable ways: they either dismiss the book as totally irrelevant and thus unworthy of serious consideration; or they find it so remarkable for its uniqueness of approach that they similarly praise extravagantly and unanalytically. This results in a kind of critical vacuum, where, for the present at least, Auchincloss' works languish.

Hopefully, the publication of this bibliography will not only draw attention to this deplorable situation but will also help rectify it. The first section, of works by Auchincloss, should illustrate graphically the range and volume of his achievements. These would be even more apparent had the many paperback reprints of Auchincloss' novels and short story collections been included. Suffice it to say that his work has sold extremely well--in hardcover and in paperback. His secure position as a "popular" writer is also evidenced by the many interviews with him which have appeared in newspapers and in such large-circulation magazines as *Life* and *People*. The second section of the bibliography should, as noted above, offer convincing testimony

regarding the respectability of Auchincloss' literary reputation
among both academic and newspaper critics. It should also focus attention on the critical problems raised by his writing. The bibliography as a whole, then, will, hopefully, cause people to begin to
take Louis Auchincloss seriously. With the recent deaths of Edmund
Wilson and Lionel Trilling, it is not too extravagant to suggest that
their logical successor as our leading man of letters, that is, a
figure who is adept at various different kinds of literary art, might
well be Louis Auchincloss. His election to the prestigious National
Institute of Arts and Letters in 1965 and the awarding to him by New
York University of an honorary Doctor of Letters degree in 1974 are
surely recognitions of this possibility.

In the first section of the bibliography, I have included only
the first American and English publications of Auchincloss' books,
subsequent English-language hardcover editions, and all foreign trans-
lations. I have not listed the many paperback editions because a complete and accurate list of these is impossible. Also, almost all the
reviews in the second section of the bibliography are of the American
or English hardcover editions.

In the second section of the bibliography, I have included
virtually any and all references which I could verify personally or
have verified for me by a librarian who had direct access to the publication involved. In the reviews section, I have included entirely
descriptive and/or very brief reviews because to have excluded them
would have had the effect of giving an unrealistic impression of the
extent of the attention given to Auchincloss' books. In general, the
length of the annotations has been determined by one or more of three
criteria: the intrinsic merit and value of the comment, the importance of the author of the comment, and the significance of the publication in which the comment appeared. The very few reviews of Auchincloss' books which can be considered significant general appraisals
of his full career are marked with an asterisk. Articles or reviews
which contain mention of Auchincloss along with other writers are
cited with the page numbers of the full piece listed first, and the
pages on Auchincloss following in brackets. The list of reviews of
The Winthrop Covenant is incomplete because that volume appeared just
as this bibliography was going to press.

The names of newspapers and magazines are listed as they appear
on the masthead, thus accounting for some minor variances and seeming
inconsistencies, as, for example, between the Tulsa *World* and the
Tulsa *Sunday World*. It is assumed that any user of the bibliography
will not be confused by such differing citations. In the cases of
syndicated reviews, I have made no effort to locate and list even a
large number of these; and I have in general fully listed only one
appearance of each such piece, with representative additional appear-
ances listed, often in incomplete form.

Anyone who undertakes a project of this sort knows that it cannot possibly be even partially successful without the assistance,

co-operation, and understanding of many people. My greatest debt is to Louis Auchincloss, who has not only encouraged me from the outset but has made my task immeasurably easier by putting at my disposal his files, his scrapbooks, and his listings of his works. His patience in answering my endless series of inquiries was remarkable; and his understanding of the length of time it has taken me to complete this work has been much appreciated. I am particularly honored that he has graced this volume with a Preface.

My other major debts are to Mrs. Joyce Hartman of Houghton Mifflin and her staff, who generously permitted me to examine their review files; to Mrs. Joanne Giza, who was originally my collaborator on this book and did well over half of the work for the first year of the project, but was then forced to withdraw due to the happy event of her pregnancy; to Mary Anne Dempsey, whose appreciation of Louis Auchincloss' works was a great inspiration to me and whose voluntary research assistance and moral support were of considerable help both emotionally and in the completion of the book; to Dr. Betty Bostetter, who unselfishly gave of her time and research skills to track down several of those elusive last-minute references which are the banes of any bibliographer's existence; and to Nancy Prothro.

Otherwise, my acknowledgements must be rendered anonymously-- to the many librarians throughout the world who answered my queries and often performed extraordinary duties in locating and verifying reviews and essays which I had first found as clippings in Auchincloss' scrapbooks and files. There would literally be no book without their help.

Finally, I am grateful to the General Research Board of the University of Maryland for a summer grant which was a great help during a very crucial period in the preparation of this book.

A. Works by Louis Auchincloss

A1   *The Indifferent Children* [Fiction]. New York: Prentice-Hall,
      1947. This edition was published under the pseudonym of
      "Andrew Lee."
   A1a   *I figli indifferenti,* tr. Giulana Veneziani Beltrami.
          Rome: Einaudi, 1949.
   A1b   Englewood Cliffs, N.J.: Prentice-Hall, 1964.

A2   *The Injustice Collectors* [Fiction]. Boston: Houghton Mifflin,
      1950. Contents: The Miracle; Maud; The Fall of a Sparrow;
      Finish, Good Lady; The Unholy Three; The Ambassadress; The
      Edification of Marianne; Greg's Peg.
   A2a   London: Victor Gollancz, 1951.

A3   *Sybil* [Fiction]. Boston: Houghton Mifflin, 1951.
   A3a   London: Victor Gollancz, 1952.
   A3b   Westport, Conn.: Greenwood Press, 1971.

A4   *A Law for the Lion* [Fiction]. Boston: Houghton Mifflin, 1953.
   A4a   London: Victor Gollancz, 1953.

A5   *The Romantic Egoists* [Fiction]. Boston: Houghton Mifflin,
      1954. Contents: Billy and the Gargoyles; The Fortune of
      Arleus Kane; Wally; Loyalty Up and Loyalty Down; The Legends
      of Henry Everett; The Great World and Timothy Colt; The
      Evolution of Lorna Treadway; The Gemlike Flame.
   A5a   London: Victor Gollancz, 1954.
   A5b   Westport, Conn.: Greenwood Press, 1970.
   A5c   "The Great World and Timothy Colt" (first appearance in
         this volume). In John Welcome, ed. *Best Legal Short
         Stories.* London: Faber and Faber, 1962. Pp. 135-171
         [under incorrect title, "The Great World of Timothy
         Colt"].

A6   *The Great World and Timothy Colt* [Fiction]. Boston: Houghton
      Mifflin, 1956.

A Bibliography of Writings By and About Louis Auchincloss

WORKS BY

A6   *(The Great World and Timothy Colt)*
      A6a   London: Victor Gollancz, 1956.
      A6b   *Timothy Colt och stora världen,* tr. Torsten Blomkvist.
          Stockholm: Bonniers, 1959.

A7   *Venus in Sparta* [Fiction].   Boston: Houghton Mifflin, 1958.
      A7a   London: Victor Gollancz, 1958.

A8   *Pursuit of the Prodigal* [Fiction].   Boston: Houghton Mifflin, 1959.
      A8a   London: Victor Gollancz, 1960.

A9   *The House of Five Talents* [Fiction].   Boston: Houghton Mifflin, 1960.
      A9a   London: Victor Gollancz, 1960.
      A9b   *Das Haus der Fünf Talente,* tr. Peter Schünemann and
          Claudia Mertz. Tübingen: Rainer Wunderlich, 1961.
      A9c   *La casa de los cinco talentos,* tr. Baldomero Porta Grau.
          Barcelona: Bruguera, 1961.
      A9d   *Dzieje jednej fortuny,* tr. Maria Zborowska. Warsaw:
          Ksiazka i Wiedza, 1972.

A10   *Reflections of a Jacobite* [Non-Fiction].   Boston: Houghton
      Mifflin, 1961.   Contents: Early Reading and Alphonse
      Daudet; Edith Wharton and Her New Yorks; The Two Ages of
      Thackeray; Is George Eliot Salvageable?; The Little Duke
      and the Great King: Saint-Simon and Louis XIV; Meredith
      Reassailed; Proust's Picture of Society; Americans in Trol-
      lope, James and Bourget: The Artist and the Crank; The
      Novel of Manners Today: Marquand and O'Hara; James and the
      Russian Novelists; Crisis in Newport--August, 1857 (with
      previously unpublished extracts from the diary of George
      Templeton Strong); A Reader's Guide to the Fiction of
      Henry James.
      A10a   London: Victor Gollancz, 1961.
      A10b   Clifton, N.J.: Augustus M. Kelley, 1973.

A11   *Edith Wharton* [Non-Fiction].   University of Minnesota Pam-
      phlets on American Writers, No. 12. Minneapolis: Univer-
      sity of Minnesota Press, 1961.
      A11a   London: Oxford University Press, 1962.

A12   *Portrait in Brownstone* [Fiction].   Boston: Houghton Mifflin, 1962.
      A12a   London: Victor Gollancz, 1962.
      A12b   *Retrato en piedra,* tr. Carlos Barrera. Mexico City:
      Diana, 1963.
      A12c   *53^e Rue,* tr. Pierre Marly. Paris: Plon, 1966.

A13   *Powers of Attorney* [Fiction]. Boston: Houghton Mifflin, 1963.
Contents: Power in Trust; Power of Suggestion; Power of
Bequest; The Single Reader; The Revenges of Mrs. Abercrombie; The Mavericks; The Power of Appointment; From Bed and
Board; The Deductible Yacht; The "True Story" of Lavinia
Todd; The Ambassador From Wall Street; The Crowning Offer.
    A13a London: Victor Gollancz, 1963.

A14   *The Rector of Justin* [Fiction]. Boston: Houghton Mifflin,
1964.
    A14a London: Victor Gollancz, 1965.
    A14b *Der Rektor,* tr. Eva and Peter Marginter. Vienna/Hamburg: Paul Zsolnay, 1965.
    A14c *El Rector de Justin,* tr. Mareia Bofill. Barcelona:
Grijalbo, 1965.
    A14d New York: Modern Library, 1967.
    A14e *Le Recteur de Justin,* tr. Jacqueline Hardy. Paris:
Gallimard, 1967.
    A14f *O Magnífico Reitor,* tr. Hélio Martins. Rio de Janeiro:
Nova Fronteira, 1969.

A15   *Ellen Glasgow* [Non-Fiction]. University of Minnesota Pamphlets on American Writers, No. 33. Minneapolis: University of Minnesota Press, 1964.

A16   *Pioneers & Caretakers* [Non-Fiction]. Minneapolis: University
of Minnesota Press, 1965. Contents: Pioneers & Caretakers;
Sarah Orne Jewett; Edith Wharton; Ellen Glasgow; Willa
Cather; Elizabeth Madox Roberts; Katherine Anne Porter;
Jean Stafford; Carson McCullers; Mary McCarthy.
    A16a London: Oxford University Press, 1966.

A17   *The Embezzler* [Fiction]. Boston: Houghton Mifflin, 1966.
    A17a London: Victor Gollancz, 1966.
    A17b *Die Gesellschaft der Reichen,* tr. Edmund Th. Kauer.
Vienna/Hamburg: Paul Zsolnay, 1967.
    A17c *O Trapaceiro,* tr. Pinheiro de Lemos. Rio de Janeiro:
Nova Fronteira, n.d.
    A17d *El Malversador,* tr. Amparo García Burgos. Barcelona:
Grijalbo, 1969.
    A17e *Ha-Moel,* tr. A. Amir. Tel Aviv: E. Lewin-Epstein, 1969.

A18   *Tales of Manhattan* [Fiction]. Boston: Houghton Mifflin, 1967.
Contents: Stirling's Folly; The Question of the Existence
of Waring Stohl; The Moon and Six Guineas; Collector of
Innocents; The Money Juggler; The Senior Partner's Ghosts;
Foster Evans on Lewis Bovee; Lloyd Degener on Eric Temple;
Cliffie Beach on Himself; The Landmarker; Sabina and the
Herd; The Club Bedroom; The Wagnerians.

A Bibliography of Writings By and About Louis Auchincloss

WORKS BY

A18   *(Tales of Manhattan)*
       A18a London: Victor Gollancz, 1967.
       A18b *Contos de Manhattan,* tr. Edilson Alkmim Cunha. Rio de
             Janeiro: Nova Fronteira, n.d.

A19   *A World of Profit* [Fiction]. Boston: Houghton Mifflin, 1968.
       A19a London: Victor Gollancz, 1969.
       A19b Boston: Lanewood Press, 1969 [Large Type Edition].
       A19c *De Profiteurs,* tr. J. F. Kliphuis. Leiden: A. W. Sijt-
             hoff, 1970.
       A19d *Die Profitmacher,* tr. Hanna Lux. Vienna/Hamburg: Paul
             Zsolnay, 1971.
A20   *Motiveless Malignity* [Non-Fiction]. Boston: Houghton Mifflin,
       1969.
       A20a London: Victor Gollancz, 1970.

A21   *Second Chance--Tales of Two Generations* [Fiction]. Boston:
       Houghton Mifflin, 1970. Contents: Black Shylock; The
       Cathedral Builder; The Waiver; The Prince and the Pauper;
       Red Light; Days of Wrath; The Prison Window; The Double
       Gap; The Collector; Second Chance; Suttee; The Sacrifice.
       A21a London: Victor Gollancz, 1971.
       A21b *Druga Szansa--Opowiadania dwóch pokoleń,* tr. Zofia
             Kierszys. Warsaw: Ksiażka i Wiedza, 1973.

A22   *Henry Adams* [Non-Fiction]. University of Minnesota Pamphlets
       on American Writers, No. 93. Minneapolis: University of
       Minnesota Press, 1971.

A23   *Edith Wharton--A Woman in Her Time* [Non-Fiction]. New York:
       Viking Press, 1971.
       A23a London: Michael Joseph, 1972.

A24   *I Come as a Thief* [Fiction]. Boston: Houghton Mifflin, 1972.
       A24a Boston: G. K. Hall, 1972 [Large Type Edition].
       A24b London: Weidenfeld & Nicolson, 1973.
       A24c *Llego como un Ladrón,* tr. Marcelo Covián. Barcelona:
             Grijalbo, 1975.

A25   *Richelieu* [Non-Fiction]. New York: Viking Press, 1972.
       A25a London: Michael Joseph, 1973.

A26   *The Partners* [Fiction]. Boston: Houghton Mifflin, 1974.
       Contents: A Kingly Crown; The Love Death of Ronny Sim-
       monds; The Peacemakers; Agreement to Disagree; The Diner
       Out; Beeky's Conversion; The Marriage Contract; Shepard &
       Howland; The Novelist of Manners; The Last of the Barons;
       Oberon and Titania; The Foundation Grant; The Merger--I;
       The Merger--II.

A26a Boston: G. K. Hall, 1974 [Large Type Edition].
A26b London: Weidenfeld & Nicolson, 1974.

A27 *A Writer's Capital* [Non-Fiction]. Minneapolis: University of Minnesota Press, 1974.

A28 *Reading Henry James* [Non-Fiction]. Minneapolis: University of Minnesota Press, 1975.

A29 *The Winthrop Covenant* [Fiction]. Boston: Houghton Mifflin, 1976. Contents: The Covenant; The Fall; The Martyr; The Diplomat; In the Beauty of the Lilies Christ Was Born Across the Sea; The Arbiter; The Mystic Journal; The Triplets; The Penultimate Puritan.

BOOKS EDITED BY LOUIS AUCHINCLOSS

A30 *The Edith Wharton Reader*. New York: Charles Scribner's Sons, 1965. "Introduction" by Auchincloss, pp. ix–xvi.

A31 *Fables of Wit and Elegance*. New York: Charles Scribner's Sons, 1972. "Introduction" by Auchincloss, pp. vii–xiii.

CONTRIBUTIONS TO BOOKS

A32 "Foreword." In Joanna Russell Auchincloss and Caroline Auchincloss Fowler, comps. *Auchincloss Family Tree--John and Elizabeth (Buck) Auchincloss--Their Descendants and Their Ancestry*. Freeport, Me.: Dingley Press, 1957. P. 3.

A33 [Letter signed "Sheridan Dale"]. In Norman Mailer. *Advertisements for Myself*. New York: G. P. Putnam's, 1959. P. 289.

A34 "The Different Grotons." In *Views From the Circle*. Groton, Mass.: The Trustees of Groton School, 1960. Pp. 241–244.

A35 "The Beginning." In Joseph Harned and Neil Goodwin, eds. *Art and the Craftsman--The Best of the "Yale Literary Magazine"--1836-1961*. Carbondale: Southern Illinois University Press, 1961. Pp. 351–352.

A36 "Veal Birds" and "A Note on Curry." In Berge Barr, ed. *The Artists' and Writers' Cookbook*. Sausalito, Calif.: Contact Editions, 1961. Pp. 169, 191.

A Bibliography of Writings By and About Louis Auchincloss

WORKS BY

A37   "Afterword." In Edith Wharton. *Hudson River Bracketed*. New York: New American Library, 1962. Pp. 408–413.

A38   "Foreword." In Edith Wharton. *The Age of Innocence*. New York: New American Library, 1962. Pp. v–xi.

A39   "Henry James and the Russian Novelists." In Louis Kronenberger, ed. *Novelists on Novelists*. Garden City, N.Y.: Doubleday Anchor, 1962. Pp. 215–225.

A40   "Introduction." In Nancy Sirkis. *Newport: Pleasures and Palaces*. New York: Viking Press, 1963. Pp. 11–13, 22.

A41   "Afterword." In Edith Wharton. *The House of Mirth*. New York: New American Library, 1964. Pp. 343–349.

A42   "Edith Wharton." In William Van O'Connor, ed. *Seven Modern American Novelists: An Introduction*. Minneapolis: University of Minnesota Press, 1964. Pp. 11–45. Reprinting of Item A11.

A43   "Introduction." In Edith Wharton. *A Backward Glance*. New York: Charles Scribner's Sons, 1964. Pp. vii–xvii.

A44   "Introduction." In Edith Wharton. *The Reef*. New York: Charles Scribner's Sons, 1965. Pp. v–xii.

A45   "The Parable of the Prodigal Son in Our Day." In his *Pursuit of the Prodigal*. New York: Lancer Books, 1965. P. 5.

A46   "Introduction." In *Three Hundred Years of New York City Families*. New York: Wildenstein Gallery, 1966. First four unnumbered pages.

A47   "Introduction." In Anthony Trollope. *The Warden and Barchester Towers*. Riverside Edition. Boston: Houghton Mifflin, 1966. Pp. v–xiii.

A48   "Afterword." In John Galsworthy. *The Man of Property*. New York: New American Library, 1967. Pp. 293–299.

A49   "Lawrence Morris." In *Memorial Book* (Association of the Bar of the City of New York). New York: Association of the Bar of the City of New York, 1968. Pp. 95–97. Obituary tribute.

A50   "Introduction." In Theodore Dreiser. *Sister Carrie*. Merrill Standard Edition. Columbus, Ohio: Charles E. Merrill, 1969. Pp. v–xi.

A Bibliography of Writings By and About Louis Auchincloss

A51   "Writing *The Rector of Justin.*" In Thomas McCormack, ed.
      Afterwords--Novelists on Their Novels. New York: Harper &
      Row, 1969. Pp. 3-9.

A52   "Charley Strong's Manuscript (1921)." In Whit Burnett, ed.
      This Is My Best. Garden City, N.Y.: Doubleday, 1970.
      Pp. 252-257. Reprinting of section of Item A14.

A53   "Introduction." In Dixon Wecter. *The Saga of American Socie-*
      ty. New York: Charles Scribner's Sons, 1970. Pp. xiii-xix.

A54   "Origin of a Hero." In Gordon Carroll, ed. *Famous Writers'*
      Manual. Westport, Conn.: Famous Writers' School, 1970.
      Pp. 31-36.

A55   "Introduction." In Henry James. *The Spoils of Poynton and*
      Other Stories. Garden City, N.Y.: Doubleday, 1971.
      Pp. vii-xiv.

A56   "Introduction." In Henry James. *Washington Square.* New York:
      Limited Editions Club, 1971. Pp. v-xii.

A57   "Wharton, Edith Newbold Jones (Jan. 24, 1862-Aug. 11, 1937)."
      In Edward T. James, ed. *Notable American Women--1607-1950--*
      A Biographical Dictionary. Cambridge, Mass.: Belknap Press
      of Harvard University Press, 1971. Vol. III, pp. 570-573.

A58   "John Sloane." In *The Century Association Year-Book--1973.*
      New York: The Century Association, 1973. Pp. 344-346.
      Obituary tribute.

A59   "Henry Adams." In Ralph Ross, ed. *Makers of American Thought:*
      An Introduction to Seven American Writers. Minneapolis:
      University of Minnesota Press, 1974. Pp. 13-48, 265-266.
      Reprinting of Item A22.

A60   "Henry Adams--1838-1918," "Ellen Glasgow--1873-1945," and
      "Edith Wharton--1862-1937." In Leonard Unger, ed. *American*
      Writers--A Collection of Literary Biographies. New York:
      Charles Scribner's Sons, 1974. Vol. I, pp. 1-24; Vol. II,
      pp. 173-195; Vol. IV, pp. 308-330. Reprintings of Items
      A22, A15, and A11, respectively.

A BIBLIOGRAPHY OF WRITINGS BY AND ABOUT LOUIS AUCHINCLOSS

WORKS BY

CONTRIBUTIONS TO PERIODICALS

Fiction

A61 "The Futility of Prophecy," *Third Form Weekly* (Groton School),
       XI (December 21, 1931), 3-5.

A62 "Agrippina," *Third Form Weekly* (Groton School), XI
       (April 22, 1932), 5-6.

A63 "The Ultimate Goal of Man," *The Grotonian*, XLIX
       (December 1932), 34-36.

A64 "To Be or Not To Be," *The Grotonian*, XLIX (March 1933),
       140-142.

A65 "Public Opinion," *The Grotonian*, XLIX (June 1933), 203-206.

A66 "The Dance," *The Grotonian*, L (December 1933), 32-36.

A67 "War Memorial," *The Grotonian*, L (December 1933), 41-44.

A68 "Mademoiselle," *The Grotonian*, L (Christmas 1933), 67-72.

A69 "Manley's," *The Grotonian*, L (February 1934), 103-108.

A70 "A Day in the City," *The Grotonian*, L (June 1934), 232-237.

A71 "Summer Day," *The Grotonian*, LI (October 1934), 5-10.

A72 "'Aida,'" *The Grotonian*, LI (Christmas 1934), 81-91.

A73 "Versailles," *The Grotonian*, LI (March 1935), 149-154.

A74 "Miss Bissell," *Yale Literary Magazine*, CI (May 1936), 28-33.

A75 "Old Retainer," *Yale Literary Magazine*, CII (November 1936),
       15-21.

A76 "The Beach," *Yale Literary Magazine*, CII (December 1936),
       4-11.

A77 "The Chelton-Pulver Game," *Yale Literary Magazine*, CII
       (March 1937), 24-32.

A78 "The Last Supper," *Yale Literary Magazine*, CIII
       (September 1937), 13-15.

Contributions to Periodicals-Fiction

A79   "Red Hair," *Yale Literary Magazine*, CIII (January 1938),
       13-14, 30.

A80   "Finish, Good Lady," *Yale Literary Magazine*, CIII
       (March 1938), 11-12.

A81   "Two Votes for Beauty," *Yale Literary Magazine*, CIII
       (May 1938), 15-16, 26.

A82   "Maud," *Atlantic Monthly*, CLXXXIV (December 1949), 38-44;
       CLXXXV (January 1950), 55-60. Collected in *The Injustice
       Collectors* (A2).

A83   "The Ambassadress," *Town & Country*, CIV (February 1950), 48-49,
       109-110, 112, 114; CIV (March 1950), 76-77, 112, 115-116,
       118-119. Collected in *The Injustice Collectors* (A2).

A84   "Finish, Good Lady," *Atlantic Monthly*, CLXXXVI (October 1950),
       38-44. Collected in *The Injustice Collectors* (A2). This
       is not the same story as Item A80.

A85   "Billy and the Gargoyles," *New World Writing*. First Mentor
       Selection. New York: New American Library of World Liter-
       ature, 1952. Pp. 34-45. Collected in *The Romantic Egoists*
       (A5).

A86   "Loyalty Up and Loyalty Down," *New Yorker*, XXVIII
       (November 15, 1952), 126-135. Collected in *The Romantic
       Egoists* (A5).

A87   "The Legends of Henry Everett," *Harper's Magazine*, CCX (Decem-
       ber 1952), 41-49. Collected in *The Romantic Egoists* (A5).

       A87a   Reprinted: Ephraim London, ed. *The World of Law--Vol-
               ume I: The Law in Literature*. New York: Simon and
               Schuster, 1960. Pp. 541-554.

A88   "Wally," *New Yorker*, XXVIII (January 17, 1953), 68-79. Col-
       lected in *The Romantic Egoists* (A5).

A89   "The Gem-Like Flame," *New World Writing*. Third Mentor Selec-
       tion. New York: New American Library of World Literature,
       1953. Pp. 136-154. Collected in *The Romantic Egoists*
       (A5).

A90   "The Fortune of Arleus Kane," *Harper's Bazaar* (London), XLIX
       (July 1953), 54-55, 71-74, 76. Collected in *The Romantic
       Egoists* (A5).

9

A Bibliography of Writings By and About Louis Auchincloss

WORKS BY

A91   "The Evolution of Lorna Treadway," *Harper's Bazaar* (London),
      L (November 1953), 84–85, 104. Collected in *The Romantic
      Egoists* (A5).

A92   "The Colonel's Foundation," *New Yorker*, XXXI (September 17,
      1955), 49–71. Collected in *Powers of Attorney* (A13) as
      "Power of Bequest."

A93   "The Adventures of Johnny Flashback," *Saturday Review*, XXXVIII
      (October 22, 1955), 11, 36–38.

A94   "The Trial of Mr. M.," *Harper's Magazine*, CCXIII
      (October 1956), 45–52.
      A94a Reprinted: Orville Prescott, ed. *Midcentury*. New York:
            Pocket Library, 1958. Pp. 73–89.

A95   "The House of Five Talents," *Good Housekeeping*, CLI
      (August 1960), 58–61, 169–182, 186–190, 195–198. Incorpo-
      rated into *The House of Five Talents* (A9).

A96   "The Whispers of Fancy," *Good Housekeeping*, CLIV (March 1962),
      76–77, 200–209, 215–218, 223–230. Incorporated into *Por-
      trait in Brownstone* (A12).

A97   "Bed and Board," *Cosmopolitan*, CLIII (September 1962), 84–89.
      Collected in *Powers of Attorney* (A13) as "From Bed and
      Board."

A98   "A Lady For All That," *Cosmopolitan*, CLIII (December 1962),
      96–101. Collected in *Powers of Attorney* (A13) as "The
      Ambassador From Wall Street."

A99   "Office Party," *Good Housekeeping*, CLV (December 1962), 66–67,
      169–175, 178. Collected in *Powers of Attorney* (A13) as
      "The Revenges of Mrs. Abercrombie."

A100 "The Deductible Yacht," *Harper's Magazine*, CCXXVI
      (February 1963), 42–47. Collected in *Powers of Attorney*
      (A13).

A101 "Venus in Sparta," *Sir*, XIX (February 1963), 14–15, 68–81,
      104, 106, 108, 110. Reprinted from *Venus in Sparta* (A7).

A102 "The Power of Appointment," *Saturday Evening Post*, CCXXXVI
      (March 9, 1963), 34–43. Collected in *Powers of Attorney*
      (A13).

A103 "The 'True Story' of Lavinia Todd," *Cosmopolitan*, CLIV
      (April 1963), 80–87. Collected in *Powers of Attorney* (A13).

A104   "Power in Trust,"
     56-62. Collected in *Powers of Attorney* (A13).
     A104a   Reprinted: *Best Modern Short Stories Selected From*
           "The Saturday Evening Post." New York: Curtis Books,
           1965. Pp. 1-15.
     A104b   Reprinted: *Res Gestae* (Indiana State Bar Association),
           XI (March 1967), 5-11.

A105   "The Senior Partner's Ghosts," *Virginia Law Review*, L
     (March 1964), 195-211. Collected in *Tales of Manhattan*
     (A18).
     A105a   Reprinted: John Welcome, ed. *Best Legal Stories*. Lon-
           don: Faber and Faber, 1970. Pp. 170-187.

A106   "The Landmarker," *Saturday Evening Post*, CCXXXVII
     (May 23, 1964), 50-53. Collected in *Tales of Manhattan*
     (A18).

A107   "Sabina and the Herd," *Saturday Evening Post*, CCXXXIX
     (January 29, 1966), 70-75. Collected in *Tales of Manhattan*
     (A18).

A108   "The Secret Journal of Waring Stohl," *Saturday Evening Post*,
     CCXXXIX (April 23, 1966), 76-84. Collected in *Tales of*
     Manhattan (A18) as "The Question of the Existence of Waring
     Stohl."

A109   "The Wagnerians," *McCall's*, XCIII (July 1966), 88-89, 111-115.
     Collected in *Tales of Manhattan* (A18).

A110   [*The Embezzler* (A17) in Serialized Form], Minneapolis *Tribune*,
     August 15, 1966, p. 52; August 16, 1966, p. 15;
     August 17, 1966, p. 15; August 18, 1966, p. 19;
     August 19, 1966, p. 22; August 20, 1966, p. 18;
     August 22, 1966, p. 25; August 23, 1966, p. 22;
     August 24, 1966, p. 18; August 25, 1966, p. 4;
     August 26, 1966, p. 42; August 27, 1966, p. 5;
     August 29, 1966, p. 27; August 30, 1966, p. 40;
     August 31, 1966, p. 24; September 1, 1966, p. 36;
     September 2, 1966, p. 15; September 3, 1966, p. 14.

A111   "The Money Juggler," *Yale Literary Magazine*, CXXXV
     (September 1966), 3-13. Collected in *Tales of Manhattan*
     (A18).

A112   "Collector of Innocents," *McCall's*, XCIV (April 1967), 102-103,
     149-151. Collected in *Tales of Manhattan* (A18).

A Bibliography of Writings By and About Louis Auchincloss

WORKS BY

A113 "The Cathedral Builder," *McCall's*, XCVI (May 1969), 88–89,
      142–146. Collected in *Second Chance* (A21).

A114 "A World of Profit," *Imprint* (Bombay), IX (June 1969), 77, 79,
      81, 83, 85, 87, 89, 91, 93, 95, 97, 99, 101, 103, 105, 107,
      109, 111, 113, 115. Excerpts from *A World of Profit*; Auch-
      incloss's name is misspelled "Lois Auchincloss."

A115 "The Waiver," *Cosmopolitan*, CLXVII (December 1969), 154–159.
      Collected in *Second Chance* (A21).

A116 "Suttee," *Virginia Quarterly Review*, XLVI (Spring 1970),
      292–310. Collected in *Second Chance* (A21).

A117 "Black Shylock," *Playboy*, XVII (April 1970), 80, 83, 84, 198.
      Collected in *Second Chance* (A21).

A118 "Days of Wrath," *Redbook*, CXXXV (June 1970), 76–77, 179–181.
      Collected in *Second Chance* (A21).

A119 "The Sacrifice," *Playboy*, XVII (June 1970), 137–138, 150,
      210–212. Collected in *Second Chance* (A21).

A120 "The Ghost of Hamlet's Ghost," *Harper's Bazaar*, No. 3115
      (June 1971), 66–69, 98.

A121 "The Diner Out," *Juris Doctor*, III (November 1973), 24–28, 30.
      Collected in *The Partners* (A26).

A122 "The Love Death of Ronny Simmonds," *Cosmopolitan*, CLXXVI
      (January 1974), 123–127. Collected in *The Partners* (A26).

Essays

A123 "Editorial," *The Grotonian*, L (June 1934), 230–231.

A124 "Editorial," *The Grotonian*, LI (October 1934), 3–5.

A125 "Editorial," *The Grotonian*, LI (November 1934), 33–34.

A126 "Editorial," *The Grotonian*, LI (Christmas 1934), 77–79.

A127 "Editorial," *The Grotonian*, LI (February 1935), 112–113.

A128 "Editorial," *The Grotonian*, LI (March 1935), 147–148.

A129 "Editorial," *The Grotonian*, LI (May 1935), 175–176.

A Bibliography of Writings By and About Louis Auchincloss

Contributions to Periodicals—Essays

A130   "Theatre," *Yale Literary Magazine*, CIII (April 1938), 20.

A131   "Edith Wharton and Her New Yorks," *Partisan Review*, XVIII
       (July-August 1951), 411-419. Collected in *Reflections of
       a Jacobite* (A10).
       A131a Reprinted: Irving Howe, ed. *Edith Wharton: A Collec-
              tion of Critical Essays.* Englewood Cliffs, N.J.:
              Prentice-Hall, 1962. Pp. 32-42.

A132   "On Meeting Authors," *Saturday Review*, XXXVII (June 19, 1954),
       13.

A133   "A Strategy for James Readers," *The Nation*, CLC
       (April 23, 1960), 364-367. Collected in *Reflections of a
       Jacobite* (A10) as "A Reader's Guide to the Fiction of
       Henry James."

A134   "Marquand and O'Hara: The Novel of Manners," *The Nation*, CXCI
       (November 19, 1960), 383-388. Collected in *Reflections of
       a Jacobite* (A10) as "The Novel of Manners Today: Marquand
       and O'Hara."

A135   "Proust's Picture of Society," *Partisan Review*, XXVII (Fall
       1960), 690-701. Collected in *Reflections of a Jacobite*
       (A10).

A136   "These I've Read and Will Read Again," *New York Times Book
       Review*, December 4, 1960, pp. 7, 48, 50 [7]. Auchincloss
       one of several writers asked which of books read during
       past year he'd reread.

A137   "Louis Auchincloss Tells About *Portrait in Brownstone*," *Wings--
       The Literary Guild Review*, Summer 1962, pp. 4-5.

A138   "Treasure Chest--Life and Fiction," *New York Times Book Review*,
       September 22, 1963, p. 2. Brief excerpt from *Reflections
       of a Jacobite* (A10).

A139   "Treasure Chest--Marquand's World and O'Hara's World," *New
       York Times Book Review*, September 29, 1963, p. 2. Brief
       excerpt from *Reflections of a Jacobite* (A10).

A140   "The World of Henry James," *Show*, IV (July-August 1964), 49-55.
       Collected in *Reading Henry James* (A28).

A141   "The Print on the Wall," *St. Bernard's Alumni Notes* (St. Ber-
       nard's School, New York, N.Y.), Christmas 1964, pp. 7-8.

A Bibliography of Writings By and About Louis Auchincloss

WORKS BY

A142   "Speaking of Books: Racine," *New York Times Book Review*, January 10, 1965, p. 2.

A143   "Speaking of Books: Saint-Simon," *New York Times Book Review*, February 21, 1965, p. 2.

A144   "Speaking of Books: Lytton Strachey Endures," *New York Times Book Review*, May 9, 1965, p. 2.

A145   "Introduction of Dr. Crocker at the Groton Alumni Dinner on Friday, April 23, 1965," *Groton School Quarterly*, XXXVII (Summer 1965), 10.

A146   "Speaking of Books: The Novel as a Forum," *New York Times Book Review*, October 24, 1965, p. 2.

A147   "Speaking of Books: The Creative Process," *New York Times Book Review*, January 9, 1966, pp. 2, 46.

A148   "Speaking of Books: Emma in the Suburbs," *New York Times Book Review*, July 17, 1966, p. 2.

A149   "Images of Elegant New York," *American Heritage*, XVII (October 1966), 48-65.

A150   "Edith Wharton and Her Letters," *Hofstra Review*, II (Winter 1967), 1-7.

A151   "Why I Am for Seymour for Congress," *Village Voice*, October 24, 1968, p. 23. Auchincloss says that this piece was "totally rewritten by Dodie Schultz."

A152   "Louis Auchincloss Tells About *A World of Profit*," *Literary Guild Magazine*, January 1969, pp. 6-7.

A153   "Speaking of Books: Nancy Mitford's Versailles," *New York Times Book Review*, December 14, 1969, pp. 2, 38.

A154   "Aristocracy Is Dead But Society Lives On," *Holiday*, XLVII (February 1970), 50-51, 102.

A155   "'Never Leave Me, Never Leave Me,'" *American Heritage*, XXI (February 1970), 20-22, 69-70. Some of this material is reprinted in *A Writer's Capital* (A27).

A156   "Speaking of Books: The Trick of Author as Character," *New York Times Book Review*, February 1, 1970, pp. 2, 38.

14

A Bibliography of Writings By and About Louis Auchincloss

A157   "In Search of Innocence--Henry Adams and John LaFarge in the South Seas," *American Heritage*, XXI (June 1970), 28-33.

A158   "Oaklawn," *Newport History--Bulletin of the Newport Historical Society*, XLIV (Winter 1971), 19-24.

A159   "Money, Vanity and Museum Boards," *New York Magazine*, IV (August 9, 1971), 6.

A160   "Fellow Louis Auchincloss Spoke at ACPC New York Luncheon," *American College of Probate Counsel Newsletter*, IX (September 1971), 2-3.

A161   "*The Blithedale Romance*: A Study of Form and Point of View," *Nathaniel Hawthorne Journal*, II (1972), 53-58.

A162   "Writer's Choice--*The Ambassadors*," *Horizon*, XV (Summer 1973), 118-119. Some of this material is reprinted in *Reading Henry James* (A28).

A163   "My Schizophrenia: Writing and the Law," *Bulletin of the Museum of the City of New York*, IV (Spring 1974), unpaged.

A164   "So Brief a Time," *Yale Alumni Magazine*, XXXVII (June 1974), 7-9. Excerpt from *A Writer's Capital* (A27).

A165   "Henry James's Literary Use of His American Tour (1904)," *South Atlantic Quarterly*, LXXIV (Winter 1975), 45-52. Reprinted in *Reading Henry James* (A28).

A165a   "Louis Auchincloss--'Life Was Simple in Lawrence," *Newsday* (Garden City, N.Y.), January 18, 1976, *LI* Magazine, p. 20.

Theatre Reviews

A166   "The Play's the Thing--Shubert Theatre," *Yale Daily News*, November 12, 1937, pp. 2-3. ["The Housemaster" by Ian Hay]

A167   "The Play's the Thing," *Yale Daily News*, November 17, 1937, p. 2. ["Love of Women"]

A168   "The Play's the Thing--'On Borrowed Time,'" *Yale Daily News*, January 14, 1938, p. 2. ["On Borrowed Time" by Paul Osborn]

A169   "The Play's the Thing," *Yale Daily News*, January 21, 1938, p. 2. [Mercury Theater production of "Julius Caesar"]

A170   "Theatre," *Yale Literary Magazine*, CIII (March 1938), 23, 36. ["The House Party" by S. N. Behrman]

A Bibliography of Writings By and About Louis Auchincloss

WORKS BY

Book Reviews

A171 [Review of *Marie Antoinette* by Stefan Zweig], *The Grotonian,*
      L (November 1933), 18.

A172 [Review of *Flush* by Virginia Woolf], *The Grotonian,* L
      (Christmas 1933), 86.

A173 "Book Reviews," *The Grotonian,* L (March 1934), 153-155. [Sev-
      eral reviews jointly signed by K. R., Jr., B. W., II and
      L. S. A.]

A174 [Review of *A Judge Comes of Age* by John C. Knox], *Virginia Law
      Review,* XXVII (December 1940), 252.

A175 [Review of *Life and Law* by Samuel Williston], *Virginia Law Re-
      view,* XXVII (February 1941), 571-572.

A176 [Review of *Holmes-Pollock Letters* (The Correspondence of
      Mr. Justice Holmes and Sir Frederick Pollock 1874-1932),
      edited by Mark DeWolfe Howe], *Virginia Law Review,* XXVII
      (March 1941), 730-732.

A177 [Review of *The Dual State* by Ernst Fraenkel], *Virginia Law Re-
      view,* XXVII (April 1941), 851-852.

A178 [Review of *The Struggle for Judicial Supremacy* by Robert H.
      Jackson], *Virginia Law Review,* XXVII (May 1941), 980-981.

A179 [Review of *The Last Resorts--A Portrait of American Society at
      Play* by Cleveland Amory, *Good Old Summer Days* by Richmond
      Barrett, and *Mount Desert--The Most Beautiful Island in the
      World* by Sargent F. Collier and Tom Horgan], *New England
      Quarterly,* XXVI (March 1953), 110-113.

A180 "The Master Journalist of American Fiction," *Harper's Magazine,*
      CCXXIII (November 1961), 124-127. [*Sinclair Lewis: An
      American Life* by Mark Schorer]

A181 "Bound for Bremerhaven--and Eternity," *New York Herald Tribune
      Books,* April 1, 1962, pp. 3, 11. [*Ship of Fools* by Kather-
      ine Anne Porter]

A182 "Old New York on Skates," *New York Herald Tribune Books,*
      September 15, 1963, pp. 8, 35. [*Those Days* by Hamilton
      Fish Armstrong]

A183　"A Jacobite Files a Demurrer," *Virginia Quarterly Review*, XL (Winter 1964), 147-150. [*Henry James and the Jacobites* by Maxwell Geismar]

A184　"The Best Man, Vintage 361 A.D.," *Life*, LVI (June 12, 1964), 19, 21. [*Julian* by Gore Vidal]

A185　"His Presidency Was a Stepping Stone," *Book Week* (Washington *Post*, New York *Herald Tribune*, San Francisco *Examiner*), April 4, 1965, p. 3. [*William Howard Taft: Chief Justice* by Alpheus Thomas Mason]

A186　"Picture Books (4-8)," *Book Week*--Spring Children's Issue (Washington *Post*, New York *Herald Tribune*, San Francisco *Examiner*), May 9, 1965, p. 4. [*Salt: A Russian Tale*, adapted by Harve Zemach, illus. by Margot Zemach and 4 other children's books. Review signed by Louis and Adele Auchincloss.]

A187　"Stuyvesant to Lindsay," *Book Week* (Washington *Post*, New York *World Journal Tribune*, Chicago *Sun-Times*), October 23, 1966, p. 14. [*The Epic of New York City* by Edward Robb Ellis]

A188　*"The Rector and the Rogue,"* *New York Times Book Review*, November 10, 1968, p. 6. [*The Rector and the Rogue* by W. A. Swanberg]

A189　*"The O'Hara Generation,"* *Literary Guild Magazine*, July 1969, pp. 3-5. [*The O'Hara Generation* by John O'Hara]

A190　*"Anthony Trollope,"* *New York Times Book Review*, May 21, 1972, pp. 49-50. [*Anthony Trollope* by James Pope Hennessy]

A191　"Diary of a Spirited Talker," *Saturday Review*, n.s. II (August 23, 1975), 42-43. [*From the Diaries of Felix Frankfurter*, ed. by Joseph P. Lash]

MISCELLANEOUS

Poetry

A192　"The Castle," *The Grotonian*, XLIX (Prize Day 1933), 241.

Drama

A193　"The Club Bedroom," *Esquire*, LXVI (December 1966), 226-229. Collected in *Tales of Manhattan* (A18).

A Bibliography of Writings By and About Louis Auchincloss

WORKS BY

Legal Decisions and Notes

A194   "Internal Revenue--Part Payment in Full Discharge of Indebtedness Where Security Depreciates Held Not Taxable Income," *Virginia Law Review*, XXVI (December 1939), 225-226.

A195   "Trade Marks and Trade Names--Corporate Name--Loss of Right to Exclusive User by Submerging Identity," *Virginia Law Review*, XXVI (January 1940), 383-384.

A196   "Refusal to Bargain Collectively," *Virginia Law Review*, XXVI (April 1940), 769-778.

A197   "Constitutional Law--Interstate Commerce--Validity of City Sales Tax," *Virginia Law Review*, XXVI (April 1940), 820-821.

A198   "Patents--Validity of Licensing System to Maintain Resale Prices Under Anti-Trust Laws," *Virginia Law Review*, XXVI (May 1940), 956-957.

A199   "Corporations in Decedent's Estates," *Virginia Law Review*, XXVII (February 1941), 497-508.

Letters to the Editor

A200   [Letter to the Editor], *New York Law Journal*, July 14, 1960, p. 4.

A201   "Writing Off Entertainment," New York *Times*, May 29, 1961, p. 18. [On the deduction allowed businessmen for entertainment]

A202   "Scale of Living," *New York Review of Books*, VI (February 17, 1966), 31. [On Edith Wharton]

A203   "Problems in Student Control," New York *Times*, May 8, 1968, p. 46.

A204   "Delicate Medical Ethics," New York *Times*, November 23, 1968, p. 46. [On whether or not doctor who treated President Nixon should have admitted doing so]

A205   [Letter About *The Rector of Justin*]. In Whit Burnett, ed. *This Is My Best--In the Third Quarter of the Century*. Garden City, N.Y.: Doubleday, 1970. P. 251.

A206   "Banana Republic Cops," New York *Times*, February 3, 1970, p. 42. [On President Nixon's uniforms for White House policemen]

18

A Bibliography of Writings By and About Louis Auchincloss

A207   "Jack the Ripper," *Life*, LXIX (December 4, 1970), 24A. [On question of whether or not the Duke of Clarence was Jack the Ripper]

A208   "Din of Subway Loudspeakers," New York *Times*, January 2, 1973, p. 34.

A209   "'Fresh Fields'" New York *Post*, September 23, 1974, p. 38. [A call for the press to stop writing about Watergate and move on to "fresh fields"]

A210   [Letter to Morris U. Schappes], *Jewish Currents*, XXIX (April 1975), 41. [On Schappes' contention that "Merchant of Venice" should not be presented today because of its anti-Semitism]

A211   Letter to the Editor, *The Circle Voice* (Groton School), VI (June 4, 1975), 4.

B. Works about Louis Auchincloss

BOOKS

B1   ADAMS, J. DONALD. "Louis Auchincloss and the Novel of Man-
     ners." In his *Speaking of Books--and Life*. New York:
     Holt, Rinehart and Winston, 1965. Pp. 11-14.
         Reprint of Adams' *Times* column (B10), with brief post-
     script on *Rector of Justin*: "The book has, in its delinea-
     tion of the central character, portraiture of a depth and
     width of perspective which this novelist has not attained
     before."

B2   "Auchincloss, Louis 1917-   ." In Carolyn Riley, ed. *Contem-
     porary Literary Criticism*. Detroit: Gale, 1975. Vol. 4,
     pp. 28-32.
         Excepts from reviews of Auchincloss's works and from
     critical articles--by Hicks, Tuttleton, Kanon, Maloff,
     Schott, Fremont-Smith, Vidal, and others.

B3   HICKS, GRANVILLE, with the assistance of Jack Alan Robbins.
     "Louis Auchincloss." In his *Literary Horizons--A Quarter
     Century of American Fiction*. New York: New York University
     Press, 1970. Pp. 185-208.
         Reprinted reviews of *Venus in Sparts* (B516), *Portrait in
     Brownstone* (B696), *Powers of Attorney* (B755), *The Rector of
     Justin* (B846), *Pioneers & Caretakers* (B940), *The Embezzler*
     (B1004), and *Tales of Manhattan* (B1093). Also includes
     (p. 185) a brief "Foreword" by Hicks, in which he admits a
     reluctance to include Auchincloss in this book because he
     seems unaware of any world other than the small one he
     writes about: "Although he is conscious of its faults, he
     never questions its values in any serious way."

B4   McCORMACK, THOMAS. "Introduction." In his ed. *Afterwords--
     Novelists on Their Novels*. New York: Harper & Row, 1969.
     Pp. vii-xvi [viii-ix].
         Brief appreciation of Auchincloss.

B5   NEWQUIST, ROY. "Louis Auchincloss." In his *Counterpoint*.
     Chicago: Rand McNally, 1964. Pp. 32-38.
         Interview which includes Auchincloss's autobiographical
     résumé, remarks on *The Rector of Justin*, his objectives as
     a writer, and his views on the modern cultural scene.

A Bibliography of Writings By and About Louis Auchincloss

WORKS ABOUT

B5a PEDEN, WILLIAM. *The American Short Story: Continuity and Change 1940-1975.* Boston: Houghton Mifflin, 1975. Pp. 54-55.

    If "at times" Auchincloss's stories "seem slightly bland and a bit too leisurely in terms of what they accomplish, they are invariably amusing, perceptive, witty." His best collection is *The Injustice Collectors*; the best story is "Greg's Peg."

B6 TUTTLETON, JAMES W. "Cozzens and Auchincloss--The Legacy of Form." In his *The Novel of Manners in America.* Chapel Hill: University of North Carolina Press, 1972. Pp. 236-261 [245-261].

    Shorter version of Tuttleton's *American Literature* essay (B94). Focus is on *The House of Five Talents* and *Portrait in Brownstone.*

B7 VOSS, ARTHUR. *The American Short Story--A Critical Survey.* Norman: University of Oklahoma Press, 1973. P. 346.

    Brief summaries of Auchincloss's short story collections.

PERIODICAL ARTICLES

B8 "About Louis Auchincloss," *Literary Guild Magazine,* January 1969, p. 7.

    Brief biographical sketch.

B9 "About the Author--Louis Auchincloss," *Wings--The Literary Guild Review,* Summer 1962, p. 6.

    Brief biographical sketch.

B10 ADAMS, J. DONALD. "Speaking of Books," *New York Times Book Review,* September 29, 1963, p. 2. Reprinted in Adams, *Speaking of Books--and Life* (B1).

    Adams begins by saying that he "would like today to prove that Louis Auchincloss is the best living American novelist." Auchincloss has "a shrewd and yet compassionate understanding of why men and women behave as they do, that I do not find equaled in the work of any other contemporary American novelist."

B11 AMIS, KINGSLEY. "Laughter's To Be Taken Seriously," *New York Times Book Review,* July 7, 1957, pp. 1, 13 [13].

    Very brief mention of Auchincloss as an American satirist.

B12 "And Speaking of Religion," New York *Daily News,* September 14, 1964, p. 31.

    Editorial appreciation of *Rector:* "the book...is warm, wise, highly dramatic and superbly written. Also, it contains some valuable insights into the thinking of intelligent Episcopalian churchmen in today's world."

A Bibliography of Writings By and About Louis Auchincloss

B13   BAKER, GEORGE. "The Author," *Saturday Review*, XXXIX
(October 20, 1956), 17.
Brief biographical note which emphasizes Auchincloss's
career as a lawyer and quotes Auchincloss's complaint that
his characters have been eclipsed by his settings.

B14   BALSAN, CONSUELO VANDERBILT. "'Portrait in Brownstone,'"
New York Herald Tribune Books, August 5, 1962, p. 11.
Letter to the Editor taking issue with Nora Johnson's
"condescending review" of *Portrait* (B700): "A novel which
achieves so true a rendering of a certain American society,
a characterization so discerning, should at least command
respect as no doubt will be the verdict of posterity."

B15   "Bard Buff," Washington (D.C.) *Post*, September 6, 1969, p. C8.
Syndicated (AP) interview with Auchincloss occasioned by
his forthcoming book on Shakespeare (A20). Focus is on
Auchincloss's theories regarding Shakespeare's sonnets.

B16   BEAM, ALVIN. "Reviewers' Choices: The Top 52," Cleveland
Plain Dealer, January 5, 1975, p. 6-G.
The Partners included on list of the year's best books.

B17   "Breakthrough in Britain," *The Bookseller*, No. 3077
(December 12, 1964), 2254.
On *Rector*: "This novel, say Gollancz, promises to be
Auchincloss's 'breakthrough' book over here. The author
has always been regarded with respect in this country but
has not hitherto achieved big sales."

B18   "Buckley Says He Was Hero in N.Y. Mayoralty Race," Washington
(D.C.) *Post*, June 8, 1966, p. D12.
Account of American Booksellers Association convention
session at which Auchincloss spoke. Very little specifi-
cally about Auchincloss.

B19   BUCKLEY, THOMAS. "Author Sees City Without a Past--Auchin-
closs, New Museum Head, Deplores Demolition," New York
Times, March 17, 1966, p. 41.
Interview centers on how New York's past is being eroded
by demolition.

B20   BUGBEE, EMMA. "1,000 at Book and Author Luncheon Hear Auchincloss, Lilienthal, Vidal," New York *Herald Tribune*,
December 1, 1964, p. 23.
Brief summary of Auchincloss's talk in which he noted
that modern writers seem to be turning away from class distinction and more and more toward the inner lives of their
subjects.

A Bibliography of Writings By and About Louis Auchincloss

WORKS ABOUT

B21   BURKE, TED. "New York: Its Men--The Planners and Achievers,"
       Town and Country, CXXXI (September 1967), 105-106, 156-157
       [157].
          Brief sketch of Auchincloss which quotes him briefly.

B22   "Choice Books For the Special Season," *Saturday Review,* LIII
       (November 28, 1970), 30, 32, 34 [32].
          Second Chance (A21) briefly mentioned in list of best
       ideas for Christmas book-buyers.

B23   COLBY, VINETA. "Louis Auchincloss," *Wilson Library Bulletin,*
       XXIX (December 1954), 284.
          Sketch of Auchincloss's life and writing career.

B24   COPELAND, EDITH. "Fiction in the United States: 1964," *Books
       Abroad,* XXIX (Spring 1965), 151-152 [152].
          Appreciation of Auchincloss and of *Rector:* "Dignity,
       taste, and precise, disciplined, crystalline prose under
       perfect control mark all of Auchincloss's work; his char-
       acters are so complex and interesting that he has no need
       of melodrama."

B25   COURNOS, JOHN. "Books Which Remain in Memory," New York *Sun,*
       December 2, 1947, p. 23.
          The Indifferent Children, "suave, witty and humorous,"
       is included on a list of the best books of the year.

B26   CROSLAND, PHILIP F. "Bruce St. John Resigns as Art Museum
       Director," Wilmington (Del.) *Evening Journal,*
       October 11, 1972, p. 59.
          Account of meeting of Wilmington Society of the Fine
       Arts at which Auchincloss gave address.

B27   DAVIS, SANDRA. "Best-Selling Novelist Louis Auchincloss--
       Urbane Echo of a Graceful Past," *Life,* LX (April 15, 1966),
       53-54, 56-57.
          Photographs of Auchincloss and his family, followed by
       quotations from him on his life, his work, contemporary
       society, and his favorite writers.

B28   "Dual Career," *New Yorker,* XXXVI (August 13, 1960), 23-25.
          Interview in which Auchincloss gives a résumé of his
       life to date and comments on *The House of Five Talents*
       (A9), his latest novel.

B29   ECKMAN, FERN MARJA. "Daily Closeup--Rector to Richelieu," New
       York *Post,* March 26, 1973, p. 33.
          Biographical sketch, interspersed with interview with

(ECKMAN, FERN MARJA)
Auchincloss, who comments on origins of his interest in Richelieu, among other subjects.

B30   EDEL, LEON. "Value of a Novel," *New York Times Book Review*, May 28, 1961, p. 24.
Letter to the Editor criticizing David L. Stevenson's review of *Reflections of a Jacobite* (B654) for its remarks on the novel of manners.

B31   EDGE, PEGGY. "WLB Biography: Louis Auchincloss," *Wilson Library Bulletin*, XXXVII (January 1963), 440.
Biographical sketch and summary of Auchincloss's writing career, with emphasis on brief quotes from reviews of his books.

B32   E[HRLICH], A[RNOLD] W. "PW Interviews: Louis Auchincloss," *Publishers' Weekly*, CCV (February 18, 1974), 12.
Auchincloss comments on New York as the setting for his novels, on his favorite contemporary American writers, on his writing habits, on Watergate, and on his dual career.

B33   EPHRON, NORA. "Closeup: Lawyer-Author," New York *Post*, August 29, 1963, p. 23.
Interview with Auchincloss, who comments on his two professions, on critics who only comment on a book's subject matter, on O'Hara, and on the novel of manners.

B34   "Fiction," *Saturday Review of Literature*, XXXIII (November 26, 1950), 16.
Brief mention, in headnote on Fiction, that Auchincloss's *The Injustice Collectors* (A2) has marked him "as one of the most talented practitioners" of the short story form.

B35   FIELDS, SIDNEY. "Only Human--Man of Letters and Law," New York *Daily News*, March 3, 1967, p. 42.
Interview with Auchincloss, who comments on his two professions, on America's classless society, and on his life.

B36   FREMONT-SMITH, ELIOT. "Books of The Times--20 Novels for Christmas," New York *Times*, December 5, 1966, p. 43.
The Embezzler (A17) is included on the list.

B37   GARY, BEVERLY. "Closeup: Lawyer-Novelist," New York *Post*, August 14, 1962, p. 25.
Interview with and profile of Auchincloss. He notes that the rich are not that different. Mention is made of Auchincloss's efforts to publish a condensed edition of Proust.

A Bibliography of Writings By and About Louis Auchincloss

WORKS ABOUT

B38   GILROY, HARRY. "150 Years Marked by Harper & Row--Publishers
       Hold a Reception at Museum of the City," New York *Times*,
       January 28, 1967, p. 25.
            Account of reception at which Auchincloss gave address.

B39   GIRSON, ROCHELLE. "Books For Spring Reading," *Saturday Re-
       view*, L (February 25, 1967), 46-47, 95 [46].
            Very brief mention of *Tales of Manhattan* (A18), forth-
       coming Auchincloss publication.

B40   GOLDSTEIN, TOM. "Law Firms Shifting From Wall St.," New York
       Times, March 7, 1974, pp. 41, 77.
            Auchincloss is one of several New York lawyers inter-
       viewed about tendency of firms to shift their offices away
       from Wall Street.

B41   GRAHAM, NAOMI R. "New Type Censorship," *Saturday Review of
       Literature*, XXX (July 5, 1947), 23.
            Letter to the Editor complaining about Merle Miller's
       review of *The Indifferent Children* (B146).

B42   GREENWOOD, CHARLES. "A Lawyer at Large," *The Law Journal*,
       n.s. CVII (November 8, 1957), 709-710.
            Most of this essay is concerned with Auchincloss's de-
       piction of an American law office. There is incidental
       mention of *Timothy Colt* (A6): "The book holds much that is
       of interest to an English lawyer."

B43   [HAMMEL, LISA]. "Members of Old New York Families Star as
       Subjects of Portraits," New York *Times*, January 13, 1966,
       p. 68.
            Auchincloss interviewed at reception before opening of
       exhibition of portraits of famous New York families which
       he organized. He comments on changes in New York society.

B44   HANSEN, HARRY. "Dutton's (House of Macrae) Is 100 and Still
       Going Strong," *Chicago Sunday Tribune Magazine of Books*,
       January 20, 1952, p. 13.
            Brief biographical sketch of and interview with Auchin-
       closs, who has just published *Sybil* (A3) and has retired
       from the practice of law to write full-time.

B45   HAVERSTICK, IOLA. "The Author," *Saturday Review*, XLV
       (July 14, 1962), 21.
            Brief interview in which Auchincloss comments on genesis
       and writing of *Portrait in Brownstone* (A12).

B46   HICKS, GRANVILLE. "Literary Horizons--The Gift of Fiction:
       1964," *Saturday Review*, XLVII (December 26, 1964), 23-24 [23].
            Very brief mention of *Rector*.

26

A Bibliography of Writings By and About Louis Auchincloss

B47   HOFFMAN, C. FENNO, JR., [Mark Krupnick, and Lura Lawton].
      "Wise Folly and Pure Manners: The Distance Between *Herzog*
      and *The Rector of Justin*," *Church Review*, XXIII (February-
      April 1965), 3-9.
         Emphasis of the essay is on *Herzog*; but it includes con-
      siderable discussion of *Rector*. Stress is on areas of com-
      parison of the two novels. Some of this essay is in the
      form of a taped conversation.

B48   HURLEY, NEIL P. "Liberation Theology and New York City Fic-
      tion," *Thought*, XLVIII (Fall 1973), 338-359 [357-359].
         Brief considerations of *Timothy Colt*, *The Embezzler*, *A
      Law for the Lion*, and *The House of Five Talents*.

B48a "Interview...Louis Auchincloss," *The Literary Guild*, May 1976,
      p. 2.
         Auchincloss comments on his dual career, on James and
      Wharton, and the notion of an American aristocracy.

B49   KANE, PATRICIA. "Lawyers at the Top: The Fiction of Louis
      Auchincloss," *Critique*, VII (Winter 1964-65), 36-46.
         Discussion of lawyers in Auchincloss's fiction and how
      his depiction of law firms constitutes a novel of manners:
      "In the legal establishment of the world of finance a wri-
      ter of Auchincloss's perceptions can find many elements to
      make the novel of manners a viable form."

B50   KATES, ARNOLD D. "Influence of the Rector," *Saturday Review*,
      XLIX (March 5, 1966), 34.
         Letter to the Editor, objecting to Granville Hicks' re-
      view of *Rector* (B846). Kates claims that the novel is not
      as remote from the everyday problems of today as Hicks
      claimed.

B51   KENNEDY, BILL. "Auchincloss: A 'Special Author,' But...,"
      Albany (N.Y.) *Times-Union*, January 15, 1967, pp. H-1, H-5.
         Interview in which Auchincloss comments on *Rector*, his
      family, literary fashions, and his preferences among modern
      writers.

B52   KENNY, HERBERT. "The World of Writers--Auchincloss Finds
      Time," Boston *Sunday Globe*, June 12, 1966, p. 20-A.
         Interview with Auchincloss who comments on his dual
      career.

B53   KERR, BARBARA. "Out of the Pages--A Lawyer's Other Best-Sell-
      ing Life," *People*, I (May 20, 1974), 58-59.
         Brief biographical sketch, with a few quotations from
      Auchincloss.

A Bibliography of Writings By and About Louis Auchincloss

WORKS ABOUT

B54   KILGALLEN, DOROTHY. "Voice of Broadway," New York *Journal-American*, June 16, 1947, p. 9.
      Brief mention that "Andrew Lee," author of *The Indifferent Children*, is Auchincloss.

B55   KOSOVER, TONI. "Louis XVII," *Women's Wear Daily*, December 18, 1968, p. 12.
      Biographical sketch and comments by Auchincloss on *A World of Profit* (A19).

B56   LEVICK, L. E. "New York...A Tale of a City," *Palm Beach Life*, XLIX (December 1966), 109-113.
      Interview-portrait, which centers on Auchincloss's Presidency of the Museum of the City of New York and on his comments on New York and art.

B57   "L. L. B.," *Virginia Law Weekly*, III (November 2, 1950), 4.
      Brief biographical sketch of Auchincloss, 1941 graduate of Virginia Law School, on occasion of the appearance of his second book.

B58   LONG, ROBERT EMMET. "The Image of Gatsby in the Fiction of Louis Auchincloss and C. D. B. Bryan," *Fitzgerald/Hemingway Annual*, IV (1972), 325-328 [325-326].
      "Auchincloss has used *The Great Gatsby* diagrammatically for *A World of Profit*, which is also concerned with social mobility and the American Dream; he has attempted to restate Gatsby's career in terms of contemporary social reality."

B59   MACAULEY, ROBIE. "'Let Me Tell You About the Rich...,'" *Kenyon Review*, XXVII (Autumn 1965), 645-671 [653-655].
      Brief discussion of *The House of Five Talents* (A9). Auchincloss is called "the coolest of writers; he is untouched by Fitzgerald's resentments, by Edith Wharton's rather romantic despair, or by the deceptive aphorisms. This makes him superbly good at looking at the rich in their own mirrors, at a kind of closet drama, at interiors--but without undertaking to relate this to any more general life around them."

B60   MacGREGOR, MARTHA. "Pity the Poor Rich," New York *Post*, September 4, 1960, Magazine Section, p. 11.
      Interview in which Auchincloss talks briefly about his dual career and about the rich.

B61   MANCINI, ANTHONY. "Daily Closeup--Protector of the Parks," New York *Post*, October 18, 1973, p. 39.
      Profile of and interview with Mrs. Auchincloss, who alludes to her husband in the course of her remarks.

B62   "Middlebury To Present Lecture By Author-Attorney Auchincloss,"
      Burlington (Vt.) *Free Press*, April 15, 1971, p. 9.
            Biographical sketch of Auchincloss who will lecture on
      Edith Wharton at Middlebury College.

B63   MORROW, SHERMAN L.   "The In Crowd and the Out Crowd," *New York
      Times Magazine*, July 18, 1965, pp. 12-14, 16, 18-19.
            Auchincloss mentioned as "In."

B64   MOSES, ROBERT.   "Bits and Pieces--Louis Auchincloss," *Park
      East*, February 21, 1974, p. 5.
            Harsh criticism of Auchincloss's work in general and *A
      Law for the Lion* (A4) in particular: "The trouble with
      Auchincloss' actors is that the bitches are too bitchy and
      the stuffed shirts too starchy."

B65   MURPHY, AGNES.   "At Home With...Mrs. Louis S. Auchincloss,"
      New York *Post*, July 8, 1967, p. 43.
            Profile-interview in which Mrs. Auchincloss talks about
      her husband and children in passing.

B66   [NEWQUIST, ROY].   "In Person: Auchincloss," Chicago's *Ameri-
      can*, December 22, 1968, Sec. I, p. 12.
            Interview in which Auchincloss comments on his role as
      a "society author" and on *The House of Five Talents* (A9).

B67   _____.   "In the Book World--In Review: Year's Top Fiction,"
      Chicago's *American*, December 20, 1964, Sec. 4, p. 10.
            Rector is one of eight novels listed and briefly
      praised.

B68   "News and Trends of the Week," *Publishers' Weekly*, CLXX
      (December 17, 1956), 2561-2562 [2562].
            Brief squib about how New York lawyers who interview job
      applicants use *Timothy Colt* (A6) as a means of separating
      the applicants. They advise those who haven't read the
      book to do so and ask those who have "what they think about
      Mr. Auchincloss' portrait of the lawyer's life."

B69   NICHOLS, LEWIS.   "Talk With Louis Auchincloss," *New York Times
      Book Review*, October 21, 1956, p. 56.
            Interview which centers on Auchincloss's dual career.

B70   _____.   "Talk With Mr. Auchincloss," *New York Times Book Re-
      view*, September 27, 1953, p. 28.
            Synopsis of Auchincloss's career to date, interspersed
      with quotes from Auchincloss.

WORKS ABOUT

B71   NORTH, STERLING. "Sterling North Reviews the Books," New York
      World-Telegram and Sun, January 18, 1952, p. 26.
            Brief mention of Auchincloss's popularity in England, of
      recent publication of *Sybil* (A3), and of Auchincloss's
      claim that America has an aristocracy.

B72   O'HARA, DENNIS. "Afternoon Sketch of Louis Auchincloss," *The
      Lynx* (Villanova University), XXXVIII (Spring 1966), 47-54.
            Interview with Auchincloss, who comments on Thackeray,
      Marquand, O'Hara, James, and Wharton.

B73   O'HARA, JOHN. "My Turn," Pittsburgh *Press*, December 20, 1964,
      Sec. 5, p. 10.
            Brief mention of Auchincloss, along with Gore Vidal and
      Cleveland Amory, as socially prominent writers.

B74   "One That Got Away," *New York Times Book Review*, December 6,
      1964, pp. 4, 60, 62, 64.
            Cass Canfield of Harper & Row (p. 60) and Charles Scrib-
      ner, Jr. (p. 64) both cite *Rector* as the one book of 1964
      which they most wished they'd published but didn't.

B75   P., I. M. "Turns With a Bookworm," *New York Herald Tribune
      Weekly Book Review*, July 20, 1947, p. 12.
            "And again, a novel called 'The Indifferent Children'
      appears, which brings in requests for copies (under a mis-
      apprehension) from 'parent' magazines, journals, and learned
      periodicals in the field of child psychology."

B76   PECKHAM, STANTON. "Readers' Roundup," Denver *Sunday Post*,
      February 6, 1966, *Roundup* Magazine, p. 43.
            Brief comment on *The House of Five Talents* (A9) and its
      similarities to *The Embezzler* (A17). Both contain an em-
      bezzling stockbroker. Auchincloss "seems to be stressing
      the point that once a man has got away with dishonesty, no
      matter how unthinkingly he may have slipped into it, there
      is no sense trying to protect him from the law."

B77   _____. "Readers' Roundup," Denver *Sunday Post*, June 19, 1966,
      Roundup Magazine, p. 12.
            Report on Auchincloss's talk and interview at American
      Booksellers Association convention and praise for Auchin-
      closs as "America's No. 1 novelist at this time."

B78   "People Who Read and Write," *New York Times Book Review*,
      March 2, 1947, p. 8.
            Squib on use of the pseudonym "Andrew Lee" for author of
      The Indifferent Children.

A Bibliography of Writings By and About Louis Auchincloss

B79   PETERSEN, CLARENCE. "Paperbacks—Magie McGee," *Book World* (Chicago *Tribune*, Washington *Post*), February 25, 1968, p. 17.
      In brief review of paperback reissue of *Tales of Manhattan* (A18), Auchincloss is called "one of the best and readable novelists in America."

B80   PETERSON, VIRGILIA. "Louis Auchincloss," *Book-of-the-Month Club News*, February 1966, pp. 4, 9.
      Profile and biographical sketch.

B81   PHIPPS, ANNA. "Fiction That Charms," *Good Housekeeping*, CLI (October 1960), 18.
      Letter to the Editor: "It has been a long time since a piece of fiction has charmed me and held my interest so much as Louis Auchincloss' 'The House of Five Talents.'"

B82   PRESCOTT, ORVILLE. "Books of The Times—Books, Christmas and 1964," New York *Times*, December 4, 1964, p. 37.
      In listing year's best books, *Rector* is included as one of five most admired and called "the best novel of the year."

B83   PRESCOTT, PETER S. "Books," *Women's Wear Daily*, December 4, 1964, p. 33.
      Brief mention of *Rector* among eight best works of fiction published during 1964.

B84   PROVEN, GRACE. "Book Marks—News About Books and Their Authors," Pittsburgh *Press*, June 1, 1947, p. 50.
      Brief note that "Andrew Lee" is the pen name of "a socially prominent New York attorney."

B85   _____. "Book Marks—News About Books and Their Authors," Pittsburgh *Press*, July 20, 1947, p. 50.
      Brief note that Prentice-Hall has been flooded with requests for review copies of *The Indifferent Children* from child-care experts under the impression that the book is relevant to their field, only to receive polite explanatory notes that "'The Indifferent Children' are all grown up." Cf. Item B75.

B86   ROLO, CHARLES J. "Louis Auchincloss," *Book-of-the-Month Club News*, July 1964, pp. 4, 12.
      Portrait of Auchincloss by a personal friend: "He has no taste for abstractions, no urge to explore the ultimate questions, no streak of philosophic despair."

A Bibliography of Writings By and About Louis Auchincloss

WORKS ABOUT

B87   SHELTON, FRANK W. "The Family in the Modern American Novel of
        Manners," *South Atlantic Bulletin*, XL (May 1975), 33-39
        [33].
            Auchincloss quoted briefly on how important a sense of
        family is to the novelist of manners.

B88   SHERMAN, THOMAS B. "Wall Street Lawyer-Novelist--Louis Auchin-
        closs Manages to Find Time For Two Exacting Careers,"
        St. Louis *Post-Dispatch*, February 27, 1968, p. 3D.
            Biographical sketch and interview.

B89   STEVENSON, DAVID L. "The Novel of Our Time," *New York Times
        Book Review*, July 9, 1961, p. 22.
            Letter to the Editor replying to Edel's letter (B30).
        Stevenson reiterates his preference for the "psychological"
        or "existential" novel over the novel of manners.

B90   STEVENSON, TOM. "Louis Auchincloss: Teller of Tales Out of
        Court," *Juris Doctor*, III (November 1973), 20-22.
            Interview-biographical sketch which stresses Auchin-
        closs's two careers and his views on the law and lawyers
        as revealed in his novels and stories.

B91   STIRBL, DAVID. "Auchincloss and Taylor," *New York Times Book
        Review*, September 27, 1970, p. 42.
            Letter to the Editor complaining about Edward Abbey's
        review of *Second Chance* (B1255): "I was heartily offended
        by Edward Abbey's...remarks on Louis Auchincloss.... Auch-
        incloss, though not one of my favorite authors, is a capa-
        ble one...."

B92   TANENBAUM, MARY. "The Tastemakers--A Couple Influenced By
        Tradition But Living For Today and Tomorrow," *Cue*, XXXVII
        (April 6, 1968), 14-15, 48.
            Interview with Auchincloss and his wife, with comments
        on Albee's plays, Auchincloss's family background, his work
        as President of the Museum of the City of New York, and on
        how he has used some of his experiences in the latter posi-
        tion in his fiction.

B93   THOMAS, PHIL. "Auchincloss' World Becomes Book--Lawyer-Writ-
        er's Profile," Jackson (Tenn.) *Sun*, April 28, 1974, p. 13-B.
            Brief syndicated profile, including short quotations
        from Auchincloss.

B94   TUTTLETON, JAMES W. "Louis Auchincloss: The Image of Lost
        Elegance and Virtue," *American Literature*, XLIII
        (January 1972), 616-632. Some of this material is included
        in Tuttleton's *The Novel of Manners in America* (B6).

A Bibliography of Writings By and About Louis Auchincloss

(TUTTLETON, JAMES W.)
Auchincloss's fiction suggests a shift in the novel of manners from social to psychological concerns. He differs from James and others of his predecessors by suggesting that the real drama of manners in the twentieth century is the pressure on the social elite to maintain an image of aristocratic elegance even though class has lost much of its importance. Thus, Auchincloss is not "taken in" by this society; he loves it as an artist loves his material.

B95   WATTS, RICHARD, JR. "Random Notes on This and That," New York *Post*, August 11, 1964, p. 14.
High praise for Auchincloss ("more readable" than James or Wharton) and for *Rector* ("the finest new novel I've read in a long time").

B96   _____. "Random Notes on This and That," New York *Post*, August 26, 1969, p. 34.
Short statement on *Motiveless Malignity* (A20): Auchincloss has placed emphasis on Shakespeare's "dramatization of the irrationality in human conduct."

B97   WEILER, A. H. "By Way of Report," New York *Times*, November 18, 1956, Sec. 2, p. 7.
Brief note that three major film companies are bidding for the rights to *Timothy Colt* (A6).

B98   WESTBROOK, WAYNE W. "Louis Auchincloss' Vision of Wall Street," *Critique*, XV (No. 2, 1973), 57-66.
Discussion of *The Embezzler* (A17) as embodiment of "the myth of the Fall of Adam, not necessarily to emphasize the idea that sin, evil, and corruption are conditions of modern urban existence, but to show how the old ideal of innocence has gone sour and how an old culture is unable to continue." Guy Prime is seen as the Adamic hero and Rex Geer as the devil figure.

B99   WHITE, G. EDWARD. "Human Dimensions of Wall Street Fiction," *American Bar Association Journal*, LVIII (February 1972), 175-180.
Examination of Auchincloss's two novels and four short story collections which deal with Wall Street lawyers. Emphasis is on four themes: "bureaucraticization, class consciousness, professional ethics and the contemporary critique of Wall Street practice by young lawyers." Thrust of the article is how does Auchincloss's fiction help us to understand Wall Street lawyers and their lives. The works

A Bibliography of Writings By and About Louis Auchincloss

WORKS ABOUT

(WHITE, G. EDWARD)
studied are *A Law for the Lion, Timothy Colt, The Romantic Egoists, Powers of Attorney, Tales of Manhattan,* and *Second Chance.*

B100   WOLFE, TOM. "Funky Chic," *Rolling Stone,* No. 152 (January 3, 1974), 37-39 [37-38].
Brief mention of Auchincloss who is quoted on writers' reluctance to write about the fashion of their own day.

YARDLEY, JONATHAN. "About Books, Greensboro (N.C.) *Daily News,* August 27, 1972, p. E3.
See B1396.

B101   "The Year in Print: A Varied Spectrum," *Newsweek,* LVI (December 19, 1960), 89-91 [89, 91].
Auchincloss's *The House of Five Talents* (A9) is ranked among the best American novels of the year.

B102   YOUNT, J. B., III. "Auchincloss, Prettyman Typify the Successful Lawyer-Author," *Virginia Law Weekly,* XIV (February 22, 1962), 2, 4.
Auchincloss is interviewed regarding the relationship of his two careers.

B103   ZOLOTOW, SAM. "Play by Louis Auchincloss Listed for TV and Stage," New York *Times,* December 13, 1966, p. 59.
Announcement of forthcoming productions of "The Club Bedroom."

BOOK REVIEWS

The Indifferent Children

B104   "Aristocracy," Atlanta *Journal,* June 8, 1947, p. 8-C.
Brief review. "The story moves from a precise, often witty presentation of life among the highly bred into the melodrama of a new era with power and authority."

B105   ATKINS, ESTELLE. Gastonia (N.C.) *Gazette,* July 26, 1947, p. 10.
Brief review. "Sparkling with wit and a punch of satire, this is a delightful first novel that is distinctly in the nature of a literary discovery."

B106   B., A. "Poor Comparison," Louisville *Courier-Journal,* June 29, 1947, Sec. 3, p. 10.

(B., A.)

Brief review. "The book, though too long and detailed, has moments of good and witty writing, but no, Prentice-Hall, not Henry James."

B107   B., W. B. "War Tragedy In Smart Manner," Kansas City *Star*, June 21, 1947, p. 12.

Book is "that rarity in fiction, a highly readable failure." Its failure lies "in its basically superficial characters, not one of whom the reader gives a hoot about."

B108   BARKHAM, JOHN. "The Bookshelf--Auchincloss Novel Re-Issue Shows Author's Mature Start," New York *World-Telegram and Sun*, December 12, 1964, p. 14.

Review of 1964 re-issue. Book, although it is "dated" and some of its dialogue "wears a musty air," is "still a solid, well-constructed novel." Its weakness, as Auchincloss realized, is in its characterization: "The author is better at creating his hero's world than in fashioning the hero himself."

B109   BAXTER, MAXINE. "Some of the Recent Novels," Cincinnati *Enquirer*, May 31, 1947, Part One, p. 5.

Novel "could almost be called a comedy of manners because it points out the shallowness and artificiality of society in trying times, yet it has tragic overtones that make it something more than just an amusing story."

B110   BEAUCHAMP, ELISE. "Good Copy," New Orleans *Times Picayune*, July 13, 1947, Sec. 2, p. 15.

"*The Indifferent Children* is not a pleasant book but it is extremely well-written and it is not going to be an ignored book, not by any means."

B111   B[ELL], E[LEANOR]. Cincinnati *Post*, July 5, 1947, p. 7. Also Covington (Ky.) *Post*, July 5, 1947.

Brief review. Book is a "diluted and self-conscious imitation of life of Henry James levels without any of the old master's finesse and perception."

B112   BELL, LISLE. "A Dilettante," *New York Herald Tribune Weekly Book Review*, June 29, 1947, p. 17.

"This portrait of the New York dilettante as a young drone--he lives in idleness, has no sting and gathers no honey--is complete and precise in irony without being a caricature." It is a first book "of which its creator should be honestly proud."

A Bibliography of Writings By and About Louis Auchincloss

WORKS ABOUT

B113   "A Book a Day," Honolulu *Star-Bulletin*, September 2, 1947,
        p. 6.
            Very brief descriptive review.

B114   "Book Notes," Allentown (Pa.) *Call*, December 14, 1947, p. 29.
            Brief descriptive review.

B115   "Booknotes," *Army Times*, June 14, 1947, p. 10.
            Very brief descriptive review: "a witty, satirical
        character study."

B116   BRIGHT, YVONNE YOUNGER. "Books on the Table--The Impossibly
        Motivated," *The Argonaut* (San Francisco), CXXVI
        (August 15, 1947), 20.
            Basically descriptive review.

B117   B[ROADDUS], M[ARIAN] H[OWE]. El Paso *Times*, July 6, 1947,
        p. 6.
            Brief review. Auchincloss is criticized for the "in-
        difference he feels for his characters." Edith Wharton
        "wrote of this people and era with contempt mixed with af-
        fection. Mr. Lee's characters could stand some of these
        invigorating emotions."

B118   BURICK, RAE. "First Novel By Young Attorney," Dayton *Daily
        News*, June 22, 1947, Sec. 3, p. 8.
            Brief descriptive favorable review.

B119   C., D. "Andrew Lee Novel Has Dickens Flavor," Hartford *Times*,
        June 14, 1947, p. 12.
            Brief review. Auchincloss "has a Dickensian flair for
        allowing his readers to 'discover' his characters. From
        the same author he seems to borrow the very effective meth-
        od of presenting a cause in the guise of entertaining fic-
        tion."

B120   CALLISON, LEE H. "Swivel Chair Sailors Had Tough War," Denver
        Post, June 29, 1947, p. 4C.
            "Some of the book is almost too good to be pure fiction
        and there are certain sections which undoubtedly resulted
        from poignant memories, good and bad."

B121   Charlotte *Observer*, June 8, 1947, Sec. D, p. 4.
            Very brief review. "The story neatly satirizes America's
        too-idle rich, the routine life of the Navy on shore, and
        such unimportant people as Beverly."

B122   CHARLTON, CATHERINE H. Savannah *Morning News*, July 6, 1947,
        p. 21.
            "The book has a very easy, readable style and the char-
        acters are drawn with great care and detail, although they
        never seem quite real." Auchincloss "seems to have some-
        thing to say, but it continually eludes the reader."

B123   COURNOS, JOHN. "Spirit of Henry James," Philadelphia *Sunday
        Bulletin*, June 15, 1947, *Book Review*, p. 3.
            Book is a "worthy candidate for the highest fiction hon-
        ors" and is "perhaps the best work of fiction so far pub-
        lished during this year." The writing is "fine" and proves
        "that traditional novels can still be written, and that the
        new material of our time is no barrier."

B124   D[ANIELS], T[HOMAS] H. "The Field of Literature: Reviews of
        Current Books," Columbia (S.C.) *Record*, July 24, 1947,
        p. 8-A.
            Descriptive review.

B125   DAVENPORT, BASIL. *Book-of-the-Month Club News*, June 1947,
        pp. 13-14.
            Although the tragic ending of the book "seems unneces-
        sary," it "remains in memory as a faithful picture of one
        type of war effort--faithful, like the wounds of a friend."

B126   DERLETH, AUGUST. "Books of Today," *Capital Times* (Madison,
        Wis.), July 2, 1947, p. 20.
            Brief descriptive review.

B127   DOYLE, PAUL A. *Best Sellers*, XXIV (December 1, 1964), 364.
            Review of 1964 re-issue. Auchincloss "overlooks the
        fact that Beverly's milieu and tastes are not as worthy of
        condemnation as the author suggests.... Down deep in his
        heart Mr. Auchincloss knows this and, consequently, his
        first novel possesses a curious ambivalence of approach.
        He intended to write a satire but it does not come out that
        way."

B128   F., E. A. "War's Challenge," Springfield (Mass.) *Republican*,
        October 5, 1947, p. 10B.
            Very brief descriptive review.

B129   F., M. Charleston (S.C.) *News and Courier*, June 8, 1947, p. 5.
            Book "gives brilliant atmospheric pictures both of New
        York circles and of American official life abroad," and the
        scenes on ship and in the tropics "are not unreminiscent of
        Smollett." Auchincloss "has the gift of bridled satire and
        a dread of sentimentality."

A Bibliography of Writings By and About Louis Auchincloss

WORKS ABOUT

B130 FIELD, LOUISE MAUNSELL. "An Engaging First Novel With a Fa-
      miliar Cast," Brooklyn *Daily Eagle*, December 24, 1947,
      p. 12.
          The faults of the novel are insignificant when "compared
      with the sympathy, understanding and imagination" it dis-
      plays.

B131 "First Novel," Honolulu *Advertiser*, March 9, 1947, Magazine
      Section, p. 10.
          Brief descriptive notice.

B132 F[OGG], M. M. Portland (Me.) *Press Herald*, June 8, 1947,
      Sec. D, p. 2.
          This is a "delightful first novel that is distinctly in
      the nature of a literary discovery."

B133 GOULD, RAY. "Sophisticated Story of a Dilettante," Montgomery
      (Ala.) *Advertiser*, September 28, 1947, Sec. D, p. 6.
          "It is a sparkling, delightful, and thoroughly sophisti-
      cated piece of writing" which "well may be compared to the
      tradition instituted by F. Scott Fitzgerald after the first
      World War."

B134 HALL, W. E. "In the World of Books--Fiction Fits Less Serious
      Mood That Goes With Vacation," Toledo *Blade*, July 25, 1947,
      p. 22.
          Very brief descriptive review.

B135 Houston *Post*, June 22, 1947, Sec. IV, p. 13.
          Brief descriptive review.

B136 "In Realm of New Books," Newark (N.J.) *Evening News*,
      September 3, 1947, p. 8.
          Brief review. Auchincloss "has developed Beverly's
      character skillfully, and his picture of the dilettante
      world of New York society and Navy offices is amusing."

B137 "In the Wharton Manner," *Christian Science Monitor*,
      June 28, 1947, Magazine, p. 10.
          Auchincloss "excels at two kinds of writing: at char-
      acter portrayal; and at allusive, bantering talk."

B138 JACKSON, KATHERINE GAUSS. *Harper's Magazine*, CXCV
      (August 1947), unpaged.
          Brief review. "The book is amusing, often brilliant,
      though the overtones have the frightening ring of deca-
      dence."

B139   *Kirkus*, XV (April 1, 1947), 197.
       Novel is called "over-diffuse" and "monotonous."

B140   L., J. "The Bookworm Turns," Panama City *Panama-American*,
       August 4, 1947, p. 7.
             "'The Indifferent Children' is a work of artlessness and
       poor writing which runs to 424 pages of sheer boredom."

B141   LA CHANCE, JEAN. "Intrigue and Tragedy Far Behind the Lines,"
       Cleveland *Plain Dealer*, June 29, 1947, p. 13-B.
             Although one might wish that Auchincloss's "satire was
       less heavy-handed," the author "has grasped the ability to
       handle a varied group of characters and make them live."

B142   LAMBRIGHT, E. D. "A Young Man's Friends," Tampa *Sunday Trib-
       une*, August 24, 1947, p. 18-A.
             Brief descriptive review.

B143   LYNN, DENISE DRYDEN. "Panama, Maine, Calif., Colo.," Hartford
       Courant, June 8, 1947, Magazine, p. 14.
             "One of the wittiest and most sophisticated novels in a
       long time,"it "does for the Second World War's 'desk-hug-
       gers' what J. P. Marquand did for 'The Late George Apley,'
       and does it superbly well."

B144   McFEE, WILLIAM. "Another Newcomer Writes an Impressive First
       Novel," Youngstown *Vindicator*, June 15, 1947, p. B-8. Also
       New York *Sun*, May 27, 1947.
             Auchincloss is "James alive to our times, aware of things
       and people James himself never even sensed but with the
       psychological alertness and a mastery of English the master
       would have enjoyed very much indeed."

B145   McKAY, MILDRED PETERSON. *Library Journal*, LXXII (May 15, 1947),
       809.
             Brief descriptive review.

B146   MILLER, MERLE. "Gilded Youth," *Saturday Review of Literature*,
       XXX (June 14, 1947), 22.
             "Mr. Lee has attempted to portray a rather unimportant
       minority in American life, and there are moments of bril-
       liance in what he has done, but, as one of his characters
       says, '...I found I had nothing to say that Mrs. Wharton
       hadn't said better.' I'm inclined to think that is true of
       Mr. Lee, too." For a response to this review, see B41.

B147   MILTON, DOROTHY B. "Book Briefs," Fort Wayne *Journal-Gazette*,
       June 8, 1947, p. 54.

WORKS ABOUT

> (MILTON, DOROTHY B.)
> Novel "doesn't move fast, it's more interested in people than the story, and it must be read carefully, as it was written.... This one doesn't begin with a bang. It definitely grows on you."

B148   MORRISON, LOUISE DOUGLAS. "Portrait of a Young Man," Nashville *Banner*, June 11, 1947, p. 16.
> Auchincloss "has established himself as a skillful comedy of manners author, though his lack of deep emotional depths makes him fall short of the mark set by Edith Wharton."

B149   *Newsweek*, XXIX (June 9, 1947), 99.
> Very brief notice: "a cool, ironic, and authentic-sounding novel" and a "witty exposé."

B150   *New Yorker*, XXIII (May 31, 1947), 71.
> Brief review. "Mr. Lee has a photographic eye and an unerring ability to set down the sort of high-class gossip that falls just short of wit, but once you have admitted, long before finishing the book, that the author can describe his art-gallery set and his wartime bureaucrats' offices with terrifying clearness, you are inclined to let it go at that."

B151   P., D. C. "Novel of a Butterfly," San Francisco *Chronicle*, June 22, 1947, *This World* Magazine, p. 14.
> Auchincloss has handled Beverly "consistently and plausibly throughout the story" and "every reader will feel he has known [him] well."

B152   P., J. R. Pasadena *Star-News*, July 13, 1947, Sec. 2, p. 22.
> Brief review. Auchincloss fails "to create interest in any one of the characters."

B153   PAPPAS, THOMAS. "Chair Commando Makes Live Novel," Memphis *Commercial Appeal*, July 20, 1947, Sec. IV, p. 12.
> This is "a sparkling and delightful story, one that should far outweigh most of the other books in the summer fiction field."

B154   PINCKARD, H. R. "Social Register Is Full of Slugs," Huntington (W. Va.) *Herald Advertiser*, June 22, 1947, p. 13.
> Criticizes Auchincloss's characters as "tedious": "the guy can write, but the self-imposed limitations of plot and cast have made it all but impossible for him to prove it."

B155   PLASKITT, COURTENAY. "Novel Is Based on Effect of War's Real-
        ism," Washington (D.C.) *Sunday Star*, June 15, 1947, p. C-3.
            "Andrew Lee carries his characters through with a rare
        degree of unity."

B156   R., E. C. New Haven *Journal-Courier*, July 11, 1947, p. 10.
            Brief review. Story "is bound to appeal to some people."

B157   RANDOLPH, PEGGY PRICE. "Loved By Women, Scorned By Men,"
        Tulsa *World*, June 8, 1947, Sec. 5, p. 3.
            Descriptive review.

B158   "The Reading Lamp," South Bend *Tribune*, July 27, 1947, Sec. 1,
        p. 8.
            Descriptive review.

B159   *Retail Bookseller* (New York), L (May 1947), 75B.
            Very brief review which calls the novel "so-so."

B160   "Reviews in Brief," Detroit *News*, June 29, 1947, Home and So-
        ciety Section, p. 17.
            Very brief review. Book is "very readable."

B161   RICHMOND, SYLVIA B. "Indifferent Author!" Chelsea (Mass.)
        Record, July 26, 1947, p. 5.
            "Mr. Lee's satirical style and keen understanding of his
        subject not only depicts contemporary society in all its
        phases, but brilliantly portrays two ways of life and how
        they differ."

B162   R[ICKETSON], A[NNA]. "Hilarious Tale Gives Satirical View of
        Navy," New Bedford (Mass.) *Standard*, June 8, 1947, p. 24.
            "A very courageous story, we'd term it, with a brilliant
        collection of character portrayals."

B163   ROBERTS, F. M. "Manhattan," *China Weekly Review*, CVI
        (July 19, 1947), 210.
            Descriptive review which emphasizes the Auchincloss-
        Edith Wharton comparison.

B164   ROBINSON, MAUDE. "Mystery Veils Novelist," Salt Lake *Tribune*,
        July 13, 1947, Sec. D, p. 6.
            Brief review. "It is a sophisticated, gracefully told
        and thoughtful tale."

B165   Rochester (N.Y.) *Democrat and Chronicle*, May 25, 1947, p. 9E.
            Very brief descriptive review.

A Bibliography of Writings By and About Louis Auchincloss

WORKS ABOUT

B166   RODGERS, RICHARD. *Ohio State-Journal* (Columbus),
            June 23, 1947, p. 8.
                Brief review. "Isolated sections are well written, but
            cliché-studded and loosely composed, most of it makes dif-
            ficult reading. The title could be a thumbnail description
            of its readers."

B167   ROYCE, JAMES. *Our Navy*, XLII (October 1947), 50-51.
                "Real Navy men will do a great deal of teeth-grinding
            over this book--if they can stay awake long enough to fin-
            ish it."

B168   "Service Life Scathed In Social World Study," Miami *Herald*,
            July 6, 1947, p. 4-D.
                Very brief descriptive review.

B169   "A Snob and Two Women," St. Louis *Post-Dispatch*,
            July 17, 1947, p. 2B.
                Very brief descriptive review.

B170   STITH, LUCIA HALL. "Novel With Jamesian Flavor," Nashville
            Tennessean, June 22, 1947, p. 29-A.
                "This story will probably be caviar to the general; but
            the *cognoscenti* may be expected to do some lip-smacking,
            behind discreet and embroidered damask table-napkins."

B171   S[URFACE], C[HARLOTTE] G. "Air of Authority," Fort Wayne
            News-Sentinel, August 2, 1947, p. 6.
                Brief review. "Having a feeling of being real and ring-
            ing true, 'The Indifferent Children' is decidedly worthwhile
            and thoroughly enjoyable reading."

B172   TANASSO, ELDA. *America*, LXXVII (July 26, 1947), 469.
                The "one flaw in an otherwise excellently thought-out
            plot and masterfully realized group of characterizations"
            is the unconvincingness of Audrey's decision to testify.
            But the "dialog all the way through snaps and crackles
            like a good fire, and the entire book is entertaining and
            unpretentiously wise."

B173   THURBER, JOHN M. "First Novel Depicts Young Officer Maturing
            in War," Buffalo *Evening News*, May 31, 1947, p. 5.
                "This work has the air of a Greek tragedy. When a char-
            acter finds the reason for his existence, he is done for,
            and we are allowed no happy ending."

B174   "Unheralded Novel By New Writer Is Delightful," Columbus (Ohio)
            Dispatch, June 1, 1947, p. 10-B.

Book Reviews-*The Indifferent Children*

("Unheralded Novel...")
Although "it carries some first-novel flaws," the book "is a delightful, completely unheralded surprise."

B175   VAN FLEET, VIRGINIA. "Lusty People, Varied Lives in New Novels," Fort Worth *Star-Telegram*, September 21, 1947, Sec. 2, p. 11.
Brief descriptive review.

B176   WARE, RUNA ERWIN. Augusta (Ga.) *Chronicle*, June 29, 1947, p. 2-B.
Book is "sophisticated" and "cleverly written." Basically descriptive review.

B177   W[ATTS], P[HYLLIS]. Boston *Globe*, July 9, 1947, p. 17.
Although Auchincloss "makes the mistake common among current fictionalists of telling the reader the impressions he wishes to get across about his characters instead of making them produce their own audience reactions," this is a "well-written first novel."

B178   W[EISSBLATT], H[ARRY] A. "Society Goes To Sea," Trenton *Sunday Times-Advertiser*, July 20, 1947, Part 4, p. 8.
It is "a story that demands reading and certainly it has life and zest."

B179   WHITE, TRENTWELL MASON. "Study of Heroes of Rear Echelon," Boston *Herald*, June 25, 1947, p. 11.
"Anyone who was attached to a desk during the recent unpleasantness will hail this novel as a most satisfying interpretation of the rear-echelon heroes."

B180   WINEBAUM, B. V. "An Isolated Self-Excluding 'Aristocracy,'" *New York Times Book Review*, June 1, 1947, p. 13.
"The novel's development suffers the autobiographical overseriousness of first novels--a desire to exhaust the material rather than the reader's sensibility." But it is "a true novel, not an expanded short story or a series of disjointed incidents thrown under one cover."

B181   *Wings--The Literary Guild Review*, July 1947, p. 11.
Brief review. "Underlying a quite wonderful sense of humor is a wise and mellow viewpoint denoting a writer, rich in human understanding, whose psychological values and motivations are sound as a bell all the way through."

A BIBLIOGRAPHY OF WRITINGS BY AND ABOUT LOUIS AUCHINCLOSS

WORKS ABOUT

B182   "Young Lawyer Publishes Novel," Indianapolis *Star*,
        June 1, 1947, Sec. 4, p. 20.
            "The author writes passable narrative and occasionally
        brilliant and blunt satire when he takes time from tireless
        psychoanalytical probing of his characters."

The Injustice Collectors

B183   A., B. "Variations on a Theme," Philadelphia *Inquirer*,
        October 1, 1950, Magazine, p. 30.
            Brief review. "It is not often that one comes across a
        collection of short stories as distinguished as those in
        The Injustice Collectors."

B184   *The Argonaut* (San Francisco), CXXIX (December 8, 1950), 19.
            Brief and essentially descriptive review. Auchincloss
        writes with "clinical coldness."

B185   *The Atlantic*, CLXXXVI (December 1950), 98.
            Brief review. "Mr. Auchincloss is cool, critical, and
        psychologically discerning. His situations are interesting
        and his prose is stylish."

B186   B. "Their Own Worst Enemies," Minneapolis *Sunday Tribune*,
        October 1, 1950, Feature-News--Section, p. 10.
            Brief review. "Auchincloss is a skilled writer with an
        obvious sympathy for and understanding of the world's mis-
        fits. But his book had best be read in short stretches.
        Read in one sitting it has the same effect as substituting
        cocktail party canapes for a full dinner."

B187   BETJEMAN, JOHN. "New Fiction--More Nancy Mitford." London
        Daily Telegraph and Morning Post, July 27, 1951, p. 6.
            "The book is American. The author has affection and not
        just a cool pity for the people he describes. The stories
        are well written and they clear one's ideas about oneself
        and other people."

B188   BRADLEY, VAN ALLEN. "Short Story Roundup--New Collections
        Include Stuart, Shaw, McCarthy," Chicago *Daily News*,
        October 25, 1950, p. 40.
            Very brief mention: "I can do without Auchincloss'
        unhappy characters, but he does write well, and subtly."

B189   "Brilliant Portraits," *Continental Daily Mail*, July 14, 1951,
        p. 38.
            Review of English edition. "Each of the stories is ad-
        mirably written, clear and smooth-flowing, without jerkiness

Book Reviews–*The Injustice Collectors*

("Brilliant Portraits,")
or slanginess. A dry wit relieves the effect which is
often pathetic but never merely mawkish."

B190   Burlington (Vt.) *Free Press*, October 18, 1950, p. 15.
Brief review of "the finest collection of short stories
to appear in a decade."

B191   BURNETT, WHIT. "The Leisure Class," *New York Times Book Review*, October 15, 1950, p. 4.
Auchincloss's "observations are sound, frequently witty,
always wry; his situations complicated and adult; and his
stories usually full-bodied and well-developed.... If
there is anything missing..., it is heart. One feels, in
the tone of these pieces, that Mr. Auchincloss does not
really like his characters any more than he likes their
Maine-New York environment."

B192   CARNAHAN, KEN. "'Wronged By the World,'" Berkeley *Daily Gazette*, October 10, 1950, p. 4.
"Mr. Auchincloss' stories...have a bad habit of trick-
ling off instead of ending on a definite note, due, of
course, to his preoccupation with people rather than incidents."

B193   Cincinnati *Times-Star*, September 27, 1950, p. 19.
Brief squib: the stories are "recommended to all who
are interested in how human beings tick."

B194   COLE, LUCRETIA. "Short Story Style No Longer Flip," Los
Angeles *News*, December 2, 1950, p. 31.
Brief favorable squib.

B195   CROFT-COOKE, RUPERT. "Our Bookshelf," *The Sketch* (London),
CCXV (September 12, 1951), 240.
Brief favorable review: "deft and urbane writing."

B196   DEDMON, EMMETT. "Distinguished Book of Short Stories Tells
What's Under the Upper Crust," Chicago *Sun-Times*,
September 26, 1950, Sec. 2, p. 5.
"Readers will be much the poorer for missing 'The In-
justice Collectors.' Wisdom, wit and gentleness do not
often travel together."

B197   DICKINSON, S. D. "With a Psychiatrist's Insight, An Artist's
Skill," *Arkansas Gazette* (Little Rock), October 8, 1950,
p. 2F.
"Auchincloss has the insight of a psychiatrist and the

A Bibliography of Writings By and About Louis Auchincloss

WORKS ABOUT

(DICKINSON, S. D.)
skill of an artist. He has been compared to Henry James.
Certainly he possesses some of the very same qualities
that made James a master. Given time and several more novels, he may well equal James in degree of artistry."

B198   DODD, ORA. Boston *Sunday Post,* October 1, 1950, p. A-2.
"Mr. Auchincloss writes smoothly, he handles his very
malleable characters with skill, and there is no great
tragedy when they allow themselves to be pushed aside,
bullied, or thwarted."

B199   E[ARLY], J. R[ICHARD]. "Of Those Who Collect Injustice," New
Bedford (Mass.) *Standard-Times,* October 22, 1950, p. 18.
"The reader will find the outline of any one of these
stories hard to remember, but the principals are so sharply
cut you will have quite a clan of faithful companions for
some time to come."

B200   EDGEMORE, ANTHONY. "Books," Birmingham (England) *Sunday Mercury,* July 8, 1951, p. 14.
Brief favorable squib: Auchincloss's prose is "superb."

B201   EDMONDSON, ARNOLD. "Art in Short Stories," Liverpool *Echo,*
June 25, 1951, p. 4.
Brief squib. "These tales, while varied greatly in
theme, share distinction of style; irony and wit are min-
gled with just the right touch of sympathy and human understanding."

B202   "Fiction--Unsatisfactory Situations," *Times Literary Supplement* (London), June 29, 1951, p. 401.
"The stories analyse the difficulties and uneasiness of
human relations, both in and out of the home.... Mr. Auchincloss is an author to watch."

B203   "Fine Study of Injustice Collectors," Pasadena *Star-News,*
September 24, 1950, p. 25.
Brief favorable review.

B204   G., H. L. "Maine Features Auchincloss Shorts," Lewiston (Me.)
Evening Journal, September 30, 1950, Magazine, p. A-8.
Brief descriptive and favorable review.

B205   HARRIS, GERALDINE C. "Impressive Short Stories," Columbus
(Ohio) *Sunday Dispatch,* October 1, 1950, p. F-7.
"This collection is distinguished by a high degree of
literary skill and a profound understanding of character.

Book Reviews-*The Injustice Collectors*

(HARRIS, GERALDINE C.)
With a fine sense of humor the author prevents his stories from being morbid."

B206 HAY, SARA HENDERSON. "Seekers of Hurt," *Saturday Review of Literature*, XXXIII (October 14, 1950), 37-38.
"'The Injustice Collectors' is the work of an extremely skilful and observant writer. These are not clinical case histories, but with the device of fiction Mr. Auchincloss puts his finger on fact. It is a tribute to the impact of these stories that one begins to speculate upon one's own propensities as a collector!"

B207 H[OLLINGSWORTH], H[ARRY] D. "Themselves Their Worst Enemies," Durham (N.C.) *Morning Herald*, October 1, 1950, Sec. IV, p. 7.
The book is recommended "for short stories of a different style, content, and situation from those you find readily in the 'popular' magazines."

B208 "In Brief," *The Observer* (London), July 8, 1951, p. 7.
Very brief review: "admirably sculptured studies."

B209 "'The Injustice Collectors' Twists Human Character Into Incongruous Shapes," Oakland (Calif.) *Tribune*, December 3, 1950, p. 2-C.
Basically descriptive favorable review.

B210 JACKSON, THOMAS C. "Some Fresh Air," Hartford *Courant*, October 8, 1950, Magazine, p. 14.
Although "the book could use some...passion and fire," the stories are "easy to read, hard to forget, and a fresh breath of literary air."

B211 JENKINS, ELIZABETH. "Books of the Day--New Fiction," Manchester (England) *Guardian*, June 29, 1951, p. 4.
Auchincloss "is a writer who enlarges the reader's sympathies."

B212 K., K. "Eight Excellent Stories," Charleston (S.C.) *News and Courier*, October 1, 1950, Sec. 7, p. 1.
"The eight stories...are almost uniformly excellent and can be warmly recommended to the most discriminating readers." Auchincloss's heroes and heroines, while they recall the figures of James, Forster, and Wharton, "are definitely our contemporaries, perfectly drawn, realistic people of today, and a great part of their insidiously fascinating tragedies lies in this fate which forces them to live in an age to which they do not belong."

WORKS ABOUT

B213   KEOWN, ERIC. "Booking Office--Mixed Bag," *Punch* (London),
        CCXXI (July 11, 1951), 52.
            In Auchincloss's stories is "none of the violence or the
        sentimentality disguised as toughness into which too many
        of his country's authors have been led; instead there is
        detachment and a wit that does not exclude compassion."

B214   M., H. "Social Misfits: Eight Portraits," Dayton *Daily News*,
        October 15, 1950, Sec. 2, p. 9.
            Brief review. "These stories are like compressed yeast--
        capable of expansion, given time to ferment."

B215   M., W. San Francisco *Chronicle*, December 10, 1950, *This
        World* Magazine, p. 30.
            Although "those who skip the foreword will...have made
        the best choice," the stories are "tenuous without being
        fragile and feminine without becoming effeminate." But
        Auchincloss has a long way to go to equal Henry James.

B216   MacGREGOR, MARTHA. "Eight Stories of Neurotics," New York
        Post, October 1, 1950, p. 18M.
            "There is nothing grim about these stories but the under-
        lying theme; the author is writing social satire, not case
        histories. He moves easily and often humorously in a priv-
        ileged world of boxes at the Met; old ladies with pearl
        chokers and paid companions; private schools and country
        places. He x-rays his characters with neat phrases and his
        dialogue is excellent."

B217   MOHLER, JACK. "Pen Dissects Self-Sadists," *Rocky Mountain
        News* (Denver), October 29, 1950, p. A-16.
            "These stories are clever without being cute, smart
        without being smart-alecky and deep without being muddled."

B218   MORTIMER, RAYMOND. "A New Storyteller," London *Sunday Times*,
        July 1, 1951, p. 3.
            Auchincloss's stories "are remarkably good just as sto-
        ries, the psychological explanation remaining implicit.
        He has concentrated on making his narrative spare and objec-
        tive: indeed, the actual writing is rather too impersonal
        for my taste, though free from awkwardness or affected sim-
        plicity. He strikes me as a born storyteller who is wise
        as well as highly intelligent."

B219   "New Novels--Miss Mitford in Paris," Glasgow (Scotland) *Herald*,
        July 26, 1951, p. 3.
            These are "some of the best short stories published for
        a long time." "Nothing quite like these stories has ap-
        peared before."

Book Reviews-*The Injustice Collectors*

B220   "New Short Stories Worthy of Attention," Washington (D.C.)
       Sunday Star, December 17, 1950, p. C-3.
              "Mr. Auchincloss has polish rare in a new writer. His
       stories, if a bit on the bloodless side, are very readable
       and insure great interest in his future work."

B221   *New Yorker*, XXVI (September 30, 1950), 102.
              Brief review. "Most of the emotional problems around
       which these stories center are somewhat stupefying, and
       suggest--as does the author's style--a conscientious study
       of the works of Edith Wharton, rather than acute and sensi-
       tive first-hand observation."

B222   Oakland (Calif.) *Tribune*, October 22, 1950, p. 2-C.
              Very brief descriptive review.

B223   O'L[EARY], M[ARY] C. "World Stories," Worcester *Sunday Tele-
       gram*, January 27, 1952, p. D9.
              Brief favorable review: "debonair, worldly stories."

B224   O'NEILL, FRANK. "Trio in 'Shorts': Stuart, Farrell and Auch-
       incloss," Cleveland *News*, November 15, 1950, p. 15.
              "The theme imposes a severe test upon the author, who
       responds with technical excellence but creates mostly a
       company of cheerless automatons."

B225   ORGILL, DOUGLAS. "Short Stories," Newcastle (England) *Journal*,
       July 24, 1951, p. 4.
              Brief squib. The stories are "urbane" and "penetrating,"
       but together "they tend to have a certain repetitive monot-
       ony."

B226   PEEL, J. H. B. "The New Books--True to Life But Not Whole of
       Life," Yorkshire (England) *Observer*, June 30, 1951, p. 4.
              Auchincloss's stories "read like a collaboration between
       Freud and Henry James. They also pose the question--must
       art become a specialized branch of psychiatry?"

B227   PETERSON, VIRGILIA. "In a World Without Passion," *New York
       Herald Tribune Book Review*, October 1, 1950, p. 12.
              "Despite his always smooth and sometimes neatly aphoris-
       tic writing, despite his knowledge of the narrow circle he
       draws with all its implied materialism and imitative aris-
       tocracy, Mr. Auchincloss has too little impact as a critic
       of man's ways. Whereas the well-bred, fastidious irony of
       an Edith Wharton fitted the times of which she wrote, that
       kind of satire applied to our day seems as anachronistic as
       the society it depicts."

A Bibliography of Writings By and About Louis Auchincloss

WORKS ABOUT

B228   PICK, ROBERT. *Book-of-the-Month Club News,* October 1950,
        p. 16.
            One finds "everywhere in this volume" an "impeccable
        taste, an unobtrusive, urbane wisdom and a subtle, melan-
        choly irony." The book "is a treat."

B229   PRESCOTT, ORVILLE. "Books of The Times," New York *Times,*
        October 3, 1950, p. 29.
            In spite of its "solemn psychiatric foundation, 'The
        Injustice Collectors' is not over-weighted with theory. It
        can be read, and I am sure will be, for its crisp, clever
        writing, for its sardonic picture of dry rot in exclusive
        circles and for its acid humor."

B230   *Psychiatric Quarterly--Supplement,* XXIV (Part 2, 1950), 360.
            "The stories are well worked out, but labor under the
        handicap of confusing the pseudo-aggressive defense with
        the underlying masochistic wish." But Auchincloss "is
        still 50 years ahead of his colleagues" as far as psycho-
        logical "insight" is concerned.

B231   QUENNELL, PETER. "One Man Tries to Change Destiny," London
        Daily Mail, July 14, 1951, p. 2.
            "Each of the stories is admirably written, clear and
        smooth-flowing without jerkiness or slanginess. A dry wit
        relieves the effect, which is often pathetic but never
        merely mawkish."

B232   RICHARDSON, JOHN. "New Short Stories," *New Statesman and Na-
        tion,* XLII (July 21, 1951), 79-80.
            This is "the best-written and most original collection
        of stories by a new writer that has been published for a
        long time. Far from being case-book clichés, Mr. Auchin-
        closs's creatures are most lifelike neurotics, and it is a
        measure of his skill that their perverse way of deliberate-
        ly twisting straightforward lives into hideously contorted
        shapes is both credible and oddly logical."

B233   ROCKWELL, KENNETH. "And So to Books--Exceptional Stories In-
        troduce New Writer," Dallas *Times Herald,* October 1, 1950,
        Sec. 7, p. 4.
            Auchincloss "has used a difficult literary form and used
        it with mastery." He is "a better psychologist than James;
        his characters are a little more important."

B234   S., I. Columbia *Missourian,* January 11, 1951, p. 6.
            "Self-torturers are a common phenomenon of this neuro-
        sis-bedeviled world, and certainly they are a fit subject

Book Reviews-*The Injustice Collectors*

(S., I.)
>
> for literature of a very high order. The author, however,
> might have been better advised if his masochists had been
> housewives and policemen rather than spinsters and million-
> aires."

B235   S[MITH], B[LANCHE] H[IXON]. "Have You Read...," Meriden
        (Conn.) *Record*, February 16, 1951, p. 6.
>
> "There is something superbly impressive about these wise
> little quiet little stories, written concisely and with ad-
> mirable taste. The volume will delight everyone interested
> in the short story form of writing."

B236   SNYDER, MARJORIE B. "Eight Superb Stories Praised," Boston
        Sunday Herald, October 1, 1950, Sec. C, p. 2.
>
> All of the stories "are distinguished by the most vivid
> phrases ever seen." "The Ambassadress" is singled out for
> special praise. The book "is better than good writing; it
> reveals a major talent."

B237   S[OLINSKI], T[ED] C. "Upper Class and Psychoses," Lexington
        (Ky.) *Herald-Leader*, November 5, 1950, p. 43.
>
> "The book is overloaded with sophistication--it leans
> too much toward one class of society. But Auchincloss does
> have a lucid and easy style."

B238   STARKEY, MARION L. "Biting Off Your Nose--Eight Very Subtle
        Short Stories About Very Complicated People," Boston *Sunday
        Globe*, October 1, 1950, p. A-35.
>
> "These are arresting stories, many of them as meaty as
> some of the short novels of James.... Unlike James' sto-
> ries, most of Auchincloss' are told with deceptive simplic-
> ity; like James' stories, each demands a re-reading."

B239   SUGENHEIMER, MARION U. "Eight Distinguished Stories," New
        Haven *Register*, October 8, 1950, Magazine, p. 8.
>
> "Certainly the locales, social backgrounds and insight
> of the stories are similar to those with which James was
> concerned. But the pace of Louis Auchincloss' work is
> swifter and there is a driven intention of reform in these
> stories such as James almost ignored."

B240   SULLIVAN, RICHARD. "8 Neurotics In Search of Injustices,"
        Chicago Sunday Tribune Magazine of Books, October 29, 1950,
        p. 4.
>
> "They are well told stories, despite a certain repeti-
> tiousness of effect which rises out of their thematic sim-
> ilarity. They all get down deep into the personalities

WORKS ABOUT

(SULLIVAN, RICHARD)
involved; they all carry a fine, full weight of conviction; and in each one there is solid craftsmanship combined with honest feeling."

B241   SYMONS, JULIAN. "A New Way to Cheaper Books," Manchester (England) *Evening News*, June 28, 1951, p. 2.
Brief favorable review. The book "contains eight stories of a highly accomplished kind."

B242   TAYLOR, MARY DARLINGTON. "Louis Auchincloss' Characters Find Own Injustices," Bridgeport (Conn.) *Sunday Post*, October 1, 1950, Sec. B, p. 4.
Descriptive favorable review: "a considerable achievement."

B243   "Two Masters," *Irish Times* (Dublin), July 21, 1951, p. 6.
"Mr. Auchincloss has a dignified and deceptively muted style, devoid of flourishes and yet packed with significance; and he deals ruthlessly in probabilities. Everything about this unusual book proclaims the serious artist."

B244   W., D. "Could Be Worse," Syracuse *Post-Standard*, October 28, 1950, p. 4.
Although "at least in these stories the themes are different from those in 'popular' magazines," they leave one "with the feeling that the author has labored over every word.... He is too artificial to be believable and the characters lack warmth."

B245   WALBRIDGE, EARLE F. *Library Journal*, LXXV (September 15, 1950), 1506.
Very brief review. "The author...contributes a style which can only be described as tone deaf."

B246   WILSON, DOROTHY D. "For Richland Readers: Notes on New Books at the Library," Columbia (S.C.) *Record*, October 12, 1950, p. 4-B.
"Belying its dreary theme, this is a lively and amusing book that sparkles with sardonic wit."

B247   WINN, ELIZABETH SMITH. El Paso *Herald-Post*, September 30, 1950, p. 4.
Auchincloss's "general attitude toward the world is benign and interested; his short story technique has the painstaking economy of expression so necessary in this medium. There is a measured cadence to his prose and a naturalness of wording that is effective in the short story form and indicates a first-rate talent."

B248   WRIGHT, JOHN A. Los Angeles *Mirror*, October 14, 1950, p. 34.
        Brief review. Auchincloss is "neither deceived nor awed
        by his subject and creates an unusual world with remarkable
        skill."

B249   ZINNES, HARRIET. "Those Who Attract Disaster," St. Louis *Post-
        Dispatch*, October 10, 1950, p. 2C.
        Auchincloss's philosophy is "dubious" and his characters
        "do not think: in their own disillusioned way...they plod
        their dull lives along. They are dreadful bores, and
        Mr. Auchincloss agrees although he lacks the irony to make
        his agreement convincing."

Sybil

B250   ABY, JANE. "Heroine Caught in Social Web," Tulsa *World*,
        January 20, 1952, Sec. 5, p. 9.
        "'Sybil' is, to me, an important novel saved only by its
        protagonist, Sybil Rodman, a most sympathetic character...."

B251   *The Atlantic*, CLXXXIX (February 1952), 85.
        Brief review. "This is a civilized novel, neither pow-
        erful nor profound, but thoroughly adult, well-written, and
        with an individuality of its own."

B252   BECK, CLYDE. "Books of the Day--Novelists of 1952 Get Off to
        Flying Start," Detroit *News*, January 27, 1952, Home and So-
        ciety Section, p. 8.
        "Mr. Auchincloss has yet to learn how to carpenter the
        novel skillfully. Too many of his chapters begin with flat-
        footed remarks.... The skillful novelist knows how to be-
        gin and end his chapters." But Auchincloss "will get
        there"; Sybil and the other characters "were as real to me
        as my friends and neighbors."

B253   BECKWITH, RUTH A. "Fashionable Girl Revolts--Clear Style
        Makes Sybil Human Heroine," *Rocky Mountain News* (Denver),
        January 20, 1952, p. 7-A.
        Brief descriptive review. Calls novel "accomplished"
        and Auchincloss's style "clear and pleasant."

B254   BELLASIS, M. "Marrying and Giving in Marriage," *The Tablet*
        (London), CXCIX (May 31, 1952), 440.
        "Mr. Auchincloss is a skilful and civilized writer, who
        has been compared to Edith Wharton. Here, at least, is one
        American novelist who is not shouting at the top of his
        voice."

A Bibliography of Writings By and About Louis Auchincloss

WORKS ABOUT

B255   Burlington (Vt.) *Free Press*, January 28, 1952, p. 14.
        Brief favorable review. Sybil Rodman is one of Auchincloss's "most sympathetic characters."

B256   C., V. Pasadena *Star-News*, January 6, 1952, p. 37.
        Brief favorable review: "a well written, plausible
        story."

B257   CARRERE, THOMAS A. "Poor Girl--Rich Boy," Charleston (S.C.)
        News and Courier, January 6, 1952, Sec. C, p. 1.
        "This is a novel in which the form outweighs the content.
        The author's prose style is a delight to read. It is a pity
        that the theme is not worthy of the beautiful style in which
        it is written."

B258   CHARQUES, R. D. "Fiction," *The Spectator*, CLXXXVIII
        (May 16, 1952), 654.
        "I must insist that *Sybil* is shockingly dull and trivial.... Mr. Auchincloss may write short stories like an
        angel, but his performance in this novel is naive and
        empty."

B259   "Clash With Convention," *Times Literary Supplement* (London),
        May 16, 1952, p. 325.
        "*Sybil* is a novel written with the cool distinction and
        the delicate sense of social differences that marked the
        short stories [*The Injustice Collectors*]; and it shows, in
        addition, a considerable power of penetration, at least
        into the mind of its principal character."

B260   C[OCHRAN], P[OLLY]. "Novelist Sketches His Social World in
        Major Work, 'Sybil,'" Indianapolis *Star*, January 27, 1952,
        Sec. 6, p. 8.
        "By not glossing over the rotten spots in this social
        group, the writer provides his reader with a realistic story, good in its naturalness and simplicity."

B261   Columbia (S.C.) *State*, January 13, 1952, p. 2-D.
        Brief review. "Words flow smoothly from this author's
        able pen, but he uses its sharp point to jab with, too; if
        the story is no masterpiece, it still is told well."

B262   DEDMON, EMMETT. "Book Week--Upper-Class Code Justified in
        'Sybil,'" Chicago *Sun-Times*, January 6, 1952, Sec. 2, p. 20.
        Auchincloss writes "with the perception of an insider
        and the detachment of the fine social novelist that he is.
        There are few novels--none of the current crop comes to
        mind as a comparison--where the reader can find such gentle
        persuasive portraits of a variety of women as here."

B263   E., R. "Girl's Struggle," Nashville *Tennessean*, January 13,
        1952, p. 15-C.
            "Mr. Auchincloss attempts to out-Marquand J. P. and
        while he does not succeed in doing this, he brings a dry
        insight into the life of a girl of family who does not be-
        long."

B264   FANE, VERNON. "The World of Books," *The Sphere* (London), CCIX
        (May 3, 1952), 196.
            Brief descriptive review. "The character studies are
        photographically sharp, and the dialogue admirably natural."

B265   FINEGOLD, HANNAH A. Providence *Sunday Journal*, January 27,
        1952, Sec. VI, p. 8.
            Auchincloss "knows this society inside out and portrays
        it with unprejudiced insight. He writes cleanly and per-
        suasively, but without force, for his craftsmanship squeezes
        out the life. And when Sybil 'dies' as a character, so does
        the novel."

B266   HILL, BOB. "Looking at Books," Spokane *Daily Chronicle*,
        January 3, 1952, p. 29.
            The "principal trouble" of the book is that there's
        "just too much cool and impersonal observation of its peo-
        ple, too little revelation of character in action."

B267   JACKSON, KATHERINE GAUSS. *Harper's Magazine*, CCIV (February
        1952), 109.
            "The novel paints a picture of what seems a devastating
        and soul-destroying way of life with so dry and pure a
        style and so sure a sense of narrative that the reader feels
        put out because it hardly seems worth writing."

B268   JOHNSON, PAMELA HANSFORD. "Study of a Marriage," *John O'Lon-
        don's Weekly* (London), LXI (May 16, 1952), 483.
            "Mr. Auchincloss's range is small, and I do not claim
        that work so disproportionate as his in its depth to its
        width is likely to increase in power: he has not the
        force of the major novelist. But I am sure he is a minor
        novelist of the first class."

B269   JULIER, VIRGINIA C. "After the Wedding," *Books on Trial*, X
        (April 1952), 287-288.
            "While this is not a 'great' novel, it is a careful,
        sympathetic study of a very real character, and it has a
        somehow fresh approach to an old problem. If Mr. Auchin-
        closs can maintain his viewpoint while he improves his
        technique, he may well prove to be a good writer."

A Bibliography of Writings By and About Louis Auchincloss

WORKS ABOUT

B270   KIKEN, JONAS. "The Upper Stratum," Denver *Post*, February 10,
        1952, p. 6E.
            "The clichés are clever and the class-pointed cynicism
        is always poignant. However, the core-reaching psychology
        that produces authenticity of character in Edith Wharton
        and James is superficially approached and emptily answered
        in the nebulous reaches of only names and scattered, unsus-
        tained emotions."

B271   KIMMEL, SUE. Laguna Beach (Calif.) *Post*, January 3, 1952,
        p. 10.
            Auchincloss "has a brilliant style and a flair for char-
        acterization."

B272   KNIGHT, CLIFF. "Eyebrow Raiser," Hartford *Courant*, January 20,
        1952, Magazine, p. 18.
            "*Sybil* is written in impeccable English, has a high
        style and, in the first part at least, a delicious humor,
        found too rarely in books today. Auchincloss is a master
        of dialogue and situation...."

B273   LAMBERT, J. W. "New Novels--Readiness Is All," London *Sunday
        Times*, April 27, 1952, p. 8.
            "Mr. Auchincloss has achieved a remarkable piece of
        character-creation; his knowledge of human nature is ob-
        viously deep, yet his attitude is uncoloured by distaste."
        Sybil "still shows the hand of the short-story writer, but
        it is in itself a novel of quality."

B274   LAWRENCE, JOSEPHINE. "Society Heroine," *Saturday Review*,
        XXXV (January 26, 1952), 12.
            "It is frankly exasperating not to be able to warm up to
        Sybil in her role of heroine. The sense of frustration is
        due in part to a peculiar vague quality that washes out
        definite impressions. Mr. Auchincloss is writing against a
        New York and Long Island backdrop, but city and shore alike
        lack authentic atmosphere."

B275   LENKEITH, NANCY. "The Burden of Pride," *New York Times Book
        Review*, January 6, 1952, p. 5.
            "Though it may lack style and humor, this first novel re-
        veals a sureness and shrewdness of intention missing in
        much recent fiction."

B276   McGRORY, MARY. Washington (D.C.) *Sunday Star*, January 6, 1952,
        p. C-3.
            "Mr. Auchincloss is very witty, very acute, and his de-
        scriptions of some of the more overpowering clan-gatherings
        among the privileged are a delight."

B277 McLAUGHLIN, ELIZABETH. *Christian Science Monitor*, April 3,
        1952, p. 14.
          Although Auchincloss's characters "seem to be all sur-
        face" and "do not come fully alive until well along in the
        middle of the book" and although Sybil never really does
        the "something very significant...that will make the whole
        book come vibrantly alive with meaning," it is nonetheless
        "an interesting novel, gracefully handled throughout."

B278 "Mr. Auchincloss On the Wealthy and the Bored," *Berkshire
        Evening Eagle* (Pittsfield, Mass.), January 12, 1952, Sec.
        2, p. 11.
          "In the end this novel boils down to a smooth, suave
        story of the tony set, presented with that narrative skill
        Mr. Auchincloss has presented before. What he needs now is
        a sharper barb to his pen."

B279 MUNN, L. S. "Comedy of Manners," Springfield (Mass.) *Sunday
        Republican*, March 16, 1952, p. 12D.
          Calls novel "delightful, refreshing and extremely enter-
        taining."

B280 *New Yorker*, XXVII (January 12, 1952), 82.
          Very brief review: "a stiffly related, rather old-fash-
        ioned novel."

B281 O'LEARY, MARY C. "Modern Comedy of Manners," Worcester *Sunday
        Telegram*, January 6, 1952, p. D9.
          Auchincloss's book "is a well concocted comedy of man-
        ners, authentic in background and peopled with all kinds of
        men and women belonging to that background."

B282 O'LEARY, THEODORE M. "Wealthy New Yorkers Don't Awe Auchin-
        closs," Kansas City *Star*, February 2, 1952, p. 16.
          "Auchincloss writes with a kind of wry detachment. His
        approach is intellectual rather than emotional.... Char-
        acterization and conversation rather than action mark his
        novel."

B283 P., M. Boston *Sunday Post*, January 6, 1952, p. 54.
          "Somehow Sybil never becomes very important to the read-
        er, though the author writes well enough to carry the story
        along. 'Sybil' is a picture in greys and pastels, and
        lacks urgency."

B284 P., W. W. "Sybil," Lewiston (Me.) *Daily Sun*, January 31,
        1952, p. 4.
          Totally descriptive· review.

A Bibliography of Writings By and About Louis Auchincloss

WORKS ABOUT

B285   PRESCOTT, ORVILLE. "Books of The Times," New York *Times*, January 2, 1952, p. 23.
Auchincloss's novel "is cold and solemn. Its heroine's emotional frustration should be important. It should be moving. But the reader's emotions, mine of course, are left untouched. 'Sybil' lacks the satirical bite, the humorous indignation, the dramatic intensity that could give a novel with such a theme the vigor and impact necessary to carry readers along with it. It is undeniably well done, but it is also quite dull."

B286   "Recent Novels," *Irish Times* (Dublin), May 17, 1952, p. 8.
Although *Sybil* "lacks the impact" of Auchincloss's short stories, it is "distinguished and intelligent" and Auchincloss writes "a cool, measured prose without a touch of histrionics and he has an unlimited interest in the behaviour of the human animal, especially when it comes into conflict with the rest of the herd."

B287   ROCKWELL, KENNETH. Dallas *Times Herald*, January 6, 1952, Sec. 2, p. 8.
Sybil "is a book to read and to treasure."

B288   ROSS, MARY. "A Fashionable Dry-Point," *New York Herald Tribune Book Review*, January 6, 1952, p. 8.
"The value of Mr. Auchincloss' novel...is that he has taken persons and circumstances that cannot be unusual in the circles of which he writes and gives them light and shade and definition by the clarity and scrupulousness with which he sees and pictures them."

B289   SCOTT, J. D. "New Novels," *New Statesman and Nation*, XLIII (May 10, 1952), 566.
Although *Sybil* has some positive points, "it isn't enough to make a novel, and for the rest, *Sybil*, while retaining its tone of urbane perceptiveness, and providing some agreeable and intelligent entertainment, does not seem to me to rise very high above the standard of fiction in the better class women's magazines."

B290   SMITH, MARJORY. "Auchincloss'· Second--Threadworn Theme Gets Rare Handling," Atlanta *Journal*, February 17, 1952, p. 7-F.
Praises novel for its "rare" handling of a "threadworn" theme. Sybil is "a jewel who continues to baffle and bemuse the reader right up through the final paragraph."

58

A Bibliography of Writings By and About Louis Auchincloss

B291   SMITH, STEVIE. "New Novels," *World Review*, n.s. XLI (July 1952), 68-72 [68-70].
"Mr. Auchincloss is a wonderfully subtle explorer of the pleasures of a really abandoned artificiality."

B292   SNYDER, MARJORIE B. "Clashes of Old Personalities," Boston *Herald*, January 13, 1952, Sec. IV, p. 15.
"Mr. Auchincloss wrote his shorter tales with a subtlety that is missing in this novel. But his 'psychological alertness,' his portrayal of the behavior pattern of old-family New Yorkers is again outstanding."

B293   SPEARMAN, WALTER. "Literary Lantern," Greensboro (N.C.) *Daily News*, January 6, 1952, Feature Section, p. 3.
Brief favorable review: "a completely convincing account."

B294   SPRING, HOWARD. "With the Rich in New York," *Country Life* (London), CXI (May 9, 1952), 1435.
"Mr. Auchincloss gives the impression of knowing these people and their lives as he knows the back of his hand." He is "certainly a novelist of a very high accomplishment within his class."

B295   STARKEY, MARION L. Boston *Sunday Globe*, January 20, 1952, p. A-31.
"A girl of Sybil's breed does not make the most sympathetic of heroines; however, she is well-placed against a world of the New York smart set that the author seems to know well, and its maneuverings make frequently for fascinating reading."

B296   SULLIVAN, RICHARD. "The Growing Up of a Poor Little Introvert," *Chicago Sunday Tribune Magazine of Books*, January 20, 1952, p. 5.
"Mr. Auchincloss' study of Sybil is careful, sympathetic, and knowing; there is a fine honesty and a sensitive understanding in this scrupulously written novel."

B297   SYMONS, JULIAN. "Life, People--and Books," Manchester (England) *Evening News*, May 8, 1952, p. 2.
Basically descriptive review.

B298   TAYLOR, HELENE SCHERFF. *Library Journal*, LXXVII (January 1, 1952), 48.
Very brief descriptive review.

A Bibliography of Writings By and About Louis Auchincloss

WORKS ABOUT

B299   TAYLOR, MARY DARLINGTON. "Louis Auchincloss Writes an Intui-
          tive and Compassionate Novel, the Story of a Moody Girl at
          War With Herself and Her Environs," Bridgeport (Conn.)
          Sunday Post, December 30, 1951, Sec. B, p. 4.
             Largely descriptive favorable review.

B300   THOMPSON, J. M. "More Novels," *Time and Tide* (London),
          XXXIII (May 24, 1952), 562.
             Descriptive review. It is a novel "with something to
          say."

B301   *Virginia Quarterly Review*, XXVIII (Summer 1952), lxiv.
             Brief review. "As a literary portrait of a shy, sensi-
          tive person, the story has a delicate perceptive quality
          that is of a high order; as a character study of one who
          might be expected to develop into a deeper and finer per-
          son, the story lacks conviction."

B302   W., W. S. "Browsing in Books," *Cavalier Daily* (University of
          Virginia), May 1, 1952, p. 2.
             "Mr. Auchincloss's writing does not betray his exposure
          to legal jargon; his survival is remarkable, as those who
          suffer through legal documents can attest. He remains al-
          ways judicious, never judicial; his one flaw, which could
          be related to legal training, is a minor one: he fre-
          quently addresses questions to the reader, a device which
          can become annoying."

B303   "Where Cuts Don't Bleed," *Time*, LIX (January 14, 1952), 94.
             "For all its urbanity, *Sybil* winds up as not much more
          than fashionable gossip, well and truly gossiped." Auchin-
          closs's "detached air" turns Sybil and her circle "into
          people talked about rather than seen."

B304   YAFFE, JAMES. "Outstanding Novels," *Yale Review*, XLI
          (Spring 1952), VI-XX [VI].
             Auchincloss shows "many faults": "his style is rather
          flat, and at times even clumsy; he has a sharp eye, but
          seldom describes what he observes with quite enough flair
          or wit"; and his heroine "is a little too sensitive to ring
          true." Nonetheless, *Sybil* is "one of the most promising
          American novels in a long time" because Auchincloss "suc-
          ceeds in giving us vivid portraits of nearly every one of
          the people in his story."

A Law for the Lion

B305   ABY, JANE. "Chronicle of Divorce," Tulsa *World*, October 11,
1953, Magazine, p. 20.
"Although it seems highly improbable that this book will
have any effect on New York's divorce laws, it is extremely
revelatory as to the existing ones."

B306   ALLEN, WALTER. "New Novels," *New Statesman and Nation*, XLVI
(September 5, 1953), 264.
Auchincloss "creates characters very deftly and illuminates them with wit, but, having invented them, he does not
seem quite to know what to do with them, and unfortunately
his heroine Eloise is the least successful of them. She is
presented as a woman bent on finding out the truth about
herself; she appears almost as a case of arrested development."

B307   BARKHAM, JOHN. "Shattered Pattern," *New York Times Book Review*, September 27, 1953, pp. 5, 38.
Although this is not "the major novel" that Auchincloss's
readers have been waiting for, "parts of it are so impressive and the work as a whole so assured, that it further
whets our appetite for the big book still to come. Any
novelist who can dare to create so cerebral a milieu--and,
withal, engage the reader's sympathies without stooping to
concessions--obviously possesses the equipment of a mature
man of letters."

B308   BISCHOFF, BARBARA M. "Trivial, Interesting," *Oregon Sunday
Journal* (Portland), November 22, 1953, Magazine, p. 9M.
This is "a trivial story, interesting and well-written
though it is." One character, "the heroine's mother, a
much-married continental soul, almost but not quite brings
the novel to life."

B309   BLYTHE, OLIVE. El Paso *Herald-Post*, September 19, 1953, p. 4.
"The importance of Mr. Auchincloss' book lies not only in
his ability to portray human nature, but also in the time-
liness of his subject matter."

B310   BRANDEIS, ADELE. "Expert Style Without Warmth," Louisville
Courier Journal, September 27, 1953, Sec. 3, p. 11.
"Mr. Auchincloss writes expertly and with style, but with
no warmth, no real sympathy for his characters except the
slightly eccentric ones.... It is just as well, perhaps,
because you never seem to care particularly about the chief
protagonists." All of Auchincloss's novels to date "are...

A Bibliography of Writings By and About Louis Auchincloss

WORKS ABOUT

(BRANDEIS, ADELE)
singularly unlovable novels about rather ungenerous or im-
perceptive people who have not enough imagination to keep
from getting involved, either in marriage, or in a liaison,
with the wrong person, thereby making a great deal of trouble for other members of their families and friends, and
extricating themselves with a resultant scandal which seems
more important than any sorrow or remorse."

B311   B[ROADDUS], M[ARIAN] H[OWE]. El Paso *Times*, September 6, 1953,
p. A-4.
The novel "offers a clever presentation of the evils of
depending too much on principles without the leavening
touch of human affection."

B312   BULLOUGH, GEOFFREY. "New Novels," Birmingham (England) *Post*,
September 15, 1953, p. 3.
Very brief review: "a well-written story which shows
that even in America divorce is not so trivial an occurrence
as Hollywood might make us suppose."

B313   CASH, THELMA. "Novel Based on Human Weakness," Fort Worth
Star-Telegram, September 27, 1953, Sec. 6, p. 3.
"There are no particular preachments in Mr. Auchincloss'
writing, although he points an accusing finger at the
American man who puts business prestige ahead of marital
happiness and who reckons his success by the fatness of his
bank balance."

B314   C[HAMBERLAIN], J[OHN] D[UDLEY], JR. Columbus (Ohio) *Citizen*,
October 4, 1953, *Citizen* Magazine, p. 41.
"This novel is a savage commentary on divorce procedure
and a sensitive exploration of four interesting people."

B315   CHARQUES, R. D. "New Novels," *The Spectator*, CXCI
(September 4, 1953), 254.
The novel "has a narrow range but is otherwise an active
piece of work, nicely observed and decorated with taking
passages of comedy. There is not a lot to say about it,
however, except that it is often, in spite of weak moments,
cleverly and entertainingly done."

B316   Columbia (S.C.) *State*, October 11, 1953, p. 2-E.
"Once in a while Auchincloss wrenches a character around
a bit arbitrarily, sacrificing life-likeness for story.
But it doesn't detract from the remarkable achievement of
the whole. This is an uncommonly successful attempt to

(Columbia (S.C.) *State)*
> point a moral by telling a tale. Make the punishment fit
> the crime, Auchincloss argues eloquently; with me on the
> jury, he'd win."

B317 C[OOPER], M[ARION]. *"A Law for the Lion,"* Lewiston (Me.)
Daily Sun, November 21, 1953, p. 4.
> Auchincloss "has a disconcerting habit of standing off at
> one side to observe his characters with a coldly objective
> eye, which has the effect of making them seem less alive and
> more like automatons whose movements are controlled and
> regulated to bring them ultimately to a planned conclusion."

B318 "The Courage of Her Convictions," *The Argonaut* (San Francisco),
CXXXII (October 2, 1953), 18.
> Auchincloss's "style is as smooth as silk, and women
> especially should like his story. He gives them more than
> an even break."

B319 D., G. Boston *Sunday Herald,* October 11, 1953, Sec. II, p. 15.
> "Mr. Auchincloss, master of the smooth and sophisticated
> phrase and situation, outdoes himself on this one and pro-
> duces an entrancing novel of conversation and character
> that is certain to delight those who have enjoyed his ear-
> lier books."

B320 DRAPER, WANETTA. "New & Readable Fiction," Colorado Springs
Free Press, September 13, 1953, "Sunday Review" Section,
p. 2.
> "This is an honest and compassionate account--one that
> doesn't end when the last page is turned, but echoes and
> re-echoes in the reader's mind."

B321 "Fiction--Mixed Marriages," *Times Literary Supplement* (London),
September 11, 1953, p. 577.
> In contrast to *The Injustice Collectors* which "indicated
> an original talent," this book is a "disappointment."

B322 FLINTAN, DONNA. "Auchincloss Controls Novel in Masterful Way,"
Los Angeles *Times,* October 4, 1953, Part IV, p. 6.
> "When a novelist does not lose control of his material--
> and that is a very rare thing--he may be labeled cold. The
> criticism can be just, because control isn't everything;
> but if the work is done from within the characters, with
> compassion and not sentimentality, there will be no sense of
> cold and sterile perfection."

WORKS ABOUT

B323   FORBES, HARRIET R. *Library Journal*, LXXVIII (September 15, 1953), 1528-1529.
       Very brief descriptive review: "light, sophisticated, yet heartwarming."

B324   G., K. "Urbane Novel Sheds No Light on Old Problem," Charlotte *Observer*, July 5, 1953, p. 14-C.
       "That there is a social problem in the book is not in dispute. That it sheds any light or contains any new approach or social impact is in serious doubt."

B325   GLASSEY, STANLEY. "A Judgment on Life," Yorkshire (England) *Observer*, September 8, 1953, p. 4.
       Brief review. "The story is extremely well told, the dialogue lively, and the characters, if a little overdrawn, convincing"; but "it is a pity...that a writer of Mr. Auchincloss's ability should have ended such an appealing story on so flat an anti-climax as the last chapter."

B326   GRIFFIN, DOROTHEA. "Two Unusually Good Novels," Nashville *Banner*, September 25, 1953, p. 28.
       The novel "is both a devastating indictment of conventional hypocrisy and a delightful social comedy."

B327   HANLEY, JAMES. "New Fiction," London *Daily Telegraph*, August 28, 1953, p. 6.
       The book "is notable for a very shrewd insight into the diversity of its characters, and its skill in handling the situations involved by their impact on one another."

B328   HAY, SARA HENDERSON. "Poor Sinner in a Labyrinth," *Saturday Review*, XXXVI (October 3, 1953), 28.
       This "is a compassionate, honest, and very moving story, but I think that, in the earnestness of his conviction, Mr. Auchincloss has sacrificed something of the leisurely elegance and urbanity of style which lightened but did not detract from the seriousness of his earlier work."

B329   HOLDEN, THEODORE L. "Rigid N.Y. Divorce Law Frame for a Social Novel," Hartford *Times*, September 26, 1953, p. 18.
       "It's an entertaining, well organized, well written story, and one that will make you think a good deal about the touchy questions Mr. Auchincloss raises."

B330   INGE, WELFORD. "Diverting, But Too Ambitious," Oklahoma City *Daily Oklahoman*, September 27, 1953, Magazine, p. 18.
       "The main flaw in this otherwise diverting novel is its pretentiousness. If the author had been content to present

Book Reviews–*A Law for the Lion*

(INGE, WELFORD)
>only a surface picture of shy, winning, naive Eloise Dil-
worth and the dilemma in which she found herself..., his
story would have gained in sharpness, clarity, and interest,
what it loses in a kind of muddled and arch superiority of
tone...."

B331 JACKSON, KATHERINE GAUSS. *Harper's Magazine*, CCVII
(November 1953), 103.
>Auchincloss's "characters sometimes lose reality by be-
ing so completely typed"; and "deep feeling is sacrificed
to satire, but it is very pretty satire."

B332 JOHNSON, MARGARET L. "Brittle People Are Dull," Richmond (Va.)
Times-Dispatch, September 20, 1953, p. 8-A.
>"Auchincloss has undoubted talent, and his writing is
very smooth. New York has its full share of the brittle,
superficial people he describes, but it seems too bad that
the reader is expected to find them justified in their
puerilities."

B333 JULIER, VIRGINIA C. "A Modern Woman and Her Discontent,"
Books on Trial, XII (November 1953), 84.
>Auchincloss "writes exceedingly well; he has an uncanny
and delicate touch at characterizing women. But if he in-
tends to take as his theme the subject of modern woman, he
should learn that she does not always consider adultery as
the solution to every problem."

B334 K., J., JR. "Never Let Go," Trenton *Sunday Times-Advertiser*,
September 13, 1953, Part 4, p. 12.
>"It is a difficult matter to make the social problems of
antiquated divorce laws into a lively novel. Mr. Auchincloss accomplished this by being fluent, witty, sympathetic,
and yet clear and coolly observant of the world he pictures."

B335 KURZ, MYRTIS T. "In Divorce--Her Loss Really a Victory,"
Birmingham (Ala.) *News*, September 27, 1953, p. D-22.
>Auchincloss "succeeds admirably in the legal scenes and
in his knowledge of personal lives of the socially elect in
New York."

B336 LAMBERT, J. W. "New Novels--The Lawyers and the Lady," London
Sunday Times, August 30, 1953, p. 5.
>Auchincloss is "a most accomplished and enjoyable writ-
er"; the novel is "a work of exceptional quality, although
in its plot it makes some concessions to the commonplace."

A BIBLIOGRAPHY OF WRITINGS BY AND ABOUT LOUIS AUCHINCLOSS

WORKS ABOUT

B337   LIGHTNER, LEONE. "New York High Life Shows Seamy Side," Wichita *Eagle*, September 27, 1953, Magazine, pp. 16, 30.
Entirely descriptive review.

B338   MacGREGOR, MARTHA. "The Moral--Let's Catch Up With Kinsey," New York *Post*, September 27, 1953, p. 12M.
"There is a colorless quality about the novel, due perhaps to the colorless personality of the heroine, perhaps to the lack of passion among these people.... This civilized frigidity is no doubt intentional and may be admirably conscientious reporting of a social scene, but it does not make an electrifying novel."

B339   McMANIS, JOHN. "Books of the Day," Detroit *News*, October 4, 1953, p. E-17.
Brief descriptive review.

B340   MORSE, SAMUEL F. "Respectability's Woes," Hartford *Courant*, September 27, 1953, Magazine, p. 18.
"With extremely little fuss and technical flurry, the author peels off the protective coating of the world he writes about. He gets down to the tender core, to the growing cells. But he is never merely ruthless nor shocking; his subtlety is that of a man interested in a story not for its incidental social and satirical aspects, but for its impact upon the characters who act it out."

B341   MUNN, L. S. "'A Law for the Lion'--Louis Auchincloss' Novel of Social Conventions Written With Clarity and Subtlety," Springfield (Mass.) *Republican*, September 27, 1953, p. 6C.
The book is "a highly sophisticated and civilized attack on outworn and hypocritical double-standard conventions, written by a novelist who possesses an ingratiating and pointed prose style impeccably suited to the material he develops."

B342   "New Fiction," London *Times*, August 26, 1953, p. 4.
Auchincloss "in the past has sometimes appeared to overreach himself" but here he "writes well within his means" and the novel is an "intelligent and pointed study."

B343   *New Yorker*, XXIX (September 19, 1953), 118.
Brief review. "This is a very capable, well-made novel."

B344   "The Novel of the Week," *Illustrated London News*, CCXXIII (November 14, 1953), 798.
The novel "is neat, subtle and, in an intellectual way, dramatic. So one can put up with its weaker side--namely, the woman it is all about."

B345   NUGENT, ELIZABETH M. *The Sign,* XXXIII (November 1953), 67.
        "More of a propagandist than a novelist, Mr. Auchincloss
        gathers together a few puppets representing New York's so-
        cial set" and presents unsavory characters who are meant to
        convince us that the divorce laws are outmoded. "So we
        must change the laws to have more Eloises, more broken
        homes, and more asylums?"

B346   O'CONNOR, RICHARD. "*A Law for the Lion,*" Los Angeles *Evening
        Herald Express,* July 18, 1953, p. B-2.
        "Auchincloss' talent, as indicated by his latest novel,
        is steadily developing and maturing."

B347   O'DELL, SCOTT. "Books in the News: Novels By Auchincloss and
        Chatterton," Los Angeles *News,* September 28, 1953, p. 16.
        Basically descriptive review.

B348   O'L[EARY], M[ARY] C. "Problems of Young Married People,"
        Worcester *Sunday Telegram,* September 13, 1953, Sec. E,
        p. 11.
        "It's the usual story. There's nothing new to the plot.
        But what attracts us is the compassion of the author. His
        perspection is startling. He strips people of their emo-
        tions before the reader's eyes, yet he does it with a sen-
        sitiveness which is not offensive. Rather the self-reve-
        lation by the characters leaves the reader with a feeling
        that some problems can be solved."

B349   PETERSON, VIRGILIA. "A Whack at False Living and False Gods,"
        New York Herald Tribune Book Review, October 4, 1953,
        p. 10.
        "What saves this book, and his work in general, from
        the sere and yellow desiccation of too much shrewdness is
        the fact that Auchincloss possesses, and is not too proud
        to show, a heart. He has compassion for his characters."

B350   POORE, CHARLES. "Books of The Times," New York *Times,*
        September 24, 1953, p. 31.
        The book "is notable for Mr. Auchincloss' capacity to
        create short dramatic scenes"; but when "it comes to
        building the full arc of a novel,...he runs into difficul-
        ties inherent in an episodic way of putting a narrative
        together."

B351   RHODES, ANTHONY. "New Novels," *The Listener* (London), L
        (August 27, 1953), 353.
        Descriptive review: a "well-told tale."

A Bibliography of Writings By and About Louis Auchincloss

WORKS ABOUT

B352   ROBERTSHAW, JAMES. "Novel Seems to Be Attack on Divorce Sys-
        tem of New York," Greenville (Miss.) *Delta Democrat-Times*,
        October 4, 1953, p. 18.
            "It is difficult to tell whether the novel is intended
        as an attack upon New York's archaic divorce laws, or a
        defense of adultery under the circumstances of the story."

B353   ROLO, CHARLES J. "Eloise and Esther," *Atlantic Monthly*,
        CXCII (October 1953), 87–88.
            This is "an interesting but uneven novel." Eloise, her
        mother, her husband, and his law partners are handled well;
        but Auchincloss's "grip slackens when he turns to Hilda and
        her romance; and his denouement, which straightens out ev-
        erything so neatly, seemed...decidedly contrived."

B354   SHUMACKER, ELIZABETH W. "Marriage Story," Chattanooga *Times*,
        October 25, 1953, p. 18.
            This is "a beautifully organized and exceptionally well-
        written novel about marriage and divorce--and consequently
        about people--a subject on and about which Mr. Auchincloss
        evidences a wonderful perception and concern."

B355   SNYDER, MARJORIE. "Procedures Hit--Characters Subdue Blow at
        Divorces," Washington (D.C.) *Post*, September 27, 1953,
        p. 6B.
            Brief descriptive review. The book "may well start a
        movement toward changes in divorce laws."

B356   SULLIVAN, RICHARD. "For Divorce--Or Against?" *Chicago Sunday
        Tribune Magazine of Books*, October 4, 1953, p. 4.
            This is "a very carefully wrought novel of contemporary
        life; a thoughtful, quiet, and composed book possessing a
        quality somewhat uncommon."

B357   TAYLOR, MARY DARLINGTON. "One Book After Another...," Bridge-
        port (Conn.) *Sunday Post*, September 13, 1953, Sec. B, p. 4.
            "There is a discernment here that has characterized all
        Auchincloss's writing. But there is a sense of hurry, not
        previously present, that suggests he may have rather dras-
        tically reduced a longer novel."

B358   TEMPLETON, LUCY. "Books Old and New," Knoxville (Tenn.) *News-
        Sentinel*, October 4, 1953, p. C-2.
            This book "is superior both in direction and style to
        any novel I have read this season."

B359   TURNER, E. S. "Some New Books," Syracuse *Herald-Journal*,
        October 25, 1953, p. 27.

(TURNER, E. S.)
"It is just a story, points a very tenuous moral, if any, but is interesting reading."

B360 VAN PATTEN, RICHARD. "Woman's Search For Individuality," Nashville *Tennessean,* September 20, 1953, p. 7-E.
"Although Mr. Auchincloss is a keen observer and able craftsman, there is very little warmth or appeal" in any of his characters. Nonetheless, this is "an urbane engrossing story" and "maintains high reader interest throughout."

B361 *Virginia Quarterly Review,* XXX (Winter 1954), xi-xii.
Brief review. "Whatever the author may lack in profundity he compensates for, by providing good entertainment with a practiced hand."

B362 WALD, ROBERT L. "On Marital Discord--Divorce Scandal Skillfully Shown," Norfolk (Va.) *Pilot,* September 27, 1953, Part 5, p. 11.
"Auchincloss emerges in this moving account of marital discord as an inordinately skillful story-teller. The background sequences flow into the critical axial scenes with a mounting urgency. And for once an author interweaves a moral into his story without making it wear like a literary hairshirt."

B363 WATSON, PHIL. "Books," San Jose (Calif.) *Mercury News,* September 27, 1953, Magazine, p. 14.
"An excellently characterized examination of a delicate social situation."

B364 WEBSTER, HARVEY CURTIS. "Some Recent Novels," *New Republic,* CXXIX (September 28, 1953), 18.
"It is not a great novel, but it is a very good one in which an author displays both his assimilation of his ancestors and his own nominal percentage of experience that is new."

B365 WIENER, MAX. "Hypocrisy in Divorce," Newark (N.J.) *Sunday News,* January 17, 1954, p. E 2.
Auchincloss "again shows that he is a sensitive and observant writer. Unfortunately, he is so overcome with righteous rage that his book tends to become polemic rather than novel, and his characters lose depth. The satire for which his stuffy set fairly cries out is deplorably infrequent. All this tends to alienate the reader and to reduce the impact of what becomes, in the end, more thoughtful tract than deeply felt life."

WORKS ABOUT

B366   "Writer of Note," Glasgow (Scotland) *Herald*, September 10,
            1953, p. 3.
                Brief review. "In its handling of a problem this is a
            novel of real distinction."

The Romantic Egoists

B367   ADAMS, ELEANOR. "Eight Who Rebelled Against Social Norm,"
            Hartford *Times*, May 22, 1954, p. 18.
                "Fortunately Mr. Auchincloss is no heavy-handed moral-
            ist. He has a sense of humor and too much sensitivity to
            spell out the folly of bucking the line."

B368   ASWELL, JAMES. "Two Works of Fiction Tread Familiar Ground,"
            Houston *Chronicle*, May 16, 1954, Feature Magazine, p. 29.
                Auchincloss writes "with clarity, much of the time with
            urbanity and often with charm."

B369   B., J. *Punch* (London), CCXXVII (September 29, 1954), 421.
                This is "an enjoyable and well-written book which might
            have been better: the 'reflections,' one feels, sharply
            focused though they are, remain mere reflections--two-di-
            mensional, and just a little too bright and glossy to be
            mistaken for the real thing."

B370   BLAKE, FRAN. "Character Revelations," Boston *Herald*, May 23,
            1954, Sec. III, p. 2.
                "This is writing as it is done, seemingly without effort
            by a master of the art not only of story telling, but of
            character dissecting. And, for all the stories with their
            cruel, pitiless, tragic nuances, the writer never once
            loses his compassion and understanding."

B371   *The Booklist*, L (June 1, 1954), 380.
                Brief descriptive review.

B372   BOWEN, ELIZABETH. "Book Reviews--Aftermath of Scandal," *The
            Tatler and Bystander* (London), CCXIII (September 29, 1954),
            620, 636 [620].
                "Here is a story-teller with a beautifully clear and di-
            rect style--a classically good English style, one might
            say. To this is added a grip of character and a feeling
            for situation akin to (though in no way imitative of)
            Mr. Somerset Maugham's.... Mr. Auchincloss is sophisticated
            in the right way; he knows several worlds well; he is a born
            assessor of men and women.... Readers who appreciate sound
            sense should seek out this novelist, if they have not yet
            done so."

A Bibliography of Writings By and About Louis Auchincloss

B373   BRADLEY, JOHN. Boston *Post*, June 6, 1954, p. A-8.
"What...enforces the effect of this book is the author's underlying compassion..., his sense of the tragic undercurrents of life, his delicate awareness of what is beneath the surface. For Mr. Auchincloss can express in cool, detached prose those inner feelings which elude so many modern writers."

B374   CAMPBELL, KEN. "Paean For Non-Conformists," Columbus (Ohio) *Citizen*, June 13, 1954, *Citizen* Magazine, p. 15.
"These characters are described by Auchincloss in a style that shows the intimacy of keen observation and close relations with his subjects. He never gets up on a soap-box, yet the message he carries, his admiration for the non-conformist, the romantic egoist, is clearly evident."

B375   COCHRAN, POLLY. "Eight Dissenters of Tradition Interest Novelist of Manners," Indianapolis *Star*, June 6, 1954, Sec. 6, p. 10.
Auchincloss "never smacks a point home; rather, he lets a situation, in all its nuances, tell the reader whatever the latter will find."

B376   CONNELL, JOHN. "Autumn Harvest," London *Evening News*, September 11, 1954, p. 4.
Very brief review. "All the stories are good; the last ['The Gemlike Flame']...is as malicious as it is masterly."

B377   COX, WILLIAM. "The New Books--Where American Fiction Is Just Catching Up," Yorkshire (England) *Observer*, October 14, 1954, p. 8.
Brief review. "The Great World and Timothy Colt" is singled out for special praise.

B378   D., A. G. "Eight Examples of Unconformists," Springfield (Mass.) *Republican*, June 13, 1954, p. 7C.
Auchincloss "has succeeded in presenting the conflicts of his eight romantic egoists as a uniform piece of work, although each chapter originally was published as a short story. But what is more important, the author also has presented a good argument against the insistence for uniformity of opinion and behavior, that the un-conformist may be exasperating, stubborn, idealistic, foolish or courageous, but he is needed by society if only as a point of reference."

A Bibliography of Writings By and About Louis Auchincloss

WORKS ABOUT

B379   De V., J. *Arizona Republic* (Phoenix), June 27, 1954, *Arizona Days and Ways* Magazine, p. 15.
        Auchincloss "appears to be a promising and gifted writer from whom a real contribution to literature may be expected."

B380   "Eight Dissenters," *Newsweek,* XLIII (May 17, 1954), 107.
        "In some of the stories, the author writes as such a relentlessly sensitive observer that the blood in his characters' veins threatens to turn into distilled water. Other Auchincloss characters, however, come immediately to life." "Billy and the Gargoyles" is singled out for special praise.

B381   "Eight Rugged Individualists," *The Argonaut* (San Francisco), CXXXIII (June 4, 1954), 21.
        Auchincloss is "an extraordinary technician, and one can quarrel with him on only one point: as yet he has not chosen a subject worthy of his skill."

B382   FANE, VERNON. "The World of Books," *The Sphere* (London), CCXIX (October 2, 1954), 36.
        Brief review: "a brilliant piece of work, readable and immensely acute."

B383   FELD, ROSE. "Chemistry of Temperament," *New York Herald Tribune Book Review,* June 6, 1954, p. 4.
        "The Great World and Timothy Colt" is "the most revealing" story in the book. Auchincloss's writing is "polished, his humor is mature, and through deliberate understatement he places his oblique accent where it belongs."

B384   FINNEY, FRANK. "About Nonconformists," Richmond (Va.) *Times-Dispatch,* May 23, 1954, p. F-7.
        Auchincloss's "talent lies in his sensitivity to the clash and balance of egos within delicately defined social situations."

B385   FLOWERS, CHARLES. "Stiff Yankee Breeze Dispels Dixie Miasma," Knoxville (Tenn.) *News-Sentinel,* June 20, 1954, Sec. C, p. 3.
        "Every story in the book is excellent."

B386   "Four Novels For Your Hammock Reading--U. S. Aristocrats," Miami (Fla.) *Herald,* June 13, 1954, p. 4-F.
        "Auchincloss writes with wit and understanding. He is one of the few present day writers to recognize that in America there still exists an aristocracy as exclusive as the one in England. At least in the eyes of those who belong to it."

72

A Bibliography of Writings By and About Louis Auchincloss

B387   FRIEDENBERG, ED. "Eight Stories in Casual Style," Winston-Salem
       (N.C.) *Journal & Sentinel*, May 23, 1954, p. C-5.
           Auchincloss's stories "are like a fast smooth plane
       where one minute you are reading a magazine and the next
       minute you are in Paris. You have moved without incident--
       a conversation, a couple of drinks, a lunch--into a new
       country, so you smile back at the hostess and say to your-
       self, 'My, isn't it grand.'"

B388   HARMON, FRED G. "Eight Rebels," Norfolk (Va.) *Virginian-Pilot*,
       July 11, 1954, Part 3, p. 10.
           "Each of the stories is complete in itself but together
       they form as poignant and well-written a treatment of non-
       conformity as this reviewer has ever read."

B389   HARTLEY, LODWICK. "Collection of Short Stories," Raleigh *News
       and Observer*, May 16, 1954, Sec. IV, p. 5.
           Auchincloss "demonstrates a high quality of storytelling;
       and all his characters have a way of coming to life with
       vividness. Among contemporary volumes of short stories
       this one should have a highly respectable place."

B390   HARVEY, ELIZABETH. "New Novels," Birmingham (England) *Post*,
       September 7, 1954, p. 3.
           Very brief descriptive review.

B391   HAY, SARA HENDERSON. "Instinctive Non-Conformist," *Saturday
       Review*, XXXVII (July 10, 1954), 35.
           "Without moralizing, Mr. Auchincloss points out essen-
       tial moralities; he has both ironic wit and sympathy, and
       he is, in addition, the master of a clean, cultivated, ar-
       ticulate literary style which...is an esthetic delight."

B392   HUMBER, NINETTE C. "Egotism Didn't Bring Happiness," Clarks-
       dale (Miss.) *Press Register*, August 28, 1954, p. 2.
           "After finishing the book, the reader has a feeling of
       actually having known the characters. Perhaps it is because
       everyone, at some time or another, has known someone like
       each one of them. More likely, it's because of the astound-
       ing insight into character Mr. Auchincloss demonstrates."

B393   J[ONES], C[ARTER] B[ROOKE]. Washington (D.C.) *Star*, May 16,
       1954, p. E-5.
           "Somehow these stories escape the artificiality that
       usually results when a story sets out to prove a point.
       Mr. Auchincloss is too skillful a writer, too close an ob-
       server, to let them fall into that trap."

A Bibliography of Writings By and About Louis Auchincloss

WORKS ABOUT

B394   L., E. "New Novels," Durham (N.C.) *Herald*, July 18, 1954,
        p. 7-IV.
             Brief descriptive review.

B395   "Long Island Set," Dallas *News*, June 27, 1954, Part VI, p. 7.
             Brief review. Auchincloss "suffers by calling so many
        other writers to mind," but "he has a mind of his own, and
        this latest volume is proof that he has emerged as one of
        the best American novelists since the war."

B396   LYNCH, MARY ELLEN. "A Procession of Underdogs: All Hounded
        Hams at Heart," Dayton *Daily News*, May 30, 1954, Sec. 3,
        p. 7.
             Auchincloss is "a fine, fine writer--funny, sad and deft.
        And despite the fact that he obviously has a rather tender
        feeling for his neurotics he manages to gently unveil them
        all as what they really are: just hams at heart."

B397   M., W. J., JR. "Eight Individuals Well Worth Meeting," Mont-
        gomery (Ala.) *Advertiser*, May 30, 1954, p. 8-C.
             "Here is a series of remarkable characterizations, eight
        individuals who are decidedly worth meeting."

B398   "Mavericks in the Social Herd," Oakland (Calif.) *Tribune*,
        July 4, 1954, p. 44-A.
             "The appeal of these stories is to the intelligence more
        than the emotions, but their prevailing note of a wry and
        wary sympathy pricks beneath the surface of sophisticated
        irony. If Auchincloss's misfits are not always in them-
        selves a jocund company, Auchincloss himself as raconteur is
        a star performer."

B399   MOORE, REGINALD. "New Novels," *Time and Tide* (London), XXXV
        (September 18, 1954), 1241.
             Brief review. Auchincloss "writes with the precision of
        an engraver."

B400   "New Fiction," *Church Times* (London), CXXXVII (November 5,
        1954), 837.
             Auchincloss "shows himself once more as a writer of un-
        usual power, with a keen eye for detail, a shrewd, witty
        but never malignant tongue, and a worldly-wise understanding
        of the manifold temptations that flesh is heir to."

B401   "New Fiction--Personal Rebellion," London *Times*, September 8,
        1954, p. 8.
             The stories are "brilliant," "of outstanding merit,"
        and "faultlessly executed." Auchincloss's writing, "in its

Book Reviews–*The Romantic Egoists*

("New Fiction--...)
   mastery of the *nuances* of New England and New York society,
   can stand comparison with Edith Wharton, if not James himself."

B402   *New Yorker,* XXX (June 5, 1954), 121.
       Very brief descriptive review.

B403   NICOLSON, NIGEL. "Mesmerised," Manchester (England) *Daily
       Dispatch,* September 10, 1954, p. 3.
          "In themselves the stories are not particularly dramat-
       ic, and have no tingling conclusions. Perhaps it is their
       very ordinariness, so perfectly described, that gives them
       a wine-like purity."

B404   NORTH, STERLING. "Book Review," New York *World-Telegram,*
       May 13, 1954, p. 26.
          "It is fairly obvious that Mr. Auchincloss' literary
       model is Henry James. Fortunately, however, his prose
       style is nearer to the crystal clarity of the early James
       than to the affectations and obscurities of James in his
       later years."

B405   P[ECKHAM], S[TANTON]. "From Prep School to Novelist's Life,"
       Denver *Post,* May 30, 1954, *Roundup* Magazine, p. 16.
          Auchincloss "is a writer of brilliant ability, and *The
       Romantic Egoists* is a volume that will have particular ap-
       peal to admirers of *New Yorker* stories wherein plot devel-
       opment is less important than incisive reporting about
       people."

B406   PICKREL, PAUL. "Outstanding Novels," *Yale Review,* XLIII
       (Summer 1954), viii-xviii [xiv].
          "As collected, the stories need more characterization of
       the narrator; he is a little too much the mouse to hold the
       book together. Yet I think this is Mr. Auchincloss' best
       work. It presents an informed, unsentimental, and unim-
       pressed view of a segment of society usually either roman-
       ticized or attacked."

B407   "A Picture of Wealthy Suavely Drawn in Book," Buffalo *Evening
       News,* May 15, 1954, Magazine, p. 7.
          Cites Auchincloss's affinities with James, Marquand,
       Fitzgerald, Glasgow, and Meredith, but notes that Auchin-
       closs's "cool blend of civilized phrasing and a not unpleas-
       ant air of disillusion is really all his own."

A Bibliography of Writings By and About Louis Auchincloss

WORKS ABOUT

B408   "Points of View," *Times Literary Supplement* (London),
            October 8, 1954, p. 637.
            "These stories might easily have been mere essays in New
        England nonconformism. Mr. Auchincloss's careful hands,
        however, extract the last drop of intellectual juice from
        each situation." This is "a work of original and unstrained
        talent."

B409   PRESCOTT, ORVILLE. "Books of The Times, New York *Times*,
            May 12, 1954, p. 29.
            These are "excellent stories in their pale, precise way,
        in the accuracy of their social reporting, in the refined
        distaste of their gentle irony. But they lack completely
        the passion, power, vitality, drama and old-fashioned punch
        that might make one remember them for a few days. One must
        admire these stories; but it is exceedingly difficult to
        feel any response to them beyond a dutiful intellectual
        respect."

B410   QUENNELL, PETER. "New Books," London *Daily Mail*, October 15,
            1954, p. 6.
            Brief review. Auchincloss's "quiet and thoughtful ap-
        proach to his subjects and the interesting variety of his
        subjects themselves make a pleasant change after the vio-
        lent primary colours and harsh light-and-shade of so much
        Transatlantic story-telling."

B411   QUINTON, ANTHONY. "The Errors of Formalism," *Encounter* (Lon-
            don), IV (February 1955), 84–88 [85–86].
            "Only one of these stories is more than adroit carica-
        ture.... But the rest...bear too noticeably the marks of
        their first appearance, they have the mechanical shine of
        the magazines for which they were created.... The Maugham-
        like finish and deadness is a disappointment after Auchin-
        closs's earlier books."

B412   "Reflections in Various Mirrors," *The Scotsman* (Edinburgh),
            September 9, 1954, p. 11.
            "As a storyteller Mr. Auchincloss is in the front rank.
        His style is strong and economical. His wit, though spar-
        ingly used, is pungent. And his penetrating intelligence
        is a constant stimulus."

B413   R[OBINSON], O[LIVE] C. "*The Romantic Egoists*," Lewiston (Me.)
            Daily Sun, June 3, 1954, p. 4.
            "Not the least factor in Auchincloss' success is his
        ability to draw his characters with honesty, accuracy and
        understanding."

B414   ROLO, CHARLES J. "Reflection in Mirrors," *The Atlantic*, CXCIV
(July 1954), 83-84.
The book is better than Auchincloss's earlier works:
"The writing is more pointed; some of the characterizations
are stronger; the storytelling has more pull and it achieves
a sharper impact." "The Great World and Timothy Colt" is
singled out as "a powerful story" and Rolo calls the book
"among the half-dozen works of fiction I have most enjoyed
this year."

B415   SCARDINO, KAY. "Reflections Seen in Conformist's Mirror,"
Savannah *News*, May 16, 1954, p. 56.
"No character is exhaustively presented in this series,
...but there is a way of characterizing which is deadly
accurate in the same way that people often reveal themselves in one sentence."

B416   SCRUTTON, MARY. "New Novels," *New Statesman and Nation*,
XLVIII (October 9, 1954), 448-449.
"It is a book of quite remarkable distinction and solid-
ity. The method is rather like Anthony Powell's--there is
a similar dry reticence, a similar quiet building up of
surprise from everyday incidents. But where Mr. Powell
sticks out his legs and beams at you, Mr. Auchincloss, being
a *New Yorker* writer, screws the pressure up until something
explodes--and in his case that something is not just another
taut nerve, it is a new idea."

B417   SHERMAN, THOMAS B. "Reading and Writing--Eight Characters Who
Lose Themselves," St. Louis *Post Dispatch*, July 18, 1954,
p. 4C.
Auchincloss "enters the lives of his characters at a
moment of crisis and though the resolution is often too
muted, too delicate to deserve the name of dramatic action,
it nevertheless leaves the reader with the feeling that
something important has happened to a human being of consequence."

B418   SHRAPNEL, NORMAN. "Books of the Day--New Fiction," Manchester
(England) *Guardian*, September 7, 1954, p. 4.
"The most developed...of the separate stories, 'The Gem-
like Flame,' puts one in mind of Mr. Maugham with its
sharp, dispassionate, almost surgical eye, and the resem-
blance is furthered by the method of narration through a
detached observer."

B419   SMITH, STEVIE. "New Novels," *The Observer* (London),
September 5, 1954, p. 11.
Auchincloss "is an author the intelligent reader may be

A Bibliography of Writings By and About Louis Auchincloss

WORKS ABOUT

(SMITH, STEVIE)
sure of enjoying. For the English, his new book provides
the usual malicious pleasure of noting slightly off-key
echoes of their own social foibles."

B420   SPRING, HOWARD. "A Dissection of Folly," *Country Life* (London), CXVI (September 23, 1954), 1015.
Basically descriptive review. Auchincloss is "a master"
at "that swift surgical dissection of folly and absurdity."

B421   STARKEY, MARION L. "Wonderful Old Ladies--Reviewer Wants
Mr. Auchincloss to Do Life Story of One of Them," Boston
Globe, May 16, 1954, p. 83.
"As usual this author writes with psychological penetration and a sociological flair that suggests Marquand."

B422   STERN, JAMES. "Reflections in a Mirror," *New York Times Book
Review*, May 16, 1954, p. 4.
"This volume reveals Louis Auchincloss as a writer of
unusual brilliance. In it he combines a Henry Jamesian
knowledge of upper-class New York society with an economy
of style, an alertness of eye, an artful disarming modesty
reminiscent of the stories of Christopher Isherwood."

B423   STEVENS, DON. "Fight Their Own Devils," Worcester *Telegram*,
May 23, 1954, Sec. D, p. 11.
Auchincloss "has smoothly and skillfully dissected
ephemeral motives and feelings, with a fine understanding.
Apparently these sharply-drawn vignettes were not done with
a typewriter, but with a scalpel."

B424   SULLIVAN, RICHARD. "Eight Fine, Precise Auchincloss Stories,"
Chicago Sunday Tribune Magazine of Books, May 16, 1954,
p. 5.
"The writing is modest, precise, and beautifully controlled. In every story, close to the end, there is an effect similar to that of a light's being quietly turned on,
to illuminate in fine, warm clarity these chosen aspects of
the world of Peter Westcott."

B425   SWAN, MICHAEL. "Fiction of the Week--Shooting Folly as It
Flies," London *Sunday Times*, September 5, 1954, p. 4.
This, Auchincloss's fourth book, "shows that he has the
intellectual reserves and staying power of an important
novelist."

B426   *United States Quarterly Book Review*, X (September 1954),
335-336.

78

A Bibliography of Writings By and About Louis Auchincloss

(United States Quarterly Book Review)
Brief descriptive review. "Along with his instinctive skill at telling stories, Mr. Auchincloss exhibits a scrupulous care for details of character."

B427 W., B. "Recent Novels," *Irish Times* (Dublin), September 25, 1954, p. 6.
Auchincloss "has done well enough for long enough to be considered one of the best, most interesting and most civilised of living American writers. If he bears a certain relationship to Henry James and Scott Fitzgerald, he has never attempted to exploit it: he is a true original."

B428 WASSON, BEN. "Shows Pathos of Ego, People in a Pattern," Greenville (Miss.) *Delta Democrat-Times*, June 6, 1954, p. 18.
"These are mature, worldly stories. One might say they are motivated by a blasé spirit, but behind the blasé there is no bathos, but, instead, a wise and wistful pathos. Poised and sure, these stories are civilized both in understanding and presentation."

B429 W[EISSBLATT], H[ARRY] A. "Reflections," Trenton *Sunday Times-Advertiser*, July 11, 1954, Part 4, p. 10.
Auchincloss "is a very talented writer. He knows which way he should write and he sticks to that form because it is possibly the easiest to pursue and it seems to be the most honest."

B430 WHATELY, ROSALEEN. Liverpool (England) *Daily Post*, September 4, 1954, p. 3.
Brief review. "Interesting and intricate, well written and carefully finished, 'The Romantic Egoists' will make its mark and only a few readers will search in vain for a man whose real self is shown in such tantalising glimpses."

B431 WIENER, MAX. "Rebels," Newark (N.J.) *Sunday News*, August 1, 1954, p. E 2.
"These...are discerning studies of eight romantic egoists unable to make the compromises which are necessary perhaps even to rebels, if they want to be effective. The author writes in clear, supple prose, with wisdom and compassion."

B432 WILSON, ANGUS. "The Short Story Changes," *The Spectator*, CXCIII (October 1, 1954), 401–402.
"Mr. Auchincloss is an arrogant neo-aristocrat and his convictions make him, I think, cocksure, lacking in compassion, and on occasion, deficient in good taste.

WORKS ABOUT

> (WILSON, ANGUS)
> Nevertheless, he is a very clever and subtle student of
> human social behavior in the widest sense and one is led
> from one story to another by the unity of mood and view-
> point to a very rewarding total effect which goes far deep-
> er than any subtle momentary flash or exact recapture of
> evanescent sensibility."

B433 WOOLSEY, BILL. "Urbane Proddings of Urban Fauna," Nashville
Tennessean, June 6, 1954, p. 27-C.
> "Conversation about one's circle of friends and acquaint-
> ances, no matter how pungent, is limited in its appeal.
> After a time, the outsider in such a conversation will turn
> his gaze to a window and watch the mundane world, where he
> feels more at home."

B434 "Word-Spinner's Delight--Essays and Short Stories," Birmingham
(England) *Mail*, October 6, 1954, p. 4.
> Brief descriptive review.

The Great World and Timothy Colt

B435 ALDISS, BRIAN W. "Life in Downtown New York," Oxford (England)
Mail, January 24, 1957, p. 6.
> Book is "a subtle study of a man forced to pursue his own
> downfall; its style is good, its characters well drawn."

B436 B[ARKHAM], J[OHN]. "Civilized Novel of Ivy Leaguers in Love
and Law," Hartford *Times*, December 8, 1956, p. 18.
> "As in his earlier novels, the prose is emollient, the
> prevailing mood urbane, and the characters highly civilized.
> However, that deeper significance we have so long sought in
> this writer's work is still absent."

B437 BLAKESTON, OSWELL. "New Novels," *Time and Tide* (London),
XXXVIII (January 26, 1957), 104.
> "The author has command of his craft, and this book
> should be more moving than it is; but it relies too much on
> best-selling contrivance. The heart-attacks, for instance,
> just have to afflict the one old lawyer who does remember
> something of his youthful ideal. The success-formula, one
> feels, has somewhat corrupted this novel."

B438 BLIVEN, BRUCE, JR. "SR's Book of the Week: 'The Great World
and Timothy Colt,'" *Saturday Review*, XXXIX
(October 20, 1956), 17.
> Although Ann and Eileen "share the fate of lacking com-
> plete literary development," one "can overlook the

Book Reviews–*The Great World and Timothy Colt*

(BLIVEN, BRUCE, JR.)
    inadequacies in Timothy's women in excitement over the drama of what goes on in Timothy's life during office hours."

B439   BOWEN, ELIZABETH. "Book Reviews--Outspoken Grief," *The Tatler and Bystander* (London), CCXXIV (June 19, 1957), 640-641, 656 [640-641].
    "Here is, probably, one of the ablest storytellers and *direct* psychologists using the English language;...here is a transatlantic writer who makes the Atlantic shrink and hardly exist." "Can it be, in part, that from his second profession Mr. Auchincloss has gained his thoroughgoing knowledge of humanity?" This book is "his masterpiece, genuine and exciting."

B440   BROOKS, JOHN. "Ideals On Trial," *New York Times Book Review*, October 21, 1956, pp. 4, 50.
    The novel "appeals in part, perhaps unintentionally, to the escapist impulse; but it also shows how traditional writing methods and social attitudes can throw a refreshing light on parts of the contemporary scene."

B441   BROWN, LOUISE FIELDING. *Book-of-the-Month Club News*, December 1956, pp. 7-8.
    Descriptive review.

B442   BRUDNEY, VICTOR. *Yale Law Journal*, LXVII (November 1957), 176-178.
    "Whatever the author may have intended to say about the trouble with the practice of law on Wall Street, the trouble in his novel is with Timothy Colt.... The level at which the author develops the story and such of the characters as may be so-called fits them for presentation in the average motion picture, but hardly for comment in the pages of this august *Journal*."

B443   BRYDEN, RONALD. "New Novels," *The Listener* (London), LVII (January 24, 1957), 165.
    The first part of the novel "achieves something remarkable and...unique"; but the last half "is conventional to banality."

B444   CEVASCO, GEORGE A. *The Sign*, XXXVI (December 1956), 62.
    "A somewhat contrived denouement mars *The Great World and Timothy Colt*, but it is nonetheless mainly realistic and convincing. Interesting throughout, it is noteworthy for probing the viciousness and amorality of two 'great worlds'--big business and high society."

A Bibliography of Writings By and About Louis Auchincloss

WORKS ABOUT

B445 CHAPIN, RUTH. "A Novel of Law and Motives," *Christian Science Monitor*, October 25, 1956, p. 4.
In this novel, "the moral problem is more crucial and hence more unifying" and the style "less uneven and more organic" than in Auchincloss's earlier work. Although Auchincloss has not yet quite reached the level of Wharton and James, "he is closing the gap."

B446 COFFEY, MARIE BUTLER. *Books on Trial*, XV (December 1956), 205-206.
Descriptive favorable review. Auchincloss "writes a revealing story with interest and authority."

B447 CONNELL, JOHN. "New Books Reviewed--Tale of Life and Love," Edinburgh (Scotland) *Evening Dispatch*, March 4, 1957, p. 10. Also London *Evening News*, February 23, 1957.
"There is a brisk, friendly sanity about Mr. Auchincloss. He writes clearly and unpretentiously; he has a heart and he is civilised. He is clearly the kind of American novelist whom English writers like; I suspect that a good many English readers will like him too."

B448 DAVENPORT, JOHN. "New Novels--Poor Little Rich Man," *The Observer* (London), January 20, 1957, p. 10.
"The novel is about money rather than power, although there is a Balzacian elaboration of the background, one of those vast law firms...which seem to English eyes such an unholy puzzle." "Few writers to-day have the knowledge or the ability to deal with life among the rich. Mr. Auchincloss has exactly the right uncensorious tone."

B449 Dublin (Ireland) *Evening Herald*, February 4, 1957, p. 26.
Brief review: "a slow-starting but excitingly developed novel of modern America."

B450 FANE, VERNON. *The Sphere* (London), CCXXVIII (January 19, 1957), 140.
Brief review. "In spite of disliking its hero only a little less than its heroine, I found this a satisfying novel."

B451 "The Fire That Illumines Life," *The Scotsman* (Edinburgh), January 17, 1957, p. 11.
"The writing's dry humour and penetrating shrewdness light a picture which, deliberately or otherwise, seems to belong to a rigidly enclosed community. But, as everybody knows nowadays, this is a small world."

Book Reviews–*The Great World and Timothy Colt*

B452   GREEN, PETER. "Recent Fiction--An Idealist Meets Temptation,"
            London *Daily Telegraph and Morning Post*, February 8, 1957,
            p. 8.
                "Within its own terms of reference this is an excellent
            novel: terse, powerful, with an emotional punch on every
            page."

B453   HARRINGTON, JOE. "Lawyer and His Conscience," Boston *Sunday
            Globe*, November 4, 1956, p. 20-B.
                Brief descriptive review: "the readable novel."

B454   "The High and the Flighty," Orlando (Fla.) *Sentinel*,
            January 13, 1957, *Florida* Magazine, p. 6-E.
                "The picture of the workings of this law firm, the office
            politics, the cases, the clients, is so extraordinarily well
            done that the book has exceptional interest. Mr. Auchin-
            closs writes with considerable skill. This is his fourth
            novel, and his best to date."

B455   HOGAN, WILLIAM. "A Bookman's Notebook--The Habit Patterns of
            a Young Lawyer," San Francisco *Chronicle*, October 26, 1956,
            p. 25.
                This "is a good novel that has atmosphere, characteriza-
            tion and fine narrative style. On top of this, Mr. Auchin-
            closs' knowledge of American habit patterns...lends the
            novel a stinging authenticity."

B456   HOLLOWAY, DAVID. "Trials of a Trustee," London *News Chronicle*,
            January 17, 1957, p. 6.
                Although this is "one of those social novels packed with
            small detail about business and personal relationships that
            the Americans do so well--Mr. Auchincloss better than most,"
            the weakness of the book "lies in the hero's overnight aban-
            doning of his rectitude and his equally sudden regaining of
            it."

B457   HOWE, MARJORIE. "New Books," Burlington (Vt.) *Free Press*,
            January 8, 1957, p. 9.
                "This is a thoughtful book about a world Mr. Auchincloss
            knows well--the world of big business, its competition and
            ruthlessness often. It's a good book and a fascinating
            one."

B458   INGE, WELFORD. "Are Males Dedicated?" Oklahoma City *Daily
            Oklahoman*, February 3, 1957, Magazine, p. 25.
                "A sharply pointed character study, this novel seems to
            be saying that men of depth and feeling and sensitivity are
            so constituted by temperament as to find it absolutely

WORKS ABOUT

(INGE, WELFORD)
imperative to be dedicated to something, if not to the moral and admirable, then to the immoral and inadmirable. But it never quite shows you why."

B459   JOHN, K. "The Novel of the Week," *Illustrated London News*, CCXXX (April 13, 1957), 602.
"Timmy's whole jag has something artificial about it, for which his own sensation of unreality is no excuse. And the characters, though subtly drawn, are often more like essays in people than elements in a story."

B460   JOHNSON, VERNON. "Books of the Day--New Novels," Manchester (England) *Guardian*, January 22, 1957, p. 4.
"On New York lawyers and business men, on their problems of ethics and conscience," Auchincloss is "brilliant and exciting too." But he is "rather less so in his love-and-marriage sections or supplements. Indeed he seems almost to have tacked these on as a makeweight or to conform to popular formula."

B461   JONES, CARTER BROOKE. "Novels Outnumbering Nonfiction This Fall," Washington (D.C.) *Sunday Star*, October 21, 1956, p. E-7.
"There are times when Timmy seems too ill-adjusted in his personal life for one of his assumed professional brilliance, when he can't seem to make up his mind about anything. But on the whole the author has drawn a persuasive portrait."

B462   KAPLAN, BENJAMIN. *Harvard Law Review*, LXX (April 1957), 1132-1135.
Auchincloss "has not dug very deep into the souls of his characters or into the professional milieu." He is also "so much concerned with the education of Colt in the cussedness of life that he has not applied his art to the *interna* of law practice as much as his lawyer-readers might like." Nonetheless, "we feel some 'shocks of recognition' and can admire some deft touches."

B463   KELLY, BERNARD. "Inside a Gray Flannel World," Denver *Sunday Post*, November 4, 1956, *Roundup* Magazine, p. 9.
The novel is "efficiently done and easy to read" and it "may paint an authentic picture"; but "what there was in Timothy Colt to charm the two women in his life is not easy to see. He seems a self-centered, bad-tempered young genius with rather easily bent integrity. The author obviously has deep sympathy for him, more's the wonder."

B464   KING, NORMAN. "Stakes Its Claim," Newcastle (England) *Journal*,
        January 26, 1957, p. 4.
            Brief review. "The book must stake its claim as the
        outstanding American novel of the year."

B465   LANE, ROBERT R. "The Fiction Shelf," Newark (N.J.) *Sunday
        News*, November 4, 1956, Sec. III, p. E2.
            "Auchincloss has told an interesting story, difficult at
        some places for those not legally-minded to follow closely,
        and far from convincing in Timmy's surrender to a longing
        for gaiety and wealth. It is fair to ask whether it is
        Timmy or the world that gets the better of the bargain at
        the end."

B466   "Lawyer in Trouble," *Newsweek*, XLVIII (October 22, 1956), 116.
            "In most hands, Timothy's tale could be intolerably
        bleak or perhaps a sermon for all young men in gray flannel
        suits. But in Auchincloss's hands, the novel is navigated
        without a nick between the busy reefs of sentimentality on
        one side and cynicism on the other. Timothy never palls,
        not because he is not dull, but because he is seen by many
        different eyes, including his own."

B467   LYNCH, JOHN A. "Novel Probes Jungle of Corporate Law," Chicago
        Sun-Times, October 28, 1956, Sec. 2, p. 10.
            The novel is "cut wholly from life. Its people are real,
        their emotions valid under the circumstances they have cre-
        ated or adopted."

B468   M[ACLAREN]-R[OSS], J. *Punch* (London), CCXXXII (January 30,
        1957), 201.
            The novel "suffers from the peculiarly American premise
        that an idealist is necessarily an ass, and the 'hick' a
        hero automatically disrupted by contact with sophisticated
        or worldly values." But "those passages concerning David,
        the homosexual interior-decorator,...exemplify the author's
        talent for portraiture at its best."

B469   METCALF, JOHN. "New Novels--Rise and Fall," London *Sunday
        Times*, January 20, 1957, p. 6.
            Although Auchincloss "has produced one of the best Amer-
        ican novels that we are likely to see in 1957," in the sec-
        ond half of the book "one begins to feel that the construc-
        tion of the story is becoming a lie; Timothy's last and most
        important decisions are not altogether a part of him."

B470   MILLAR, RUBY. "Novels," *The National and English Review* (Lon-
        don), CXLVIII (February 1957), 94-97 [94-95].

A Bibliography of Writings By and About Louis Auchincloss

WORKS ABOUT

(MILLAR, RUBY)
"This is a book which can be read equally for its story,
for its social comment, and for its exploration of personality; it is a model of what the novel should be."

B471 MILNE, ANGELA. "Getting Away From It All," *The Sketch* (London), CCXXVI (February 27, 1957), 224.
The second half of the novel is less successful than the
first; but Ann "is a fine character study."

B472 "Mixed Fiction," *Time*, LXVIII (October 22, 1956), 120-122.
Descriptive review. Timothy is "dull."

B473 NANCE, G. L. Richmond (Va.) *Times-Dispatch*, November 4, 1956,
p. 10-L.
Brief descriptive review: an "interesting story."

B474 "New Books," *The Queen* (London), CCIII (January 22, 1957), 44.
Brief review. "It gives a convincing picture of the
business world in New York, the characters are both interesting and plausible, and the author has wisely been content
to write a well-constructed novel without attempting to blow
it up into a social survey."

B475 "New Fiction--Crisis For a Lawyer," *Church Times* (London), CXL
(February 8, 1957), 5.
"It is a satisfying piece of work, and is distinguished
by a mature understanding of character and motivation. It
is also extremely readable, with the interest held trium-
phantly to the last page."

B476 "New Novels--Cold As Charity," Glasgow (Scotland) *Herald*,
January 24, 1957, p. 3.
Brief review. "The lively figures on Mr. Auchincloss's
canvas add up to a cunningly detailed picture of the higher
reaches of New York society."

B477 O'LEARY, THEODORE M. "A Lawyer's Morals Fail to Stand Up,"
Kansas City *Star*, November 17, 1956, p. 15.
"The law background" of the novel, "as well as the views
it affords of the vacuousness of New York society, are the
novel's strong points, rather than its character portrayals...."

B478 O'NEILL, FRANK. Cleveland *News*, October 22, 1956, p. 13.
"A taut novel that holds one's interest all the way."

Book Reviews—*The Great World and Timothy Colt*

B479 PRESCOTT, ORVILLE. "Books of The Times," New York *Times*,
October 22, 1956, p. 27.
"This smooth and glossy novel is everything a technically
expert work of fiction should be--in its adroit craftsmanship, its natural dialogue and its neat structure." But
Timothy Colt "is so stubborn, foolish and self-centered that
his affairs become just a little tiresome."

B480 *Publishers' Weekly*, CLXX (September 24, 1956), 1626.
This is Auchincloss's "best novel to date" and one "which
should appeal to men who, perhaps, do not usually read fiction, and to women readers as well."

B481 "The Pursuit of Power," *Times Literary Supplement* (London),
January 25, 1957, p. 45.
Auchincloss's characters "tend to appear as symbols of
the various virtues or vices they represent, and thereby to
lose some of their interest as individuals. Timothy Colt
himself...comes out, too, as a somewhat submerged individual. But Mr. Auchincloss has the born storyteller's gift
of making us deeply concerned about what happens to his
characters even when conscious of their, and his, shortcomings."

B482 QUENNELL, PETER. "Timothy Colt's Energy Will Leave You Limp,"
London *Daily Mail*, January 17, 1957, p. 6.
This is "a well-written and carefully detailed story that
could have been produced only in America."

B483 QUIGLEY, ISABEL. "New Novels," *The Spectator*, CXCVIII
(January 18, 1957), 90-91.
"Mr. Auchincloss's scope and subtlety together, the
piercing exactness of his observation, the sustained excellence of his style, above all the weight of personality--
that indefinable but measurable quality--all set him far
beyond, say, Marquand.... It is hard, in fact, to think of
any living fellow-countryman of his with whom to compare
him; and among the dead the only one that comes to mind as
a possible source of comparison--not, I hope, too extrava-
gantly--is James."

B484 R[AE], D[OUGLAS]. "Don't Take It All Too Seriously...," Aber-
deen (Scotland) *Press and Journal*, February 15, 1957, p. 7.
"Yes, the pattern is as conventional as a missive of let.
But the dialogue is as fresh and crisp as this morning's
rolls. The author has an ear for animated, if sometimes
lawyeresque, conversation."

A Bibliography of Writings By and About Louis Auchincloss

WORKS ABOUT

B485   RICHARDSON, MAURICE. "New Novels," *New Statesman and Nation*,
        LIII (January 19, 1957), 77-78 [78].
            Brief mention. "There is nothing obvious or banal about
        it, and it is written in a firm, clear, unmodern English
        style. The legal and commercial detail is copious but
        clear."

B486   R[OBINSON], O[LIVE] C. *"The Great World and Timothy Colt,"*
        Lewiston (Me.) *Daily Sun*, January 3, 1957, p. 4.
            "The bones of the plot have been served before. It is
        the Auchincloss garnish with its portion of thoughtful un-
        dertones, its dash of philosophy, and with just a suspicion
        of elusive genius that makes of 'The Great World and Timo-
        thy Colt' something for the mind to savor--a modern fable
        for an intellectual sophisticate."

B487   ROGERS, W. G. Pasadena *Star-News*, November 14, 1956, "Living"
        Section, p. 9.
            Brief descriptive favorable review.

B488   ROLO, CHARLES J. *The Atlantic*, CXCVIII (November 1956),
        110-111.
            Brief review. Auchincloss "is writing like and rather a
        little better than his renowned and unnamed competitors."

B489   ROUTLEY, ERIK. "Erik Routley's Fiction Reviews," *British
        Weekly*, CXXXIX (February 7, 1957), 2.
            "For serious readers who want to understand human nature,
        American or British or any other kind," this novel "is re-
        quired reading. Quite first-rate."

B490   SHAFFER, PETER. "Disrespect in Fiction," *Truth* (London),
        CLVII (January 18, 1957), 69.
            "Mr. Auchincloss knows his city and his professional men,
        and the fruit of his assurance is a patient, studied, ob-
        servant and graciously balanced variation on the trusty old
        American theme of 'selling out.'"

B491   SHORE, SHERMAN. "Novel Accents Great World of Ambition,"
        Winston-Salem (N.C.) *Journal & Sentinel*, January 13, 1957,
        p. C-5.
            Auchincloss's novel "is perhaps more impelling than ex-
        citing, although once it gets under way there is no lagging
        in interest."

B492   SNYDER, MARJORIE B. "Distinguished Novel," Boston *Sunday Her-
        ald*, October 21, 1956, Sec. I, p. 6.
            "It is a dramatic novel; a distinguished novel; not only

Book Reviews—*The Great World and Timothy Colt*

(SNYDER, MARJORIE B.)
   a commentary on the practice of law but also on the practice of living."

B493   SPRING, HOWARD. "From Idealism to Roguery," *Country Life* (London), CXXI (January 17, 1957), 123.
   Although this is Auchincloss's "most ambitious novel," there is "a sense of the author moving a character as he would move a counter in a game, rather than of a human being slowly sapped and undermined by the circumstances of his life." But "there can be nothing but admiration" for Auchincloss's depiction of the "great world" into which Timmy sold himself.

B494   SULLIVAN, RICHARD. "A Young Lawyer's Moral Problems," *Chicago Sunday Tribune Magazine of Books,* November 4, 1956, p. 4.
   "Eminently readable, even engrossing, and loaded with sharply, brightly realized characters, this novel seems intended as a kind of latter day morality story; yet its moral implications do not provide a steady illumination but only a fitful flickering; and the result is a somewhat tentative parable."

B495   TILLES, SAMUEL. *"The Great World and Timothy Colt,"* Los Angeles *Evening Herald Express,* December 31, 1956, p. B-2.
   "If Auchincloss...cannot be credited with an original idea, his backdrop is both vivid and dramatic.... His characters bring less response, varying between colorless Colt and his wife, and caricatures of New York society."

B496   TRAVEN, HUGH. "Mermaids and Sea Monsters Again," Manchester (England) *Evening News,* January 19, 1957, p. 2.
   Although this is "an exceptionally fine novel," Auchincloss's skill "does not hide a certain naïveté which is also fairly typical of this sort of novel."

B497   "Vogue's Book-bag," *Vogue* (London), CXIII (March 1957), 212.
   Very brief review. "The book becomes a documentary of an ethical landslide."

B498   WALSH, WILLIAM J., S. J. *Best Sellers,* XVI (December 1, 1956), 305-306.
   "An absorbing, adult novel which never descends to obscenity or indecencies of detail, *The Great World and Timothy Colt* should establish the reputation of Mr. Auchincloss as a writer well above the average and close to the tradition set by J. P. Marquand."

89

A Bibliography of Writings By and About Louis Auchincloss

WORKS ABOUT

B499   WEST, ANTHONY. "At Home and Abroad," *New Yorker*, XXXII
        (November 10, 1956), 219-224 [219-220].
            The novel is "an acute study of the working of a compul-
        sion not to succeed." It is also a "deceptively unassuming
        and exceptionally comprehensive study of the wealthy middle
        ground of New York's social fabric." Auchincloss "creates
        a surprising number of fully realized and lucidly drawn
        characters."

B500   WHATELY, ROSALEEN. "The Inner Conflict of a Brilliant Lawyer,"
        Liverpool (England) *Daily Post*, January 23, 1957, p. 6.
            "Every character in the book is an individual and the
        play of personality upon personality, the effect of various
        emotions upon certain people, the resulting action and the
        inevitable outcome are all worked out with the scrupulous
        care and by the light of the inspiration of the craftsman
        who is also an artist."

B501   WILLIS, KATHERINE TAPPERT. *Library Journal*, LXXXI
        (September 15, 1956), 1992.
            Brief descriptive review. "It is a familiar story--
        well told--and to be bought for the lovers of the Marquand
        type of tale."

B502   WILLY, MARGARET. "New Novels," Birmingham (England) *Post*,
        January 22, 1957, p. 3.
            Brief review. "The insidious corruption of the talented
        and ambitious man, almost before he realises what is happen-
        ing to him, is delineated with shrewdness and subtlety."

B503   WILSON, SLOAN. "One Manhattan Marriage," *New York Herald
        Tribune Book Review*, November 18, 1956, p. 12.
            The book "is obviously an honest attempt to deal with
        complex people under pressure. The trouble is that when
        the chips are down, the main characters act with a perver-
        sity which the reader never understands deeply enough to
        pity. The perversity is probably realistic, but for this
        reviewer, it led only to exasperation."

Venus in Sparta

B504   ALLEN, WALTER. "New Novels," *New Statesman*, LVI (September 13,
        1958), 356-357.
            "Mr. Auchincloss is very adroit; he writes an extremely
        polished professional novel.... But he seems to me to have
        nothing new to add about this, mainly, I think, because
        Farish is a dummy."

B505   BALLENTINE, RUTH. "Tragic Novel Scans Morals," Memphis *Commercial Appeal*, October 5, 1958, Sec. IV, p. 10.
       "This is a mordant and often shocking study of a man who conforms completely to the moral code of a social class. It is also a blue-print of the immorality of this class, considered definitely in, in America today." It is a "fine tragic novel."

B506   BRYANT, JACK. *Library Journal*, LXXXIII (August 1958), 2176.
       Brief descriptive review: "a cynical and polished commentary on affairs, both love and business, and also on the well-intentioned relationship of a graying business executive to his misunderstood, liberal son."

B507   BURNS, JOHN A. "Underneath, Despair," Baltimore *Sun*, October 5, 1958, Sec. A, p. 9.
       Although this is "an ugly and at all times believable story," one criticism "can be leveled at the author--his clinical detachment for his characters leads the reader to a similar detachment--one never really cares what happens to Michael Farish."

B508   CHAFFEE, NORMAN. "One Man's Three Loves," Tulsa *Sunday World*, September 28, 1958, Magazine, p. 24.
       "Louis Auchincloss handles a delicate situation in a superb manner, and in the end gives us a Farish who in sacrificing everything finds a sort of reality."

B509   CONNELL, JOHN. "Macbeth on Wall St.," London *Evening News*, December 18, 1958, p. 4.
       "Of all contemporary American novelists Louis Auchincloss is the one whom I admire most, whose work as it develops interests me most." *Venus in Sparta* is "a remarkable achievement."

B510   CULLIGAN, GLENDY. "Just Browsing--Awareness Banishes Injustice," Washington (D.C.) *Post and Times Herald*, September 21, 1958, p. E6.
       Brief descriptive review.

B511   DAVENPORT, JOHN. "New Novels--Sublime and Ridiculous," *The Observer* (London), September 7, 1958, p. 17.
       Very brief descriptive review.

B512   "Fiction--Business Before Pleasure," *Times Literary Supplement* (London), September 26, 1958, p. 541.
       Auchincloss "is among the best prose writers of his country, incapable of writing a dull or ugly sentence, and the

WORKS ABOUT

("Fiction--Business Before Pleasure,")
excellence of his latest novel lies in its manner rather
than its matter."

B513   G[REENWOOD], W[ALTER] B. "When Failure Threatened, Love Was
No Antidote," Buffalo *Evening News*, October 11, 1958, Magazine, p. 6.
Auchincloss records the lives of the wealthy "with the
urbanity and subtlety that their manner demands. His style
fits the subject beautifully, although the subject may be a
little too special for the general reader."

B514   GUTWILLIG, ROBERT. "Honorable Failure," *Commonweal*, LXIX
(December 12, 1958), 296-297.
This novel is Auchincloss's "most ambitious and best
book"; but it fails "intelligently and honorably," princi-
pally because Farish "is not a sympathetic enough person."
Auchincloss is "one of our better novelists, just on the
verge of writing a really successful book."

B515   H[ALL], B[ARBARA] H[ODGE]. "Society Explored--Auchincloss'
Book Strong," Anniston (Ala.) *Star*, January 18, 1959, p. 18.
"It is not a pretty story, but undeniably a powerful
one."

B516   HICKS, GRANVILLE. "Literary Horizons--The Fiction of Business," *Saturday Review*, XLI (September 20, 1958), 18. Reprinted in Hicks, *Literary Horizons* (B3).
Auchincloss "is a deft prober, and he shows us how a
sense of inadequacy and guilt can be created and how it can
shape a life."

B517   HOWE, MARJORIE. "New Books," Burlington (Vt.) *Free Press*,
September 24, 1958. p. 13.
"Mr. Auchincloss presents a society composed entirely of
most immoral, unattractive people, with not a single re-
deeming person. He is a brilliant writer but this book is
not one of his best."

B518   HUGH-JONES, SIRIOL. "Books I Am Reading--Ulysses Retells His
Story," *The Tatler* (London), CCXXIX (September 17, 1958),
541.
Brief review. "The semi-hero is glum and grey, but the
book is hypnotically readable."

B519   JOHNSON, VERNON. "New Novels--Down Among the Zombies," Manchester (England) *Guardian*, September 23, 1958, p. 4.
Although Auchincloss is "still most polished and expert
in his writing, his plotting, his characterisation," his

(JOHNSON, VERNON)
    hero "gives the impression time and again that he is nothing
    but a dummy manufactured with the most exquisite cunning,
    that he has been built up from some couchside case history
    rather than taken direct and warm and kicking from life."

B520   K., D. I. Wilmington (Del.) *Morning News*, September 22, 1958,
        p. 7.
        This is Auchincloss's "most important and vital work to
        date" and "one of the better novels of the fall season."

B521   KENNEDY, MILWARD. "Novels," *National and English Review* (Lon-
        don), CLI (November 1958), 210-211.
        "Only as the book draws to its close, following an af-
        fair of real passion, is the reader tempted to feel that
        Michael is stepping out of character; but the author has an
        ironical twist in store."

B522   *Kirkus*, XXVI (July 15, 1958), 521.
        "Auchincloss, always expertly at ease in the high soci-
        ety he frequents, combines its cachet with a smoothly, if
        not deeply, moving story."

B523   "Love Affairs Spark Novel," Wichita *Eagle*, February 1, 1959,
        Magazine, p. 14.
        Brief review. Auchincloss "is a good writer and his
        novel is readable although it is hard to tell just what he
        is trying to prove."

B524   McG[RORY], M[ARY]. "Contemporary Morality Is Auchincloss'
        Theme," Washington (D.C.) *Sunday Star*, October 5, 1958,
        p. E-7.
        "Mr. Auchincloss' message is a trifle murky, although
        his writing is not."

B525   MARQUAND, JOHN P. *Book-of-the-Month Club News*, September 1958,
        pp. 9-10.
        "*Venus in Sparta* is as ironic a book as its title--a
        sympathetic and telling study of human weakness, both trag-
        ic and amusing and written with the skill that has already
        made its author one of our more promising younger novelists.
        If the motivations of Mr. Farish are sometimes obscure,
        there are ample compensations in this highly vital and re-
        freshing piece of fiction."

B526   METCALF, JOHN. "In the Footsteps of Hemingway," London *Sunday
        Times*, September 7, 1958, p. 7.
        "Mr. Auchincloss handles the whole thing with a deal of

WORKS ABOUT

(METCALF, JOHN)
professional excitement; but...he makes a nonsense of it all in the long run by putting a big, cunning thumb on to one side of the scales."

B527   MIZENER, ARTHUR. "Young Lochinvar Rides to Defeat," *New York Times Book Review*, September 24, 1958, p. 4.
"With this novel," Auchincloss "confronts defeat, though he is only beginning to see all that defeat means to him." Although the story "is drastically foreshortened" and "we do not learn enough from the Mexican episodes--which are meant to reveal the sources of his despair--really to feel it," *Venus in Sparta* "has the most important subject Mr. Auchincloss has yet tackled and is a big step forward for a writer who commands his experience as very few of our younger writers can."

B528   MOONEY, HARRY, JR. "Disillusion Analyzed," Pittsburgh *Press*, September 21, 1958, Sec. 5, p. 12.
"As a novel, it is soundly and carefully plotted, its characters are delineated with complete and honest understanding, if not with any notable amount of sympathy. And it is written in the flat, beautifully controlled language of understatement." But Auchincloss's great talents demand "that he strike out into newer, deeper areas in which he can develop more meaningful themes."

B529   "New Novels: Tracts for the Times," *The Scotsman* (Edinburgh), September 27, 1958, p. 16.
"There is some fine portraiture in this study of strange human relationships, especially among members of the older generation, sketched with an accomplished pen."

B530   NICHOLSON, GEOFFREY. "New Novels--No Spartan He," *The Spectator*, CCI (September 12, 1958), 352.
Although this book reminds us that Auchincloss is "at his most accomplished in the short story," "whether he is writing novels or short stories, there are not many of his contemporaries that one would choose to put above him in a review."

B531   "Novelist Who Can Bring the Past to Life," London *Times*, September 11, 1958, p. 11.
Brief review: "a polished and very well observed" novel.

B532   O'G., F. E. *Best Sellers*, XVIII (November 15, 1958), 321.
"It is altogether a fine and well written novel. ...I am not convinced, however, that Auchincloss really saw the same problems in the beginning of his novel that he saw in

(O'G., F. E.)
his ending of the novel. I feel that he knew the eventual
destination of Michael, but somehow could not get Michael
to walk there. And so Michael is pushed. For a brilliant
writing job, a rather sad relative of failure."

B533   PICKREL, PAUL. "Two at the Crossroads," *Harper's Magazine*,
CCXVII (October 1958), 90-93.
Auchincloss "seems to be afraid of wasting a word, and
so there is a kind of nervous haste in the book. A slower,
more relaxed narration would give the story greater stature.... But in spite of these mild strictures, *Venus in
Sparta* is the best novel Auchincloss has so far written."

B534   PRESCOTT, ORVILLE. "Books of The Times," New York *Times*,
September 19, 1958, p. 25.
Auchincloss "certainly disapproves of Michael's conduct
and of the false standards or lack of them that corrupt
him. But his disapproval is not brightened by wit or by
the clean cut of satire. It is not made eloquent by indignation."

B535   REES, GORONWY. "New Novels," *The Listener* (London), LX
(September 18, 1958), 435.
"*Venus in Sparta* is so well constructed, so economical
and so well written that it could hardly be read without
pleasure; all that might mar it is a lingering doubt whether
Mr. Auchincloss' characters, so carefully hand picked as it
were, really repay the great talent he expends upon them."

B536   REYNOLDS, JERRY. "Safari Through Emotions," Des Moines *Sunday
Register*, December 7, 1958, p. 21-G.
Brief descriptive review. The book is "an interesting
study in despair and infidelity (fogged somewhat by per-
turbing flashbacks)...."

B537   ROBINS, MICHAEL. "Skilled Tale of Silent Self-Murder," Chicago
Sun-Times, October 26, 1958, Sec. 3, p. 5.
"Aside from its somewhat unreal picture of Mexico and
its echo of D. H. Lawrence, 'Venus in Sparta' is a fascinating novel of a man frustrated by his assumed roles of success and manhood."

B538   ROUTLEY, ERIK. "Fiction," *British Weekly*, CXLII (September 18,
1958), 2.
Very brief descriptive review.

WORKS ABOUT

B539   S., R. Kansas City *Star*, October 25, 1958, p. 7.
        "This book is a fascinating study, though perhaps too brief. You wonder if any man's life can be dissected adequately in 280 pages.

B540   SNYDER, MARJORIE B. "Fiction Worthy of Note--Distinguished," Boston *Sunday Herald*, September 21, 1958, Sec. I, p. 7.
        "It all adds up to being the finest of Auchincloss novels, penetrating and utterly absorbing."

B541   STATON, RUTH J. "What Made One Citizen Run Wild," Roanoke *Times*, September 14, 1958, p. B-10.
        Descriptive review.

B542   SULLIVAN, RICHARD. "Tale of a Mixed Up Sinner," *Chicago Sunday Tribune Magazine of Books*, September 28, 1958, p. 7.
        Farish "remains a dimmed down character analyzed rather than rendered; and the novel he anxiously tries to dominate is--in terms of Auchincloss' total work to date--a disappointment."

B543   T., C. San Francisco *Chronicle*, October 19, 1958, *This World* Magazine, p. 22.
        "Louis Auchincloss writes so well that it is to be wished he had chosen as a hero a man for whom one could feel admiration or sympathy. Not that Michael Farish lacks reality. There is a little of Farish in us all."

B544   *Time*, LXXII (October 20, 1958), 110.
        Although Michael Farish "may be weak and a little foolish, a man fixed by his background and fleeced by his women," Auchincloss "pleads his case effectively" and "secures his own expanding niche in American letters."

B545   W., E. "Auchincloss Novel Reveals Man's Struggle With Self," New Haven *Register*, September 28, 1958, Magazine, p. 8.
        "It is unfortunate that Auchincloss chooses the flashback as his main technical tool: this technique coupled with his businessman hero makes the reader feel he has read this book several times before."

B546   WEEKS, EDWARD. *The Atlantic*, CCII (December 1958), 93-94.
        This novel is "the strongest, and...the most interesting" Auchincloss has written. Although Michael Farish's dilemma is not developed enough, the book "shows an advance in vigor and intensity in the work of a novelist who has always been and remains fastidious, perceptive, and intelligent."

Book Reviews-*Pursuit of the Prodigal*

B547   WISE, MARVIN. "The Overcivilized Man of Our Upper Echelons,"
        Dallas *Morning News*, October 19, 1958, Sec. 5, p. 9.
             Auchincloss's "picture of the overcivilized man of the
        upper echelons of our society is bleak and despairing. We
        may quarrel with Mr. Auchincloss's views but not with his
        vision."

Pursuit of the Prodigal

B548   "The Affluent Society," *Time*, LXXIV (September 14, 1959),
        108-110.
             Auchincloss "knows his forms and his upper-crust Long
        Islanders"; but, while Reese's predicament is real, "he
        himself is sometimes the sort of hero scissored by children
        from the backs of cereal boxes."

B549   "All This and Hell Besides," *Times Weekly Review* (London),
        March 17, 1960, p. 10.
             "At the beginning *Pursuit of the Prodigal* promises to be
        a witty and ironic study of atavism, but as it proceeds
        Mr. Auchincloss writes less incisively and seems to be ac-
        quiring new characters rather for their usefulness in the
        plot than for any real interest in them."

B550   BISCHOFF, BARBARA. "Good! Good! Good!" *Oregon Journal* (Port-
        land), September 6, 1959, p. 6.
             "This is good, good, good and also thrice exasperating."

B551   BROOKS, RAE. "Books in Brief," *Harper's Magazine*, CCXIX
        (November 1959), 114.
             "The book gleams with style and polish, and the intelli-
        gence that went into its making is everywhere evident."

B552   BROWN, EARLE. Washington (D.C.) *Post*, December 6, 1959, p. E7.
             Brief review: "a fine new novel."

B553   BROWN, LOUISE FIELDING. *Book-of-the-Month Club News*,
        September 1959, pp. 11-12.
             "Serious topics can often be treated best by a liberal
        application of irony and satire, and the enlargement of
        Mr. Auchincloss' talent in this direction makes for lively
        reading."

B554   BRYDEN, RONALD. "Childe Colin," *The Spectator*, CCIV
        (March 4, 1960), 329.
             "Louis Auchincloss's novels are what good *New Yorker*
        stories would become if they grew up...." But Auchincloss's
        "brilliant parochialism" irks this reviewer "slightly" this
        time.

WORKS ABOUT

B555   BURNETTE, FRANCES. *Library Journal*, LXXXIV
        (September 1, 1959), 2518.
                Brief review. Although "characterization is weak [Amos
        Levine is "the only really convincing character in the
        book"], the author's accomplished narrative style makes it
        an absorbing story."

B556   CAMPBELL, PRISCILLA T. "A Man of Principle," Worcester *Tele-*
        gram, September 13, 1959, Sec. B, p. 9.
                The novel is "fascinating but baffling." "Is Reese's
        surrender meant to indicate a hauling down of his flag in
        deference to his love for his wife? Or has he decided that
        it is 'realistic' and 'adult' to lower his standards to
        those of his wife and business partner? Or has he just
        plain given up?"

B557   CHAPIN, VICTOR. "The Integrity of Love," *New Leader*, XLIII
        (June 27, 1960), 27-28.
                This is Auchincloss's "best" novel because "he has a-
        chieved a balance and perspective that gives his familiar
        material a new vigor and spontaneity, and, best of all, a
        broader sympathy."

B558   DeMOTT, BENJAMIN. "Monge and Other Destinations," *Hudson Re-*
        view, XII (Winter 1959-60), 618-626 [623].
                In the first sixty pages of the book, Auchincloss
        "seemed about to bring off an extraordinary stunt, that of
        setting a brute--not a comedian, or a mere British Decent,
        but a thoroughly nasty man--down in the dull unsuspecting
        world just described.... But the stage proved to be a
        stage: the nasty hero dwindles into a stereotype (The Eth-
        ical Lawyer) and Auchincloss remains what he was--a writer
        close to the dead center of American novelistic competence.
        Like Cheever among others he is precise in his awareness of
        the location of those who presently long to go elsewhere
        and see visions, but unlike Cheever he does not finally
        possess the gift of intensifying dissatisfaction."

B559   ELLIOTT, GEORGE. "Real Gardens For Real Toads," *The Nation*,
        CLXXXIX (November 14, 1959), 345-350 [349-350].
                "Within the fictional comedy of manners," Auchincloss is
        "the best since the early Marquand." This novel "is nearly
        first-rate of its kind, though not quite," because "rather
        more often than is good for his book, Auchincloss relaxes
        into such shoddiness as spite against a character (especial-
        ly the protagonist's first wife) and a certain banality of
        style (especially in some of the social conversations)."

B560   "Family Favourites," *Times Literary Supplement* (London),
        March 18, 1960, p. 173.
            Although "one does not care what happens to Reese, be-
        cause the author is morally as confused about Reese as
        Reese is about himself," the novel "has great virtues."
        Auchincloss is "a fine technician. He manages his people,
        his settings and his action with a skill that appears ef-
        fortless." Esther is "a fascinating villainess"; but it is
        "the measure of his limitation at the present stage of his
        development that Esther is only a villainess and not a hero-
        ine."

B561   FINK, MICHAEL. "Well-Born Knight Who Rebels--Somewhat," Prov-
        idence *Sunday Journal*, September 20, 1959, p. W-16.
            "The tone of this novel comes through as sincere but
        naive. The plot, characters, and values are not exciting.
        If we are not to read about ourselves, and most of us are
        not Reese Parmelees, let us read about wonderful people with
        whom we can identify, not the kind that represents the
        American male as a compromise between dreary fact and drear-
        ier fancy."

B562   FLINT, R. W. "Fiction Chronicle," *Partisan Review*, XXVII
        (Spring 1960), 374-378 [375-377].
            Auchincloss is a "neglected novelist," perhaps because
        what he "lacks is a sufficient excuse for being a *novelist*
        at all." But he is "a remarkably fine satirist, affection-
        ate, observant, penetrating, but he lives only in his di-
        gressions...." There is "a gloomy anthracite good humor
        and independence in Auchincloss that justifies a much better
        reputation than he apparently has."

B563   FURBANK, P. N. "New Novels," *The Listener* (London), LXIII
        (March 17, 1960), 511.
            Auchincloss "seems to me a worthy minor successor of
        Henry James and Edith Wharton, and I enjoyed his new novel
        a great deal."

B564   GEISMAR, MAXWELL. "A New Social Environment," *New York Herald
        Tribune Book Review*, September 13, 1959, p. 8.
            This is "an entertaining, highly readable, good novel
        that is not without wisdom and conviction." But it "doesn't
        add up to the kind of serious literature which Mr. Auchin-
        closs' talent entitles him to--and holds him responsible
        for."

B565   GRIFFIN, DOROTHEA. "Witty Dissection of Upper Class Manners
        and Morals," Nashville *Banner*, September 18, 1959, p. 24.

A Bibliography of Writings By and About Louis Auchincloss

WORKS ABOUT

(GRIFFIN, DOROTHEA)
"There are some delightfully ironic passages which deal both with life at Parmelee Cove and with the artistic New York fringe set, but Reese, as a person, often eludes the reader."

B566 HASKIN, WAYNE. "The Wealthy Beatnik," Houston *Post*, January 17, 1960, *Houston Now* Magazine, p. 33.
This novel could not have prompted the high praise of Auchincloss as "one of our very best young novelists."

B567 HOWE, MARJORIE. "New Books," Burlington (Vt.) *Free Press*, September 2, 1959, p. 13.
"This is a fine, mature novel with rich character portrayals."

B568 HUGHES, RILEY. *Catholic World*, CXC (January 1960), 253.
Brief descriptive review.

B569 JANEWAY, ELIZABETH. "Rich Boy Meets Girl," *New York Times Book Review*, September 13, 1959, pp. 4, 46.
"I do wish Mr. Auchincloss would take his interest and understanding of people into a milieu that would not make him feel obliged to surround them with a world he seems to believe his readers expect. I think a new, stranger world might quicken the sharp observation he commands. It might even persuade him to let his characters flower into complete, absorbing liveliness."

B570 JORDAN, JENICE. "Nothing Seems to Suit Him," Columbus (Ohio) *Dispatch*, October 18, 1959, TAB Section, p. 10.
Auchincloss's "plot is ironically revealing of human nature so it's a pretty good book."

B571 KEOWN, ERIC. "New Fiction," *Punch* (London), CCXXXVIII (March 16, 1960), 399.
"This novel has a professional skill and finish that puts it far above the common run."

B572 KIRSCH, ROBERT R. "The Book Report—The Story of a Wealthy Rebel," Los Angeles *Times*, September 24, 1959, Part III, p. 5.
"Despite the sense of disappointment at the end, Auchincloss is skilled enough as a storyteller to retain page-to-page interest. The weak ending is more a betrayal of his main character than a failure of talent. It is almost as though Reese Parmelee overwhelmed his creator and, in punishment, the author imposed his will upon the fictional man."

Book Reviews-*Pursuit of the Prodigal*

B573   KOCH, LEWIS Z.   "Auchincloss Novel Is a Well-Made Rarity,"
       Chicago *Sun-Times,* September 20, 1959, Sec. 3, p. 4.
       "The author deserves high praise for giving us a novel
       that is at all times penetrating, interesting and consist-
       ently well written."

B574   MOONEY, HARRY, JR.   "Author Does It Again, But It's Much the
       Same," Pittsburgh *Press,* September 13, 1959, Sec. 6, p. 7.
       The "central difficulty" in the novel is the characteri-
       zation of Reese Parmelee: "Since he is shown in rebellion
       against a whole segment of society, he needs to be a con-
       siderably more powerful and interesting figure than Mr. Auch-
       incloss ever manages to make him." Auchincloss "remains an
       impressively gifted writer. But he needs to break new
       ground to win through to a deeper and more persuasive view
       of life."

B575   *New Yorker,* XXXV (November 7, 1959), 236-238.
       "Mr. Auchincloss's work is impressively authentic in de-
       tail and atmosphere, and his story--pale, smooth, and ex-
       pertly managed--holds one's interest from its disheartened
       beginning until its ending...."

B576   "Pursuit of One Who Fled From Woman's World," Buffalo *Evening
       News,* September 12, 1959, p. B-6.
       The "novel provides lively and colorful reading. Auch-
       incloss is perceptive and highly intelligent."

B577   "Quits World of Plenty to Fashion New Life," Cleveland *Plain
       Dealer,* September 27, 1959, p. 42-E.
       Brief UPI syndicated review. "The author gives the nu-
       merous problems besetting such a busy life some penetrating
       attention although there seem to be some unmotivated acti-
       vities. But maybe that's life."

B578   RICHARDSON, MAURICE.   "New Novels," *New Statesman,* LIX
       (March 12, 1960), 374.
       "Nicely written as ever with some entertaining social
       scenes, this is yet rather far from Mr. Auchincloss's best
       book."

B579   ROGERS, W. G.   "The Bookshelf--An Honest Lawyer and His
       Shackles," New York *World-Telegram and Sun,*
       September 11, 1959, p. 27. Also Charleston (S.C.) *News and
       Courier,* September 6, 1959, p. 9-C.
       "Auchincloss's novel is again marked by the most adept
       writing. No other novelist handles the lawyer so well; no
       other handles this social stratum better."

A Bibliography of Writings By and About Louis Auchincloss

WORKS ABOUT

B580   ROLO, CHARLES. *The Atlantic*, CCIV (September 1959), 93-94.
        "Auchincloss' primary interests are those of the psycho-
        logical novelist rather than the social critic." He "has
        concerned himself largely with people whose conformity or
        non-conformity is a destructive compulsion." In this novel,
        his resolution of the plot seems "not in keeping with the
        book's insights. For the rest, the people and the settings
        are admirably drawn, and the story is engrossing."

B581   S., C. H. "No Villains, Heroes In Auchincloss Book," Durham
        (N.C.) *Herald*, October 25, 1959, p. 5D.
        Although the plot is "monotonous," Auchincloss "shows
        considerable writing skill."

B582   SCOTT, J. D. "A Page of New Fiction--How to Tame Rebels,"
        London *Sunday Times*, February 28, 1960, Magazine, p. 18.
        Auchincloss "is a novelist who possesses not only ele-
        gance and perception, but sufficient creative power to
        endow his characters with the unfathomable quality of true
        humanity; we believe in Reese because we don't quite un-
        derstand him." But this novel "is not quite successful;
        in the last resort Reese's fight seems something of a sham
        fight: there isn't really much difference, and from the
        point of view of dramatic effect there isn't *enough* differ-
        ence, between the Parmelee Cove people...and Reese him-
        self."

B583   SHERMAN, THOMAS B. "Reading and Writing--The Triangular Para-
        ble of Reese Parmelee," St. Louis *Sunday Post-Dispatch*,
        August 30, 1959, p. 4D.
        Descriptive review. Auchincloss "has given his theme
        an interesting modern setting and has exploited it with
        skill. As in all good stories the characters come alive."

B584   SNYDER, MARJORIE B. "Passion For Truth," Boston *Sunday Herald*,
        September 13, 1959, Sec. VI, p. 2.
        "It is a novel that may make you impatient with managing
        women and sympathetic with the men who are strong enough to
        stand on their own feet. One of Auchincloss' best."

B585   SULLIVAN, RICHARD. "A Heel in a Curiously Motivated Society,"
        Chicago Sunday Tribune Magazine of Books,
        September 20, 1959, p. 3.
        "Louis Auchincloss, as always, writes with precision and
        quiet authority."

B586   TILFORD, JOHN E., JR. "An Auchincloss Novel Rated at C-Plus,"
        Louisville *Courier-Journal*, September 20, 1959, Sec. 4,
        p. 7.

A Bibliography of Writings By and About Louis Auchincloss

(TILFORD, JOHN E., JR.)
Though Auchincloss "writes pretty well in a low-keyed way,...he contributes little distinction of style, wit or wisdom to his analysis of these subjects; and he scarcely makes his major characters seem very solid or their problems very significant."

B587 *Virginia Quarterly Review*, XXXVI (Winter 1960), x.
Brief review: a "pleasant book about sometimes unpleasant people."

B588 WEINBERGER, CASPAR WILLARD. "A Novel of Recognizable People," San Francisco *Sunday Chronicle*, September 27, 1959, *This World* Magazine, p. 20.
"There is little that is unpredictable in the story, but its chief merit lies in its very realistic depiction of some very real people and its records of their quite believable conversations."

B589 WILSON, SLOAN. "Parmelee's Contempt," *Saturday Review*, XLII (September 12, 1959), 25, 48.
"Mr. Auchincloss has the mind and the courage of a first-rate novelist. An examination of the body of his work gives the feeling that he is still growing. If he can rid himself of his aloofness to his characters, he will certainly graduate from being one of our very best young novelists, which he most certainly is, to just plain one of the best."

The House of Five Talents

B590 ARIMOND, CARROLL. *Extension* (Chicago), LV (December 1960), 22.
"*The House of Five Talents* is an excellent novel of admirable clarity considering its scope in time and intertwining of its characters. The story flows along chronologically with such depth and intimacy with a now nearly extinct social level that the reader is made to feel these are genuine, not fictional, recollections."

B591 "Bankbooks & Backgrounds," *Time*, LXXVI (September 12, 1960), 112, 114.
Auchincloss "seems unaware that his people are increasingly dull anachronisms. His careful, courtly prose almost manages to confer dignity, but in the end his novel is like the great Newport mansions it recalls--elaborately ornamented in its façade, too dry and dusty inside for a modern generation to bother about."

WORKS ABOUT

B592   BLAKESTON, OSWELL. "Lunacy and Sensibility," *Time and Tide*
        (London), XLII (February 10, 1961), 215.
             Brief mixed review. Auchincloss "can exploit the theatre
        of stock situations and add witty lines to create a solid
        enough entertainment for the reader without as much as a
        railroad to his name."

B593   BOROFF, DAVID. "Saga of the Silver Spoon Set," *Saturday Re-
        view*, XLIII (September 10, 1960), 25.
             "Unillusioned though he is, Mr. Auchincloss takes the
        mystique of class quite seriously. This is the source of
        the novel's authenticity—and its weakness. For the per-
        sonalities on whose vagaries he dwells so lovingly are
        faintly absurd.... The prose is a model of urbanity and
        control. But, ultimately, Auchincloss is defeated by the
        very inanition he is describing."

B594   B[RADBURY], M[ALCOLM]. "New Fiction," *Punch* (London), CCXL
        (March 1, 1961), 369-370.
             The book is "very good" but Auchincloss too often "falls
        for the picturesqueness of the society" he satirizes; and,
        unlike in a James or Wharton novel, the morals do not matter
        so much and the moral victories are gained through chance
        rather than being planned.

B595   CHAMBERLAIN, JOHN. "Reading for Pleasure—Money's Impact,"
        Wall Street Journal, September 13, 1960, p. 18.
             Descriptive review. "As Louis Auchincloss realizes, it's
        the individual that counts.... Since character is basic,
        Mr. Auchincloss lets character spin the plot."

B596   CHANDLER, DAVID. *America*, CIV (October 1, 1960), 22-23.
             "The technique of a memoir is a large challenge to style,
        and Mr. Auchincloss has perhaps met the challenge too well.
        Perhaps he has fitted Augusta's mask too closely; the novel
        has the short-comings of a *grande dame*. Its intended cre-
        scendi, when Augusta faces injustice, are querulous; its re-
        pose is often opinionated and starchy. The book suffers
        from its narrator's regality."

B597   CHAPIN, VICTOR. "What the Rich Can't Buy," *New Leader*, XLIII
        (October 31, 1960), 24-25.
             "*The House of Five Talents* is a masterful novel and...
        just misses being a great one.... Perhaps it is because
        this novel stirs the intelligence but not the imagination.
        It is perceptive, instructive, amusing, revealing; but it
        moves us only briefly."

B598   CHARLES, GERDA. "New Novels," *New Statesman*, LXI
(February 3, 1961), 186-187.
"Witty, clear-eyed, just, examining but never cold,
Mr. Auchincloss shows us this world in depth, wrapped about
in a light, pure, warm understanding, like cashmere." The
one great "fault of this otherwise distinguished, subtle
book" is that "the elements of tragedy and height are missing as they are not for instance in James, however urbane
his tone."

B599   DeMOTT, BENJAMIN. "Fiction Chronicle," *Partisan Review*, XXVII
(Fall 1960), 748-754, 757-759 [751-753].
"Auchincloss has found a figure on whom to center his
affection, and as a consequence his book is at moments
touching, but he has not really risen above the somnambulant
middle consumer. His book is, in sum, a disappointment.
Its project of distinguishing the heroic past from the mea-
sly present...issues only in withered stereotypes.... And
of them all the spiky old maid of such promise turns out at
last to be chief."

B600   "The Difference Is Money," *Newsweek*, LVI (September 12, 1960),
104-105.
Although Auchincloss is "a good deal less subtle than the
labyrinthine James and less bleakly tragic than Wharton at
her best, he remains a social novelist of rare sophistication and potency."

B601   DOLBIER, MAURICE. "Daily Book Review--'The House of Five Talents,'" New York *Herald Tribune*, September 9, 1960, p. 19.
This is Auchincloss's "most ambitious novel." It is
also "a good novel, but in its opening pages it seemed to
promise to be more than that.... I suspect that Aunt Augusta, despite her most honest efforts at impartiality, is
too much a Millinder, and that her story and theirs might
have been more sharply and searchingly told by a non-Millin-
der, say, Mr. Auchincloss."

B602   DUNN, ESTHER CLOUDMAN. "Novel of a Family and a Great Fortune," *New York Herald Tribune Book Review*,
September 11, 1960, p. 5.
"Suffice it to say not only the major characters but the
secondary figures, the art critics, the interior decorators,
the thin, cigarette-smoking, predatory females, all come to
life in a line or two of mercilessly selected detail."

B603   FANE, VERNON. *The Sphere* (London), CCXLIV (February 4, 1961),
188.
"Here is a writer of really great style; he can, in one

A Bibliography of Writings By and About Louis Auchincloss

WORKS ABOUT

(FANE, VERNON)
economical phrase, point out the essence of a person's nature; and of fantastically acute perceptions, whether he is
writing about men or women."

B604   "Fascinating Chronicle," *Christian Century*, LXXVIII
(January 25, 1961), 117.
"This is a well written novel offering a fascinating
although ultimately depressing glimpse of the Fifth Avenue
and Newport side of American life."

B605   FITZGIBBON, WILLIAM C. "Books of The Times," New York *Times*,
September 10, 1960, p. 19.
This is "an excellent novel, an absorbing and enlighten-
ing exploration of its subject."

B606   GRIFFIN, LLOYD W. *Library Journal*, LXXXV (August 1960), 2810.
Brief favorable review: "a finished piece of work in
the James-Wharton-Marquand tradition."

B607   GRIGSON, GEOFFREY. "A Fly Like Thee," *The Spectator*, No. 6919
(February 3, 1961), 158.
Very brief review: "a neat, sentimental, sub-Galsworthi-
an smooth-over."

B608   HOWARD, ELIZABETH JANE. "An Ocean of Gold," *The Queen* (London), CCXVIII (February 15, 1961), 26, 30.
This is "a remarkable and fascinatingly readable novel"
which shows Auchincloss's "sure and acute sense of period."
It is "a brilliantly good book."

B609   JANEWAY, ELIZABETH. "Augusta Millinder Looks Backward," *New
York Times Book Review*, September 11, 1960, p. 5.
"Calmly, objectively, tolerantly," Auchincloss "explores
a world that may be past but is not alien.... By so doing
he gives us what we depend on good novels for--the chance
to understand our experiences through the lives of others,
to extend our ability to judge the world as we extend our
knowledge of it."

B610   *Kirkus*, XXVIII (July 1, 1960), 526.
"It is, all in all, more grandiose than the earlier Auchincloss novels and Miss Gussie lends her own dignity to that
of the era she represents and commemorates. But one is left
with the small suspicion that the best brahmins are not the
most interesting people."

A Bibliography of Writings By and About Louis Auchincloss

B611   KOCH, LEWIS Z. "View of the Rise and Fall of a Family," Chicago *Sun-Times*, October 9, 1960, Sec. 3, p. 5.
    "The characters in [Auchincloss's] last novel lived with deep crisis and emotion; these characters seem to be more surface, their emotions stilted." But "even with these drawbacks, the book is better than much of the current fiction."

B612   LISTER, RICHARD. "Aunt Gussie Really Made Her Money Work-But It Didn't Always Do Her Much Good," London *Evening Standard*, January 31, 1961, p. 17.
    Descriptive review. "Three generations of the family are revealed to us, not very deeply but very entertainingly...."

B613   MIZENER, ARTHUR. "Some Kinds of Modern Novel," *Sewanee Review*, LXIX (Winter 1961), 154-164 [158-159].
    "As with any novelist of manners,...[Auchincloss's] problem is to achieve depth of insight and range of judgment without going outside the limits of socially possible attitudes, and for this purpose Gussie Millinder is admirable."

B614   MORTIMER, PENELOPE. "Fiction of the Week--Not Tempted By Reality," London *Sunday Times*, January 29, 1961, Magazine, p. 27.
    "This is not a novel. It's an affliction. The only question which I would like answered is--in heaven's name, *why?*"

B615   "New Novels: The Indomitable Irishry," *The Scotsman* (Edinburgh), February 4, 1961, Magazine, p. 4.
    Descriptive favorable review. "The story of a family, brilliantly told, this is also an account of a long and intricate chapter of American social history."

B616   *New Yorker*, XXXVI (November 26, 1960), 237-238.
    Brief descriptive review: "a consistently entertaining family chronicle."

B617   O'BRIEN, E. D. "A Literary Lounger," *Illustrated London News*, CCXXXVIII (February 18, 1961), 280.
    "I was much impressed with *The House of Five Talents*.... Mr. Auchincloss is a really accomplished writer."

B618   PAULDING, GOUVERNEUR. "The Four Hundred," *The Reporter*, XXIII (September 15, 1960), 55.
    This "is not merely a pleasant exercise in nostalgia and a parade of New York and Newport pageantry but also stands as a novel of character."

A Bibliography of Writings By and About Louis Auchincloss

B619   PHELPS, GILBERT. "Toujours Tristesse," *John O'London's* (London), IV (February 16, 1961), 181.
        Auchincloss is "a distinctive and original novelist" and the characterization of Aunt Gussie "*nearly* achieves greatness"; but "the book lacks that juxtaposition of 'pity and terror' leading to a 'purgation' of the emotions which Aristotle laid down as the mark of true tragedy."

B620   PHINNEY, ALLISON W., JR. *Christian Science Monitor,* September 8, 1960, p. 11.
        Auchincloss "is a highly talented writer. His style is literate and flowing. He is at his best with bright, illuminating metaphors and similes. Best of all, he shows a great capacity for self-knowledge and growth. Parts of this work certainly fulfill critics' earlier expectations that he would tend to close the gap with such novelists as Marquand and Wharton." But "there is still a maturing of purpose to come" because Auchincloss is "still slightly aloof."

B621   PICKREL, PAUL. "Old Lady's Home," *Harper's Magazine,* CCXXI (October 1960), 102, 104.
        This book is Auchincloss's "most successful so far." He has "tried less for dramatic effect in this than in some of his books" and "he is at his best not so much when he is trying for the big scenes as when his work is more essayistic."

B622   PONT, MANARD. "Auchincloss' Latest Entry In the Literary Arena Is a First-Stringer," San Francisco *Sunday Chronicle,* September 18, 1960, *This World* Magazine, p. 22.
        This "is a brilliant, crystal portrait of a frustrated, confused and insecure woman whose only avenue of expression is meddling--with uniformly unhappy results--into the lives of her relatives."

B623   REDMAN, BEN RAY. "The Bookshelf--The Impact of Riches on Five Generations," New York *World-Telegram and Sun,* September 12, 1960, p. 21.
        Descriptive review.

B624   SHRAPNEL, NORMAN. "The Cream of the Mink," Manchester (England) *Guardian,* February 3, 1961, p. 6.
        Auchincloss has achieved what many American writers attempt but few succeed at--"the big dynastic novel"--because he has brought to the task "a special sort of curiosity, a mixture of intelligence and devotion and controlled ruthlessness."

B625   SULLIVAN, RICHARD. "Tight, Richly Textured Story of 4 Generations of Wealth," *Chicago Sunday Tribune Magazine of Books*,
September 11, 1960, p. 3.
      This novel looks "like the final culmination, to date,
of its author's considerable powers." Each major character
is "a memorable portrait" and the writing is "always graceful, precise, and beautifully controlled."

B626   "Unquiet Americans," *Times Literary Supplement* (London),
February 10, 1961, p. 94.
      "As a tribute to a whole epoch of American life it is
fitting enough, but as a dissection of a fascinating world,
it is too loose, too passive, too self-important."

B627   *Virginia Quarterly Review*, XXXVII (Winter 1961), viii.
      Brief review. "It is a good novel which carries the
reader along with interest and absorption."

B628   WALKER, GERALD. "The Not-So-Idle Rich," *Cosmopolitan*, XLIX
(September 1960), 27.
      "This is literature at its highest, most serious level,
which is both illuminating and amusing as it examines a
very special slice of high-life.... It is possible that
Mr. Auchincloss is unmatched by any American writer in his
brilliance of phrasing and in his ability to sum up a character in a deft, succinct sentence or two."

B629   WEEKS, EDWARD. "A Story of a Fortune," *The Atlantic*, CCVI
(December 1960), 114, 116.
      This is Auchincloss's best novel and he is best in it
"with the women." The "heart of the story" is "the exuber-
ant and decorative first half."

B630   WYNDHAM, FRANCIS. "New Novels--A Family and a Fortune," *The
Observer* (London), January 29, 1961, p. 29.
      Descriptive favorable review.

Reflections of a Jacobite

B631   BROTHERS, S. C. "At James' Shoulder," Houston *Post*,
April 30, 1961, *Houston Now* Magazine, p. 37.
      Descriptive review.

B632   BURGESS, CHARLES E. "James Is His Guidepost To Novel of Manners," Peoria (Ill.) *Journal Star*, May 20, 1961, *Weekender*
Magazine, p. B-6.
      Auchincloss's essays, "thoroughly readable, are an ad-
mirable guide for the student of social literature."

A Bibliography of Writings By and About Louis Auchincloss

WORKS ABOUT

B633   CHASE, MARY ELLEN. "Writing and Writers In a Jamesian Disciple's View," *New York Herald Tribune Book Review*, April 23, 1961, p. 29.
     "I haven't enjoyed so keenly any reflections on the novel since E. M. Forster's irreplaceable *Aspects of the Novel*." Auchincloss's "most marked service...lies in the advice given in his final chapter on the best way to read Henry James himself."

B634   F., H. Columbus (Ohio) *Dispatch*, May 14, 1961, TAB Section, p. 13.
     Brief descriptive review. The essays are "readable."

B635   FECHER, CHARLES A. "New Books in Review--Studies of the 'Novel of Manners,'" Baltimore *Evening Sun*, May 5, 1961, p. 28.
     This is "an admirable job.... As a rule, creative writers do not make outstanding critics, but [Auchincloss] is certainly an exception."

B636   "For Browsing," *Times Weekly Review* (London) April 12, 1962, p. 10.
     Brief review. Auchincloss is "forthright and stimulating when necessary; his merit is that he likes most of what he writes about."

B637   GRAY, JAMES. "Storyteller's Guidebook," *Saturday Review*, XLIV (June 3, 1961), 38.
     "Auchincloss writes with the quiet enthusiasm of a person who has never even heard the dismal cliché that the critical faculty kills the creative, or its even more obtuse counterpart that the creative impulse stands in sullen fear of the critical."

B638   H., A. F. "Some Opinions on Novelists," New Haven *Register*, July 9, 1961, Magazine, p. 9.
     "Probably few scholars will disagree with the opinions expressed in these thirteen essays and all should enjoy the charming, witty discourses based on an intimate knowledge of the subjects' works and lives."

B639   INGLESBY, EDITH. "Novel of Manners Analyzed From Thackery [*sic*.] to O'Hara," Savannah *Morning News*, May 14, 1961, Magazine, p. 12.
     Auchincloss "is never pontifical. He does not overwhelm one with analysis of technique; but his essays are penetrating, clear and always engaging.... he has done the reading public a very good turn."

Book Reviews-*Reflections of a Jacobite*

B640   *Kirkus*, XXIV (February 15, 1961), 188.
        "It is not, and not intended to be, a broad critical
        survey--but its wit, ease, ability to convey personal in-
        terpretations remind us that Mr. Auchincloss is cultured,
        intelligent, thoughtful, well-read."

B641   LIBAIRE, BEATRICE B. *Library Journal*, LXXXVI (April 15, 1961),
        1595.
        Brief review. "These pieces will be enjoyed by those
        already familiar with the writers discussed, but the art-
        fully simple style and the enjoyment of reading they so
        clearly express will surely lead new readers to discover
        for themselves the pleasure awaiting them in books they
        have overlooked."

B642   LID, RICHARD W. "Two Obsessed, 19th Century Novelists--And a
        Literary Tour," San Francisco *Sunday Chronicle*,
        June 18, 1961, *This World* Magazine, p. 25.
        Auchincloss is "at his shrewdest" with O'Hara and Mar-
        quand, and this is "a volume of good essays."

B643   McLAREN, MORAY. "No Pretender He," *The Tablet* (London),
        CCXVI (April 7, 1962), 331.
        "An engaging and civilised book."

B644   "Middleman," *The Economist* (London), CCII (March 31, 1962),
        1223.
        "It is a book worth reading, as good reviews and still
        more retrospective articles are worth reading. There is
        nothing remarkably original in it, but there are fresh com-
        binations of ideas, and it turns one back to the authors
        about whom he writes."

B645   MILLER, PERRY. "Around the Orb of James," *Christian Science
        Monitor*, May 25, 1961, p. 7.
        Auchincloss's "collection of essays should be catalogued
        as a picture gallery designed to set the stage for an inter-
        view with Mr. James." Auchincloss "has the frankness that
        comes from assured position, along with the easy skepticism
        of an aristocrat who distrusts all aristocracies."

B646   MORTIMER, RAYMOND. "Manhattan Master," London *Sunday Times*,
        March 18, 1962, Magazine, p. 30.
        "Relishing Mr. Auchincloss's accomplishment in fiction...,
        I welcome his first venture into criticism. The economy so
        admirable in his previous works was carried too far in his
        last novel...and I now similarly wish that he had made each
        of these essays twice as long. This complaint is also, of
        course, a tribute to the interest of his opinions."

A Bibliography of Writings By and About Louis Auchincloss

WORKS ABOUT

B647   O'BRIEN, E. D. "A Literary Lounger," *Illustrated London News*,
        CCXL (April 7, 1962), 556.
            Very brief descriptive review: particular praise for the
        Trollope chapter.

B648   PITNEY, JULIE. "Have You Read?" Bernardsville (N.J.) *News*,
        May 25, 1961, Sec. 1, p. 7.
            "Mr. Auchincloss's critical essays are excellent. His
        candid appraisals will serve to whet the appetite of the
        tyro as well as to further enlighten those familiar with the
        social novelists discussed."

B649   PRICE, R. G. G. "The Ghost of Henry James," *Punch* (London),
        CCXLII (April 4, 1962), 551.
            Brief review. "The book is to be recommended less as a
        coherent body of critical doctrine than for the amateur vir-
        tues of zest, variety and freshness."

B650   REYNOLDS, J. F. "Reading for Fun," *Irish Times* (Dublin),
        March 24, 1962, p. 8.
            Auchincloss is praised for enjoying literature and ex-
        pressing that kind of appreciation in his book.

B651   ROLO, CHARLES. "The Creative Critic," *The Atlantic*, CCVII
        (May 1961), 102-103.
            Auchincloss's "pieces have the informal flavor of a live-
        ly *causerie*, and yet they come as close as the essay can to
        achieving the form of a story." The book is "the most at-
        tractive and discerning collection of literary essays that
        has come my way in quite some time."

B652   SMITH, GROVER. *South Atlantic Quarterly*, LXI (Spring 1962),
        288.
            Brief descriptive review.

B653   SPRING, HOWARD. "Some Reflections on Henry James," *Country
        Life* (London), CXXXI (April 5, 1962), 801.
            "It is good talk about books--the sort of undidactic but
        illuminating talk that could pass between friends. So dif-
        ferent from the talk of critics laying down the law about an
        art to which they have nothing of their own to contribute."

B654   STEVENSON, DAVID L. "A Mannered World," *New York Times Book
        Review*, May 14, 1961, pp. 4-5, 16.
            The reviewer objects to Auchincloss's great praise for
        the novel of manners and to his insistence that it is,
        "someway, the truly correct novel." For a reaction to this
        review, see Edel (B30); and also Stevenson's rejoinder (B89).

A Bibliography of Writings By and About Louis Auchincloss

B655　TOYNBEE, PHILIP. "Whimsical Bookman," *The Observer* (London),
March 18, 1962, p. 29.
Auchincloss's tone is often too "cheery and familiar"
and he is "too imprecise, too genial, too unimpassioned."
These criticisms do not negate the fact that "the general
merit" of Auchincloss "is that he approaches novels of the
past with a novelist's mind and eye."

B656　"Two American Causeurs," *Times Literary Supplement* (London),
May 4, 1962, p. 318.
Descriptive review. "Naturally enough, Mr. Auchincloss's
best remarks are struck from him by writers he admires."

B657　VAN DER KROEF, J. M. "Opinions on Viewers of Foibles," Bridgeport *Sunday Post,* August 13, 1961, Sec. C, p. 5.
Descriptive mixed review.

B658　*Virginia Quarterly Review,* XXXVII (Autumn 1961), cxxiv, cxxvi.
Very brief review. "This is a stimulating book which
deserves a wide audience."

Edith Wharton

B659　HICKS, GRANVILLE. "Literary Horizons--The Newest Pamphlet-
eers," *Saturday Review,* XLIV (November 11, 1961), 23.
"Auchincloss is cool and detached, sometimes amused but
never unkind. The adroitness of his portrayal adds further
distinction to an excellent piece of work." In this instance, "the right critic has found both the right subject
and the right form."

B660　RUSSELL, H. K. *South Atlantic Quarterly,* LXI (Autumn 1962),
543.
Very brief review. Auchincloss's "comment on 'the flavor
of a historical novel' in the novel of manners is useful beyond his immediate subject."

B661　WALTON, GEOFFREY. *Modern Language Review,* LXI (April 1966),
302.
"Despite waste of space on personal details which are not
made relevant, the pamphlet is a pleasant piece of populari-
zation and one hopes that it will contribute to the rehabil-
itation of a great writer."

A Bibliography of Writings By and About Louis Auchincloss

WORKS ABOUT

Portrait in Brownstone

B662   ADAMS, THEODORE F.   "Brownstone Era: Auchincloss Traces Growth
        of Old New York Family," Richmond (Va.) *News Leader*,
        July 18, 1962, p. 9.
        Descriptive review.

B663   ASHBOLT, ALLAN.   "Patrician Look at Upper Crust Life in Ameri-
        ca," Sydney (Australia) *Morning Herald*, December 29, 1962,
        p. 11.
        Auchincloss "is getting beyond the point where he can
        safely be called a minor novelist." This novel "has the
        trappings of melodrama and backstairs gossip, and often
        enough it would appear that he sees it only in those terms.
        But the fact that he is writing about these people as an
        insider gives the novel a certain strength and authentic-
        ity."

B664   ASWELL, MARY LOUISE.   "Brownstone Society," *The New Mexican*
        (Santa Fe), July 29, 1962, *Pasatiempo* Magazine, p. 12.
        "The older members of the Denison clan could play their
        part in 'The Age of Innocence,' though compared to Mrs.
        Wharton's dramatis personae they remain puppet figures.
        The younger members, however anachronistic they may seem in
        this age of the atom, show their descent not only genealog-
        ically but stylistically. And that is no mean accomplish-
        ment."

B665   ATWOOD, LOIS D.   "Maybe He Dislikes People?" Providence *Sun-
        day Journal*, July 22, 1962, p. W-16.
        "Essentially the problem may be that Auchincloss, like
        many of his characters, does not like human beings. To
        write serious satire this is not necessary. But to write
        entertaining novels I am beginning to be convinced that it
        is necessary."

B666   BARKHAM, JOHN.   "Novelist of NYC," Houston *Post*, July 22, 1962,
        Houston Now Magazine, p. 31. Also Newport News (Va.) *Daily
        Press*, July 22, 1962.
        Auchincloss "is a studied stylist, pondering his moves
        and documenting them in scenes that are securely underpinned
        before the curtain is raised. The viewpoints change without
        disturbing the narrative flow. The prose is always cool,
        detached, unemotional. The sentences are neatly balanced,
        the metaphors always apposite."

B667   BARRETT, WILLIAM.   "Once Affluent Society," *The Atlantic*, CCX
        (August 1962), 142-143.
        This is "one of the best studies of the older and more

114

(BARRETT, WILLIAM)
affluent society of New York," although Auchincloss makes
the Denisons much more interesting than the Hartleys.

B668   BASS, IMOGENE. "Family Feuds, Loves, Money," Tulsa *Sunday World*, September 9, 1962, *Your World* Magazine, p. 14.
"The portrait of the Denison family is not always a
pretty sight but, in perspective, it is fascinating."

B669   BOND, ALICE DIXON. "New Novel Has Authority, Validity," Boston
Sunday Herald, July 15, 1962, Sec. IV, p. 7.
Auchincloss "has given us not only a finely wrought and
polished book but a meaningful one as well as it examines
the power of tradition, training and family solidarity
pitted against the fluidity of a changing society and does
so in intimate, human, and interesting terms."

B670   BRADBURY, ANNE. "Brownstone Saga," Seattle *Post-Intelligencer*,
August 25, 1962, p. 8.
Brief review. The book is "superbly written."

B671   BRADY, CHARLES A. "Worthy Saga Offers Study in Varieties of
Human Conduct," Buffalo *Evening News*, July 7, 1962, p. B-8.
The book is a "thoroughly satisfying family saga" which
is "very likely" Auchincloss's "best book to date and may
well be remembered as its author's 'Age of Innocence.'"

B672   B[UCHAN], B[LISS] S. "Family Saga," New Orleans *Times Picayune*, August 12, 1962, Sec. 3, p. 18.
The book "is pleasant to read for its style alone. Its
characters are not really very interesting or convincing,
however, and one is left with the impression that Auchincloss had nothing very demanding to say when he wrote this
novel."

B673   BURGESS, ANTHONY. "New Fiction--American Dream-Boats," *The
Observer* (London), September 23, 1962, p. 25.
"Whether we like it or not, this most accomplished novel
presents the real twentieth-century world, very sharply,
very subtly, very elegantly."

B674   BURGESS, CHARLES E. "'Drammer' Lurks Behind Brownstone Fronts
In Novel By Auchincloss," Peoria (Ill.) *Journal Star*,
August 18, 1962, *Weekender* Magazine, p. C-10.
Auchincloss "seems to have taken as his fictional task
the portrayal" of the New York social community. "He does
it well, and makes of it as valid and worthwhile a cycle as
O'Hara's of Pennsylvania, Marquand's of Boston or Faulkner's
of Jefferson...."

A Bibliography of Writings By and About Louis Auchincloss

WORKS ABOUT

B675   BUTCHER, FANNY. "The Warmth of Family Traditions From Child-
        hood to Middle Age," *Chicago Sunday Tribune Magazine of
        Books*, July 15, 1962, p. 3.
            When this novel "is good it is very good. The author
        has a sensitive eye for human foibles, a sensitive ear for
        conversation, and a sensitive mind that ferrets out human
        emotions." If it "were more technically cohesive, it would
        be a fine novel instead of just a good one."

B676   CAIN, LILLIAN PIKE. "Is It Another Best Seller?" Worcester
        Sunday Telegram, July 15, 1962, p. 12 E.
            "This novel might be compared to a Picasso portrait in
        which one object is seen from several sides. Each section
        adds a colorful and distinctive touch to the final compo-
        site picture. The book...will be widely known and dis-
        cussed."

B677   CHASE, ILKA. "Books--The Ida Denison Saga," *Cosmopolitan*,
        CLIII (August 1962), 16.
            "Whether by design or oversight, Mr. Auchincloss has
        stinted on his background. The actual setting of New York
        City is weak, and the events might just as well be taking
        place in St. Louis, San Francisco or Philadelphia. But this
        is a small reservation."

B678   *Christian Century* LXXIX (October 17, 1962), 1266.
            Descriptive brief review: a "competently written novel."

B679   *Christian Science Monitor*, November 29, 1962, p. 7B.
            Brief review. "For readers who can overlook the sugges-
        tiveness and vulgarity of certain parts of this novel, it
        elsewhere offers brilliant atmosphere....with a sort of
        fond musing on the interplay of family character and maneu-
        verings for positions of personal and financial ascendancy."

B680   CLARKE, MARION TURNER. "New Books in Review--Four Recent Nov-
        els," Baltimore *Evening Sun*, July 30, 1962, p. A 16.
            "Not only has the setting authenticity and charm, but
        Mr. Auchincloss's ability to turn a phrase makes the book
        delightful reading."

B681   COFFIN, EMILY. "New York's Society Is Subject of Study,"
        Savannah *Morning News*, August 26, 1962, Magazine, p. 8.
            Auchincloss's "style continues to be masterful. But in
        this instance the story is not very interesting because it
        has been told so often, and the characters behave in such
        stereotyped fashion that the unraveling of the plot seems to
        go on forever."

B682   COOK, BRUCE A. "Ghostly Voices Haunt This Author," Chicago
       Sun-Times, July 29, 1962, Sec. 3, p. 3.
           "It is tempting to read this novel of Ida Trask's strug-
       gle against the Denisons as a dramatization of the author's
       own struggle against the domination of James and Wharton.
       I'm pulling for Auchincloss."

B683   CORDDRY, MARY. "Life Among the Rich," Baltimore *Sun*,
       July 22, 1962, Sec. A, p. 5.
           Descriptive review. "A perceptive and able writer has
       selected a group of divergent personalities, confined them
       for life to the same limited society, and produced a com-
       fortable blend of depth and entertainment."

B684   CORMIER, ROBERT. *The Sign*, XLII (November]962), 64.
           This is "an old-fashioned novel in the best sense of the
       word, an unhurried, wise, and often witty story." Auchin-
       closs "is the logical successor to John P. Marquand, if not
       already his master."

B685   COURNOS, JOHN. "Nothing to Cry Over--Auchincloss Explores
       Self-Imposed Trials of Old N.Y. Society," Philadelphia
       Evening Bulletin, July 14, 1962, p. 6.
           "If Auchincloss is brilliant in portraying society of
       older days, he is less convincing in his attempts to realize
       the lower levels which today we lump under the term of
       'beatnik.'" Auchincloss "produces in his readers laughter,
       where James merely induced smiles. On the other hand,
       James did somehow manage to maintain his mirth in a low key
       from beginning to the end, while Auchincloss too often
       switches from laughter to realism, a genre in which he is
       by no means master."

B686   CROWNFIELD, MARGARET. "A Fine Novel: Ida and the Dennisons
       [*sic*.]," Greensboro (N.C.) *Daily News*, July 15, 1962,
       p. C3.
           This "is in no sense a moralizing book. Its tone is
       calm, objective and tolerant." It has "an unmistakably
       masculine strength, in spite of complete understanding of
       the feminine leading character."

B687   CRUTTWELL, PATRICK. "Fiction Chronicle," *Hudson Review*, XV
       (Winter 1962-63), 589-598 [594].
           Brief review. "This is good standard Auchincloss....
       This writer, you feel, really *knows* the people he writes
       about. Knows them, gets on well with them, but is quite
       independent enough to judge them: indeed, the picture he
       draws of intricate networks of selfishness and domination,
       deceptions and self-deceptions, is rather horrifying."

A Bibliography of Writings By and About Louis Auchincloss

WORKS ABOUT

B688   FASS, MARTIN. "Soap Opera Level Raised," Los Angeles *Times*,
         June 17, 1962, *Calendar* Magazine, p. 15.
              "This is a tastefully written popular novel, with a long
         look at wealthy women."

B689   FOOTE, IRVING F. "Generation in Middle Captures Concern," At-
         lanta *Journal and Constitution*, July 8, 1962, p. 8-D.
              Descriptive review.

B690   GARNER, EDWARD. "Brownstone Browsing," Raleigh *News and Ob-
         server*, February 10, 1963, Sec. III, p. 5.
              The novel "picks up a better pace, becomes more interest-
         ing, and holds the reader's interest" after Dorcas is born.

B691   GEORGI, CHARLOTTE. *Library Journal*, LXXXVII (June 15, 1962),
         2396.
              Brief review. Auchincloss "is undoubtedly one of the
         ablest current American exponents of the novel as a craft"
         and this book is "highly recommended."

B692   GRANT, WILLIAM A. "Pleasant Leisureliness," Louisville *Cour-
         ier-Journal*, July 8, 1962, Sec. 4, p. 7.
              "The story does not generate very much excitement, and
         its main characters become rather uncharacteristically
         Jamesian in the book's closing pages. But these are minor
         shortcomings in a novel where the author's attention is
         fixed not so much on a few individuals as on a shifting
         pattern of upper middle-class family relationships."

B693   GROSS, SHELLEY. "A Brownstone's Facade of Faces," San Francis-
         co *Examiner*, July 8, 1962, *Highlight* Magazine, p. 6.
              "Refreshingly stuffy, this is a novel to read while re-
         laxing on the beach. It offers relief from today's psycho-
         logical novel dripping with Freudianisms."

B694   GRUMBACH, DORIS. "Fiction Shelf," *The Critic*, XXI (August-
         September 1962), 66-67 [66].
              "I admire Mr. Auchincloss's narrative skill and his
         craftsmanship, the ease with which he moves back and forth
         in time without disturbing the eventual fabric of the sto-
         ry. It may be nineteenth-century in tone, but it's more
         satisfying than much this century has produced."

B695   HALL, BARBARA HODGE. "'A Quiet Book'--Life Flows On In Brown-
         stone," Anniston (Ala.) *Star*, August 26, 1962, p. 11B.
              This "is a quiet book, but a true-to-life book, and
         above all, the work of a most capable and accomplished
         writer."

B696 HICKS, GRANVILLE. "Literary Horizons--The Good Society of
      Stocks & Bonds," *Saturday Review*, XLV (July 14, 1962), 21,
      33. Reprinted in Hicks, *Literary Horizons* (B3).
         "What distinguishes the novel...is its subtlety. ...the
      insights of an Auchincloss have their importance for us.
      The questions he raises are not cataclysmic, but they are
      persistent."

B697 HOWE, MARJORIE. "New Books," Burlington (Vt.) *Free Press*,
      July 25, 1962, p. 13.
         "Again Auchincloss takes the people and the city he
      knows so well and makes them come alive before our eyes."

B698 HUSTON, McCREADY. "A N.Y. Galsworthy," San Francisco *Sunday
      Chronicle*, July 8, 1962, *This World* Magazine, p. 29.
         "Auchincloss is a study. He has mannerisms which some
      editors would strike and write 'Get with it,' on the margin.
      Yet one does not condemn them too quickly. The danger is
      he may be a fox, 'having us on,' tongue in cheek. Certain-
      ly he is here to stay."

B699 JANEWAY, ELIZABETH. "Ugly Duckling in a Gilded World," *New
      York Times Book Review*, July 15, 1962, pp. 1, 29.
         "Within his chosen limits, Mr. Auchincloss writes per-
      ceptively and most amusingly of the pleasantly ordered, if
      provincial, life of New York before the wars." He "has
      something important to tell us about what we have lost in
      losing a world where a sense of belonging could sustain the
      individual and where tradition and convention might limit
      one's possibilities, but could also give support and signi-
      ficance to the lonely and lost."

B700 JOHNSON, NORA. "They Had It Made," *New York Herald Tribune
      Books*, July 22, 1962, p. 6.
         This is "a modern Victorian novel": "Even the prose is
      cozy, and the conversation has a Victorian flavor that odd-
      ly hangs on into the scenes of 1950."

B701 *Kirkus*, XXX (May 1, 1962), 431.
         "The ironic implications aside, this is a poised and
      polished story which benefits greatly from its background.
      Auchincloss has reproduced it with authority without dimin-
      ishing its aura...."

B702 LERNER, LAURENCE. "New Novels," *The Listener* (London), LXVIII
      (October 4, 1962), 533-534 [534].
         The "distorted time scheme" is "highly inappropriate to
      this very conventional novel." Auchincloss "writes well

WORKS ABOUT

(LERNER, LAURENCE)
   because he manipulates the novelist's counters so well: he
   never explores. The language at the climaxes is always
   slightly melodramatic, and everything is predictable except
   when it is clearly trying to be unpredictable."

B703   LESLIE, ANDREW. "New Fiction--A Cold Eye on Life," Manchester
   (England) *Guardian*, September 28, 1962, p. 7.
      Brief review. The novel "is too perfunctory about its
   people to be among [Auchincloss's] best." Nevertheless, it
   is "stylish and interesting."

B704   McDONOUGH, JAMES P. *Best Sellers*, XXII (July 15, 1962),
   161-162.
      This novel "is in the tradition of the early Henry James
   with the same highly cultivated style and the same adept
   management of plot and character."

B705   MacMURRAY, ROSE. "The Craft of Fiction--Novels Defy Dog Days,"
   Washington (D.C.) *Post*, July 15, 1962, p. G7.
      "Much worldly wisdom and profound thinking has been dis-
   pensed via Mr. Auchincloss's skillful understatement. As
   always, he presents the admirable answer to the soap opera,
   with his civilized yarns for and about adults and their ex-
   pedient decisions."

B706   MORTON, ROBERT. "Books Roundup," *Show*, II (August 1962), 95.
      "Auchincloss has lost none of his skill at sketching the
   glittering surface of upper-class life, but his concern for
   his characters and the forces which shape them in the closed
   world of an elite society has deepened."

B707   MURRAY, JAMES G. "The Art of Reading--'Portrait in Brownstone,'" *Long Island Catholic* (Rockville Centre, N.Y.),
   August 2, 1962, p. 4.
      Although "no great book will ever come from material
   that seems somehow trivial" and Auchincloss's "own gifts
   are not quite up to making mountains out of molehills,"
   nonetheless this novel is "excellent in all its parts."

B708   "New Novels," *Times Weekly Review* (London), September 27, 1962,
   p. 13.
      Brief descriptive favorable review.

B709   *New Yorker*, XXXVIII (August 18, 1962), 97-98.
      Brief review. "It must be an accident that a writer as
   gifted as Mr. Auchincloss should have produced a book as
   uninteresting as this."

B710   O'LEARY, THEODORE M.   "The Good Old Brownstone Days," Kansas
        City *Star*, July 15, 1962, p. 12D.
            "The niche that Auchincloss occupies in the museum of
        contemporary literature may be off in a side room but, as
        any visitor to art galleries knows, some of the most pleas-
        ing and precious things aren't always in the main exhibi-
        tion area."

B711   OLYPHANT, WINIFRED R.   *Nevada State Journal* (Reno),
        September 16, 1962, p. 8.
            "'Portrait in Brownstone' is pleasant, well-mannered and
        has an easy style. It is a relief from the violence and sex
        emphasis of so much of current fiction."

B712   "Other New Novels," *Times Literary Supplement* (London),
        October 12, 1962, p. 797.
            Brief review. "If *Portrait in Brownstone* has the quali-
        ty of social history--albeit shot through with passion--it
        is thanks to the author's disarming skill. But there should
        be no mistaking the fact that his achievement is that of a
        creator not an annalist."

B713   PASLEY, VIRGINIA.   "The Recreation of an Era: A Family Saga,"
        Newsday (Garden City, N.Y.), July 14, 1962, p. 23.
            "The picture of life in a particular stratum of New York
        society from the turn of the century almost to the present
        is convincing and always interesting."

B714   PAULDING, GOUVERNEUR.   "A Constant Woman," *The Reporter*, XXVII
        (September 13, 1962), 44, 46.
            Descriptive favorable review. "The story of Ida is sim-
        ply the story, movingly retold, of the good woman of all
        times."

B715   PECKHAM, STANTON.   "A Vanishing Breed of New York," Denver
        Sunday Post, July 8, 1962, *Roundup* Magazine, p. 13.
            "This is not a great novel. It is, however, one that
        has qualities that might prove enduring as an understanding
        picture of a family way of life, a class of society, and an
        era of metropolitan living soon to be forgotten. As such,
        it just might be more of a literary accomplishment than to-
        day's readers may realize."

B716   PHINNEY, A. W.   "'Is It Splendid Drama? Or Is It Corn?'"
        Christian Science Monitor, July 12, 1962, p. 7.
            At its best, this novel contains "writing of balanced,
        graceful dignity," "some brilliant atmosphere"; but, at its
        worst, "there is opportunistic plotting" and "signs of
        haste, awkwardness, and apparent dallying with popular fa-
        vor."

A Bibliography of Writings By and About Louis Auchincloss

WORKS ABOUT

B717   PICKREL, PAUL. "The Changes That Time Brings," *Harper's Magazine*, CCXXV (August 1962), 91.
        This is "an accomplished piece of fiction, consistently entertaining and uniformly excellent in observation and style. Yet it is not as impressive an accomplishment as it ought to be or as it might have been. There is a promise of largeness in the novels of Auchincloss that they never quite achieve."

B718   PITNEY, JULIE. "Have You Read?" Bernardsville (N.J.) *News*, July 26, 1962, Sec. 2, p. 2.
        Descriptive review: "an interesting and well-written novel."

B719   "The Plot Thickens," *Newsweek*, LX (July 16, 1962), 82-83.
        Auchincloss's "character drawing runs toward the stereotype, so that the figures behind the brownstone often seem cut from cardboard. Furthermore, his dialogue becomes stilted and stagy, suggesting a Social Register soap opera."

B720   POORE, CHARLES. "Books of The Times," New York *Times*, July 10, 1962, p. 31. Also Omaha *World-Herald*, July 22, 1962.
        "Mr. Auchincloss tells his story with the precise tracing of family convolutions that might be appropriate to a will-settlement proceeding in court. There is no madness in this method. It gives qualities of surprise if not suspense to old wives' tales."

B721   PRICE, R. G. G. "New Fiction," *Punch* (London), CCXLIII (October 3, 1962), 504.
        Brief review. "These bankers and lawyers and their intelligent, underoccupied women are described interestingly and judged firmly but not unkindly and if somehow their troubles do not seem very urgent they do make elegant and enjoyable patterns."

B722   REID, MARGARET W. "Auchincloss Excells In Character Development," Wichita Falls (Texas) *Times*, July 8, 1962, Magazine, p. 4.
        Descriptive review: "a most absorbing novel."

B723   RICHARDSON, MAURICE. "Upper Crusts," *New Statesman*, LXIV (September 21, 1962), 370-371 [370].
        "The early 20th-century parts [of the novel] are the best, with some delightful reconstructions of rich life in New York before 1914"; but the book as a whole is not properly "knitted together despite all the weaving that goes on."

A Bibliography of Writings By and About Louis Auchincloss

B724 RIORDAN, HELEN. "'Portrait in Brownstone' Family Novel Praised," Fort Wayne *News-Sentinel*, July 14, 1962, p. 4.
Although the changing point of view is "one flaw in the writing of this novel" and is "disconcerting," Auchincloss writes "in such a way that the reader will feel himself to be a part of" the Denison family.

B725 S[MITH], B[LANCHE] H[IXON]. "Have You Read," Meriden (Conn.) *Record*, August 1, 1962, p. 7.
This is the best novel of the year so far and is "a fascinating story about interesting people expertly characterized, and all in beautiful and impeccable English."

B726 SMITH, RUTH. "A Feeling for Virtue," Orlando (Fla.) *Sentinel*, October 28, 1962, *Florida* Magazine, p. 27-E.
"It is the point of view of the author...which makes the ups and downs of this family so engrossing, for he knows his social background well, and can write of it without satire, with subtle nuances which reveal the personal relationships with authenticity and reality."

B727 STARKEY, MARION L. "New York's Marquand?" Boston *Sunday Globe*, July 15, 1962, p. A-72.
This is a "fine novel" and "an engrossing family history." Auchincloss "tells a story more swiftly, and perhaps with less intricate sociological detail than Marquand."

B728 STIX, FREDERICK W. "Honorable Ancestors Beget Weak Progeny," Cincinnati *Enquirer*, July 28, 1962, p. 6.
"Auchincloss is no stylist, but a pedestrian writer. The world in which he is interested can--as has been shown--be made to be of intense and of lasting interest but not unless a writer is willing or able to come to grips with characters who live, and move, and have their being."

B729 STOCKTON, ZENOBIA. "Auchincloss Writes of Family Life," Charleston (S.C.) *Evening Post*, August 17, 1962, p. 10-C.
"Excellently written as this book is, with good characterization, the reading of the book evokes a negative response."

B730 THAYER, HARRIET M. "A Family Ordained to Prosper," Milwaukee *Journal*, July 8, 1962, Part 5, p. 4.
"A novel can hardly succeed unless the reader feels concern for the characters, especially for the protagonist. Concern such as this must be based on affection, and affection on some admirable traits, of which cleverness is a minor one."

A Bibliography of Writings By and About Louis Auchincloss

WORKS ABOUT

B731   THORPE, DAY. "The Privileged Class in Brownstone," Washington
        (D.C.) *Sunday Star*, July 15, 1962, p. C-5.
            "The writing is fluid and easily readable; the outstand-
        ing talent of Mr. Auchincloss' is the creation of situations
        convincing in dialogue and impressive in their implication
        of the background and character of the participants."

B732   TOWNSEND, MARION. "A Portrait of an Age," Charlotte (N.C.)
        Observer, July 15, 1962, p. 7-D.
            Auchincloss is so aloof that "we sometimes do not care
        enough about the characters' trials and successes," but "at
        his best he is like James,...in his sensitive understanding
        of their relationships."

B733   *Virginia Quarterly Review*, XXXVIII (Autumn 1962), cv.
            Brief review. "Once begun, this tale from the workshop
        of a naturally gifted narrator is hard to put aside."

B734   VOGEL, CAROLINE M. "The Making of a Dowager," Hartford *Courant*,
        July 8, 1962, Magazine, p. 14.
            "The moral in this novel is to be found in the delinea-
        tion of character, the subtle observation and candid insight
        which strip the dullness from his conservative, ultra-re-
        spectable characters."

B735   WOODBERRY, CAROL A. El Paso *Herald-Post*, July 14, 1962,
        p. A-4.
            "As a story, 'Portrait in Brownstone' may have a personal
        application for few; but many will read it and become ab-
        sorbed by the craftsmanship of its author and his acute ob-
        servation of underlying truths."

Powers of Attorney

B736   ABRAHAMS, ROBERT D. *Temple Law Quarterly*, XXXVII (Spring 1964),
        365.
            "Read as literature, the 12 related stories which make up
        the book display the highest degree of writing talent. Un-
        fortunately, it seems to this reviewer the author lacks
        compassion for the people about whom he is writing.... For
        the sake of our profession, the writer hopes the picture is
        not accurate. For the sake of American Letters, he hopes
        Mr. Auchincloss will continue to create his superb prose."

B737   ADAMS, ROBERT. "Books," *Esquire*, LX (October 1963), 26, 30,
        32 [26].
            "Mr. Auchincloss tells a brisk, terse story in an unusu-
        ally flat style. But there's a curious, uncontrolled moral

(ADAMS, ROBERT)
  trouble in the atmosphere--caused, I think, by the fact that
  Mr. Auchincloss has picked up the short-story form pretty
  much where Somerset Maugham found and left it, i.e., with a
  set of easy moral calesthenics to do, and some limited rewards and punishments to be handed out at the end. His
  trouble is that the formula won't fit the circumstances."

B738 BARRETT, WILLIAM. "Well-Bred Jungle," *The Atlantic*, CCXII
    (September 1963), 125.
      "One of our most intelligent and adult novelists,
    Mr. Auchincloss succeeds by sheer substance rather than
    frills; and if at times he seems to be writing as stolidly
    and impassively as a lawyer making a brief, his material is
    good enough to carry the day."

B739 *Best Sellers*, XXIII (October 15, 1963), 261-262.
      Brief review. The stories "are expertly written and
    should please most readers."

B740 BONNER, RUTH. "Books In Town," Brattleboro (Vt.) *Daily Reform-
    er*, February 19, 1964, p. 4.
      "Mr. Auchincloss is thoroughly at home in the legal world
    of most of his book, and this is not surprising. But he is
    also aware of the undercurrents, the open secrets, the char-
    acters and the subtle quirks of attitude that one finds
    among older people in a summer resort town."

B741 BOYDEN, WILLIAM C. "Complexities of Life at Law," Chicago
    Sun-Times, August 18, 1963, Sec. 3, p. 2.
      This book "should be a must for all lawyers, particular-
    ly for those who have struggled with the complexities of a
    large law office. For the general reader the book is an
    amusing peek behind the curtain that shields the legal pro-
    fession from the vulgar curiosity of the masses."

B742 BROPHY, BRIGID. "A Sight of Intriguers," *New Statesman*, LXVI
    (October 25, 1963), 578-579 [578].
      "Occasionally Mr. Auchincloss approaches an expansive,
    Old School sentimentality about his Co., but he is always
    snatched back by his irony, which has a near-Maupassant
    edge."

B743 BUCKNER, SALLY. "Explorations in the Legal Jungle," Greens-
    boro (N.C.) *Daily News*, September 22, 1963, Sec. B, p. 3.
      "Actually, the form matters very little, since Auchin-
    closs is primarily interested in characterization rather
    than style. His writing is clear and straightforward; his

A Bibliography of Writings By and About Louis Auchincloss

WORKS ABOUT

(BUCKNER, SALLY)
portraits, on the other hand, are as complex as any honest study of human behavior must be."

B744 BURNS, WARREN. *Financial Analysis Journal*, XIX (November-December 1963), 111.
Brief favorable review: "relaxing reading."

B745 COOKE, ANNE. "Law Firm Setting of Stories," Washington (D.C.) *Sunday Star*, August 25, 1963, p. C-6.
Auchincloss's "style is straightforward, his character-drawing as naturalistic as fine color photography, and his sense of 'story line,' leading always to a convincing climax, unerring." Auchincloss's work is compared to de Maupassant's.

B746 ELIAS, VERONICA. "Victorian Spirit Infuses Tales of Law Firm on Wall Street," *The Daily Egyptian* (Southern Illinois University, Carbondale), February 19, 1964, p. 6.
"Throughout the book one finds touches of plausibility which promise to impart to the reader a basic perception of human nature, only to be immersed each time with accurate but painstakingly contrived dialogue and observations of character which are more laudable in their literacy than in their credibility."

B747 EYRICH, CLAIRE. "Attorney's Struggles Shown Inside and Outside the Law," Fort Worth *Star-Telegram*, September 1, 1963, Sec. 4, p. 10.
"The author's style is amiable and tolerant, but he never fails to drive home his legal point with a sureness which is both ingenious and fascinating."

B748 "Fiction--Wig and Pen," *Times Literary Supplement* (London), October 25, 1963, p. 868.
"The professional detail...is immaculately turned, the tone of voice engaging without ever seeming to solicit, the matter so often the curse of distinguished advocacy--never quite living up to the manner.... how one wishes the distinguished poker-face would crack occasionally to reveal just a hint of how much irony, indignation and social concern the client is actually paying for."

B749 FRIEDE, ELEANOR KASK. *Book-of-the-Month Club News*, August 1963, p. 10.
"This is a remarkably even collection: each story is more than competently written, and perfected in a gentlemanly manner at a leisurely pace. All are recommended to the connoisseur of the well-turned short story."

126

A Bibliography of Writings By and About Louis Auchincloss

B750   GEISMAR, MAXWELL. "Life at 65 Wall St.," *New York Times Book Review*, August 18, 1963, p. 4.
"Mr. Auchincloss is a good technician; he *believes* in the literary world he is creating; and he succeeds, at least momentarily, in casting his spell over us."

B751   GERMAIN, C. A. "Law Office Intrigue Makes Good Stories," Green Bay (Wis.) *Sunday Post-Crescent*, September 8, 1963, p. 17.
"An observant and gifted writer has compiled another book to be enjoyed."

B752   "Green Goods & Grey Men," *Time*, LXXXII (October 25, 1963), 112.
"Auchincloss works out a dozen neat but wholly unreal fictional theorems. They are good stories in the sense that the recognizable counters are moved to the appropriate squares." But, while it "may be sound law, it is fictional malpractice."

B753   GREGSON, LILLIAN. "Books 'n Stuff," *North DeKalb Record* (Chamblee, Ga.), August 29, 1963, p. 4.
Auchincloss "is so adroit a craftsman that his polished style combines ease and grace."

B754   H., W. "Law, Politics, Raw Ambition in Wall Street," Augusta (Ga.) *Chronicle*, November 24, 1963, p. 3-E.
"Even those who have no specific interest in the internal structure and struggles of the law firm will find the quality of human relations omnipresent and, liberally laced with questions of human values, the superb characterizations joining to create a very readable fictional work."

B755   HICKS, GRANVILLE. "Literary Horizons--Fiction Brief of a Law Factory," *Saturday Review*, XLVI (August 17, 1963), 15-16. Reprinted in Hicks, *Literary Horizons* (B3).
"Auchincloss is perhaps not so good a short story writer as he is a novelist, but he can tell an effective and engaging tale."

B756   HIGGINS, JUDITH. *Club Dial* (White Plains, N.Y.), XXXVIII (January 1964), 35, 38.
"If you like New York and appreciate a brief behind the scenes look at the Wall Street lawyers who are one-half corporation spokesmen, and one-half tax expert, you'll have trouble putting this one down on your night table."

B757   HOWE, MARJORIE. "New Books," Burlington (Vt.) *Free Press*, August 21, 1963, p. 13.

A BIBLIOGRAPHY OF WRITINGS BY AND ABOUT LOUIS AUCHINCLOSS

WORKS ABOUT

(HOWE, MARJORIE)
>Very brief favorable review: "an excellent group of related short stories."

B758   HOYT, ELIZABETH N. "The Old School," Cedar Rapids *Gazette*, October 6, 1963, p. 2C.
>"Mr. Auchincloss bows to no other author in the final analysis. He is his own man and a most admirable one at that. Sharply drawn characters, intriguing situations and, above all, splendid writing, make 'Powers of Attorney' a fine novel."

B759   HUBLER, RICHARD G. "Portrait of Attorney Slickly Drawn," Los Angeles *Times*, August 18, 1963, *Calendar* Magazine, p. 19.
>The book "seems a breather for" Auchincloss's "talents. It is surface stuff.... The very competence of the writing seems to tell against the author; the thin gruel of emotion is not enough to satisfy the reader."

B760   IGOE, W. J. "International Vaudeville," *The Tablet* (London), CCXVIII (April 11, 1964), 412.
>Brief favorable review. "The author is excellently entertaining."

B761   "Inside Wall Street," *Newsweek*, LXII (August 19, 1963), 82-83.
>"The reader of these tales will find that he has obtained an expert and piquant view of upper-crust lawyers, their clients, and, for that matter, their office help."

B762   LAVINE, SIGMUND A. "Lawyer With Short Stories," Worcester *Sunday Telegram*, August 18, 1963, p. 10 E.
>"While there is nothing profound about any of these accounts of office politics, legal battles plotted, won and lost, all of them make enjoyable reading."

B763   LODGE, DAVID. "Tropic of Boredom," *The Spectator*, CCXI (November 1, 1963), 567.
>"The predictability of Auchincloss's final endorsement of the Organization Men over the others is perhaps a little disturbing, but he usually contrives to give the former a scare, a paralysing moment of self-doubt. Technically, the stories are models of how to create a world with a minimum of fuss."

B764   LOSCHE, GEORGE F. *New Jersey State Bar Journal*, VII (Winter 1964), 1081, 1095.
>The book "reflects a faithful image of the innermost workings of the minds, feelings and actions of the people who constitute the large law offices of New York City."

A Bibliography of Writings By and About Louis Auchincloss

B765 MacFARLAND, PERRE. "New Looks at Doctors and Lawyers," Nashville *Banner*, September 6, 1963, p. 28.
Descriptive review.

B766 MACKELL, PETER R. D. "Wall Street Law Firm," Montreal *Gazette*, December 7, 1963, p. 30.
"It is a real, but limited, peek into a rather esoteric world. Mr. Auchincloss once more demonstrates the mastery with which he can dissect a tiny, and special, slice of society today."

B767 MARSHALL, PHILIP G. "Inspecting the Law Factory," Milwaukee *Journal*, August 11, 1963, Part 5, p. 4.
"Both lawyers and nonlawyers will like this book. The reviewer wonders though, whether women readers will like the female character delineations as well as he did."

B768 MURRAY, JAMES G. "The Art of Reading--No Summer Doldrums For Book Lovers," *Long Island Catholic* (Rockville Centre, N.Y.), August 15, 1963, p. 19.
The "little gimmicks" on which the stories hang "are altogether too neat, pat, and slick." Auchincloss "has too much talent and insight to have to stoop--and these stories stoop just a bit." Nonetheless, it is "an interesting collection by an underestimated writer of better than average ability."

B769 O'BRIEN, E. D. "A Literary Lounger," *Illustrated London News*, CCXLIII (November 9, 1963), 790.
"The result here, so far as the reader is concerned, is a collection of delicately malicious little stories which are most enjoyable--and a determination never to be so unfortunate as to require the services of an American lawyer."

B770 O'LEARY, THEODORE M. "What a Varied-Spectacle Life Can Be!" Kansas City *Star*, September 1, 1963, p. 12E.
"Auchincloss knows these people well and he is not much inclined to challenge their values although he is not above laughing a little at both them and those values."

B771 O'NEILL, JOHN. Atlanta *Journal and Constitution*, September 1, 1963, p. 12-D.
"Mr. Auchincloss writes knowledgeably of his situations with an ironic eye for lawyers' pretensions and a clear one for their sordidness, although usually with a sense of their ethical efforts. But as an old-time admirer of Ephraim Tutt and Perry Mason, I was disappointed."

WORKS ABOUT

B772   PAULDING, GOUVERNEUR. "The Mannerly Lawyer," *New York Herald Tribune Book Review*, August 18, 1963, p. 4.
        "It is clear that Mr. Auchincloss' sympathies lie with the stately and largely imaginary New York past but he is no antiquarian and these expert stories, like his novels, show his belief that the qualities he admires can live on in our times."

B773   PECKHAM, STANTON. "Polished Portraits From 65 Wall St.," Denver *Sunday Post*, August 25, 1963, *Roundup* Magazine, p. 12.
        "This is good polished fiction of a sort that is too rare in current writing, and it is good to see it back again."

B774   PHILLIPS, JERRY J. "Case For White in 'Grey' Zone," Chattanooga *Sunday Times*, September 29, 1963, p. 18.
        Auchincloss is an author "who is poignantly aware of the predomination of grey in all our values and who is passionately, if frustratedly, seeking to prove that at least a significant component of the grey is really white."

B775   PHINNEY, A. W. *Christian Science Monitor*, August 22, 1963, p. 11.
        "Perfectly right touches are strewn like so many interesting props through plots with different endings, accurate but contrived dialogue, and plausible but literary observations of character."

B776   PITNEY, JULIE. "Have You Read?" Bernardsville (N.J.) *News*, October 10, 1963, Sec. 2, p. 3.
        Auchincloss "has clearly combined his talents as lawyer and author and produced a highly readable collection of stories."

B777   POORE, CHARLES. "Books of The Times--Gentlemen Lawyers Out For a Fee," New York *Times*, August 15, 1963, p. 27.
        "'Powers of Attorney' is a mine of good stories and Mr. Auchincloss tells them well."

B778   PRESLAR, LLOYD. "Tales of Attorneys," Baltimore *Sun*, August 18, 1963, Sec. A, p. 5.
        Auchincloss is, "without challenge, the nation's best writer of light fiction about lawyers--uh, pardon, attorneys."

B779   PRICE, R. G. G. "New Fiction," *Punch* (London), CCXLV (November 6, 1963), 688.
        Brief review. The book "provides both sharp, lively entertainment and some implicit comment on the shift from

(PRICE, R. G. G.)
money as an object of personal acquisition and whim to money as the material for an elaborate game between the corporate trusts and the fiscal establishment."

B780　RIES, BERNARD. Washington (D.C.) *Post*, September 8, 1963, p. G9.
"One encounters here two disquieting notes not apparent in Auchincloss' earlier work--a curiously aseptic treatment of emotional passages that often leaves his characters bloodless, and a tendency to sound, at times, as floridly formal as a parody of a Victorian novel."

B781　R[OBINSON], O[LIVE] C. "Books and Authors," Lewiston (Me.) *Daily Sun*, August 22, 1963, p. 4.
Descriptive review.

B782　ROGERS, W. G. "The Bookshelf--A Sheaf of Stories By a Master Narrator," New York *World-Telegram and Sun*, August 15, 1963, p. 19. Also St. Petersburg (Fla.) *Times*, August 18, 1963, Leisure and Arts Section, p. 8.
Auchincloss "tells his stories with a quiet, unfailing assurance. You don't throw your hat in the air, but you doff it most respectfully."

B783　ROWLAND, STANLEY J., JR. "A Common Concern," *Christian Century*, LXXXI (March 4, 1964), 307-308 [308].
Brief review. "Auchincloss deftly employs the element of quiet surprise, and his writing frequently manifests incisive insights into character."

B784　SAVINO, GUY. "Lawyers Provide Stories," Newark (N.J.) *Sunday News*, August 4, 1963, Sec. 4, p. W12.
Too many of the stories are "laced" with "unbelievable stuff" and the "trivia of slick magazineship."

B785　SCHLESINGER, TOM. "In the Jungle of the Law," Norfolk *Virginian-Pilot*, December 8, 1963, p. B-6.
"The book is filled with intriguing stories about people as human beings, and the author tells them in a straightforward manner without flounce or fluster."

B786　SMITH, GOLDIE CAPERS. "Doors of a Law Firm Open Wide," Tulsa *Sunday World*, September 8, 1963, *Your World* Magazine, p. 13.
"The brevity of the sketches scarcely permits more than surface characterization, and the personalities that do emerge are not calculated to strengthen the reader's confidence in the profession of law...."

A Bibliography of Writings By and About Louis Auchincloss

WORKS ABOUT

B787   SMITH, MILES A.   "Salty Characters Turn Up in Book By Auchin-
       closs," Jackson (Tenn.) *Sun*, September 29, 1963, p. 1-C.
       Also Anniston (Ala.) *Star*, September 22, 1963.
              "The author knows his law so well that he guides you
       easily into the legal battlefields, without getting techni-
       cal. But he obviously knows people too, and it is the peo-
       ple you will remember."

B788   SNYDER, MARJORIE B.   "Legal Eagle's Dozen," Boston *Sunday Her-
       ald*, August 18, 1963, Sec. I, p. 2.
              Brief favorable descriptive review.

B789   SOMERVILLE, COL. D. S.   "With Finesse and Wit," Hartford *Cour-
       ant*, September 8, 1963, Magazine, p. 13.
              The "real merit" of the book is "the ability of a writer
       to bring to his work a profound understanding of human na-
       ture, to sense the fears and hopes and strengths and frail-
       ties of people and deftly to delineate them in word and ac-
       tion."

B790   SONNENSCHEIN, HUGO, JR.   "Some Legal Briefs," Detroit *Free
       Press*, September 1, 1963, Sec. B, p. 5. Also Toledo *Blade*,
       September 1, 1963, Sec. A, p. 17.
              "Noted as James became for his realistic treatment of
       characters, it may be doubted if his delineation surpassed
       that of Mr. Auchincloss; here are the identical skills of
       detachment and minute observation, suffused with a humor
       and tolerance which, while trenchant, are never tedious."

B791   S[PARROW], P[REP].   "Inner Workings of a N.Y. 'Law Factory,'"
       Fayetteville (N.C.) *Observer*, September 8, 1963, p. 3D.
              "Mr. Auchincloss here draws some interesting characteri-
       zations and presents a convincing picture of a big law firm
       that enjoys success, although its progress is hampered by
       individual weaknesses, greed, unbridled ambition and incom-
       petence."

B792   SPOERRI, JAMES F.   *American Bar Association Journal*, XLIX
       (October 1963), 1007.
              Auchincloss is "an accomplished novelist" and "a prac-
       ticing lawyer, with experience that enables him to depict
       the scene and the varied personalities with conviction and
       verisimilitude; indeed, the unlikelihood of some of the in-
       cidents is not realized until the reader escapes from the
       spell."

A Bibliography of Writings By and About Louis Auchincloss

B793   SULLIVAN, RICHARD. "Assorted Legal Adventures," *Chicago Sunday Tribune Magazine of Books*, August 18, 1963, p. 4.
        "It always is satisfying to read a story which is
        charged, between the lines, as it were, with authority.
        And authority of this kind--the tone of complete convic-
        tion--rises out of both skill and knowledge, out of both
        experience in managing words and close awareness of subject
        matter."

B794   TALBOT, VIRGIL. "Book of Short (and Legal) Stories Entertaining," *Northwest Arkansas Times* (Fayetteville),
September 27, 1963, p. 5.
        Descriptive review: "satisfying entertainment."

B795   WAGENKNECHT, ROBERT E. *Library Journal*, LXXXVIII
(September 1, 1963), 3099-3100.
        Brief review. "The best stories...are those which...
        explore the personality of a single character and often end
        with his having a completely new understanding of him-
        self.... Mr. Auchincloss is adept at presenting human be-
        ings with all their peculiarities and foibles in a most un-
        derstanding and sympathetic manner."

B796   WELLEJUS, ED. "Ed Wellejus' Bookshelf," Erie (Pa.) *Times-News*,
October 6, 1963, p. 11 E.
        Descriptive favorable review.

B797   WOODBERRY, CAROL A. El Paso *Herald-Post*, August 24, 1963,
p. A-4.
        "Written as it is with compassion, humor, and tolerance
        for the basic mixture of greed and integrity in human na-
        ture, this book will surely be yet another triumph for its
        author."

The Rector of Justin

B798   A[CKERMAN], J[OHN] H. "'The Rector of Justin' Impresses Reviewer," New Bedford (Mass.) *Standard-Times*, July 26, 1964,
p. 34.
        Descriptive favorable review: "a moving, beautifully-
        crafted, superbly-written novel."

B799   ADAMS, ROBERT M. "Saturday Night and Sunday Morning," *New
York Review of Books*, II (July 9, 1964), 14-16 [14-15].
        Auchincloss "writes, like a latter-day Trollope, a pseu-
        do-critique of commercialism which collapses docilely as
        soon as one perceives it as being launched from a platform
        provided by commercialism itself. Like Mr. Auchincloss's
        blunted little semi-ethical studies of legal mores, the

WORKS ABOUT

(ADAMS, ROBERT M.)
present novel is fake criticism, moral calesthenics for the already-palpitating. It is a shame, too, for the man has intelligence; but really good novels can't be written by men who are afraid to ask the questions that hurt."

B800   ADAMS, DR. THEODORE F. "Fiction: Auchincloss Tells of Justin's Rector," Richmond (Va.) *News Leader*, July 1, 1964, p. 11.
"Here is a good story, well told. Though some will find it a little tedious and involved at times, it comes to a satisfying and rewarding conclusion...."

B801   ALEXANDER, JAMES E. "Novel Mirrors Narrators Through Subject," Pittsburgh *Post-Gazette*, July 18, 1964, p. 17.
This novel "shows Auchincloss still to be a master of upper-class ambiance, probably the book's strongest point."

B802   AMEN, CAROL. "Book Review," Fremont (Calif.) *News Register*, July 21, 1964, p. 5.
"It is refreshing to read a decent American novel, well written without prudishness, yet devoid of the currently stylish gutter vocabulary and thinking."

B803   BALLIETT, WHITNEY. "Books--A Model Novel," *New Yorker*, XL (August 1, 1964), 76-77.
"A model novel, its poise and taste and intelligence strike one on every page, as do its unerring knowledge and literary skill." Its only failing is the "unrelieved collection of whole or partial misfits" which make Prescott "godly and historical and distant" rather than "chiselling and honing him down to human proportions."

B804   BARKHAM, JOHN. "Auchincloss' Finest Novel--Fastidious Craftsman Writes Portrait of a Dedicated Cleric," Toledo *Blade*, July 12, 1964, Sec. B, p. 5. Also Eugene (Ore.) *Register-Guard*, July 19, 1964; Freeport (Ill.) *Journal-Standard*, July 16, 1964; Lewiston (Idaho) *Tribune*, July 12, 1964; Newport News (Va.) *Daily Press*, July 26, 1964; Honolulu *Star-Bulletin*, July 18, 1964; Wichita Falls (Texas) *Times*, July 19, 1964; Grand Rapids *Press*, July 12, 1964.
"This kind of leisurely, fastidious craftsmanship may be passé for some, but what a pleasure it is to read again." This is Auchincloss's "most enduring achievement to date."

B805   BARRETT, ELDON. Seattle *Post-Intelligencer*, August 15, 1964, p. 9.
"The characterizations are finely drawn and the reader

(BARRETT, ELDON)
gets the inside dope on how private boys' schools are really run. But I say again: so what? Auchincloss is more interesting than his book."

B806   BARTON, JAMES M. *Reading Guide* (University of Virginia Law School), XXII (April 1967), 18-20.
Although the book is "distractingly contrived," Auchincloss "has created a memorable and thought-provoking central character."

B807   BAUER, MALCOLM. "Headmaster Hero of New Novel of Character," Portland *Sunday Oregonian,* July 19, 1964, Sec. 1, p. 37.
This "must certainly be numbered among the most enduring and rewarding novels of the year."

B808   BERNKOPF, ELIZABETH. "An Old-Fashioned Treat--West of Boston," Boston *Sunday Globe,* July 19, 1964, p. 57.
"Here is intellectual excitement, both devotion and hypocrisy, more than a touch of irony and individual failures and successes that fit into no stereotyped formulas. All are presented with polished brilliance that adds up to high achievement. 'Rector of Justin' is a novel that adds luster to the literature of our time."

B809   BIENEN, LEIGH BUCHANAN. "New American Fiction," *Transition* (Kampala, Uganda), V (No. 20, 3, 1965), 46-51 [48].
This "is finally a pleasant and not very profound nineteenth century novel in the present, a novel which presents little threat to either reader or author. And that is probably the source of its appeal."

B810   [BLINDER, RABBI ROBERT J.] "'The Rector of Justin' Is Subject of Book Review," Vicksburg (Miss.) *Sunday Post,* November 8, 1964, Society Section, p. 9.
Descriptive favorable review which is condensation of oral review delivered by Rabbi Blinder.

B811   BOARDMAN, KATHRYN. "An Excellent Novel of Enduring Quality," St. Paul *Pioneer Press,* August 2, 1964, Women's Section, p. 13.
"So skillful a writer is Auchincloss that he produces a kind of narrative tapestry with this novel."

B812   BOGER, MARY SNEAD. Charlotte *Observer,* August 2, 1964, p. 4-B.
Although it is "controlled and literate," the novel's "main flaw is that the whole is not as good as the parts. The character of Dr. Prescott is thoroughly drawn, but the reader does not change and grow with the man. From the

A Bibliography of Writings By and About Louis Auchincloss

WORKS ABOUT

(BOGER, MARY SNEAD)
first page, the involvement is lacking. There is no rapport, no sense of immediacy. It is the difference between taped television and live theatre."

B813 BOND, ALICE DIXON. "The Case for Books--Two Novels Outstanding," Boston *Sunday Herald*, September 13, 1964, Sec. 6, p. 2.
"This is a book of genuine stature, lucid, compelling, and eminently palatable."

B814 "Books," *Extension* (Chicago), LIX (November 1964), 8.
The book lacks "empathy"; for the reader "never really *cares* what happens to" Dr. Prescott. But where it "falls short as an exciting biography of a man, it scores as a sound evolutionary story of an institution...."

B815 BROOKS, JOHN. *Teachers College Record* (New York, N.Y.), LXVI (January 1965), 369-370.
Although the novel is "cleanly and deftly written, full of well-drawn characters, spiced with wit and irony, suffused with its author's intelligence," Auchincloss has "too scrupulously" avoided "identifying himself with any of the people who tell Dr. Prescott's story." Auchincloss "has effaced himself to the point of invisibility--and irresponsibility."

B816 BROPHY, BRIGID. "Great Man," *New Statesman*, LXIX (January 29, 1965), 170.
"It is an attempt at an 'old-fashioned novel'--one that could be read aloud; but while it catches the slowness it misses the density of the 19th-century manner, because it avoids any theme...which should be as cogent for its characters as James's themes for his."

B817 BROWN, JOHN MASON. "'Witty, Perceptive and Beautifully Written,'" *Book-of-the-Month Club News*, July 1964, pp. 1-3.
This is "the richest" of Auchincloss's books and "one of the best school novels that I have ever read. Its concern may be a small pond, but Mr. Auchincloss drops a big stone into it and the ripples spread far and wide."

B818 CALDER-MARSHALL, ARTHUR. "New Novels," *Financial Times* (London), January 28, 1965, p. 24.
Brief review. Auchincloss's "delicate prose can curl like a whip-lash, so civilised that he can accept and evaluate barbarity."

B819   CALDWELL, DAVID S. "Ecclesiastical Ham Done to a Turn," Pittsburgh *Press*, July 19, 1964, Sec. 5, p. 10.
       "Ignoring the novel's contrived structure (no easy task), Auchincloss has a fine tale to tell."

B820   "Cardboard Dragon," *Times Educational Supplement* (London), February 5, 1965, p. 318.
       Brief review. Although the novel is not "negligible" and the theme is "splendid," the "pace is slow, the treatment at times insipid. Sometimes the pomposities seem almost a parody."

B821   CARTER, PETER. "A Whole Life," Newark (N.J.) *Sunday News*, August 2, 1964, Sec. 4, p. E 8.
       "The novel has a grand panorama. The central character is drawn with loving care and great compassion. Auchincloss surely is one of the profoundest of this country's modern writers. He merits comparison with Henry James."

B822   "A Case of Forced Faith," *Time*, LXXXIV (July 24, 1964), 88–89.
       This is a "much meatier" novel than Auchincloss's earlier ones. Although he "may seem to have expended too much sound and fury over something so small in the universe as a prep school," Auchincloss "writes in the manner of Henry James, finding great moral dilemmas in small events."

B823   COLBY, VINETA. "Auchincloss, Novel: Artificial and Clumsy," *Park East* (New York, N.Y.), I (September 17, 1964), 5.
       Auchincloss "is not half so good a novelist as his admirers proclaim" and this novel lacks "style and character." Dr. Prescott emerges as "a consummate bore" and the narrators are "equally preposterous."

B824   CONNOLLY, CYRIL. "Champion of the Old School," London *Sunday Times*, January 24, 1965, p. 43.
       This is "an outstanding example of what might be called the conservative novel, the novel considered primarily as a form of entertainment, rather than a capsule or bathysphere engaged on desperate exploration." Auchincloss "leaves behind a pleasant academic aroma and respect for a well-told story, and perhaps a regret that he did not delve one layer deeper and question a little more thoroughly the whole principle of muscular-Christian education in a money-ridden and violent world."

B825   COOPER, PAT OUTLAW. "Many Images Make Up a Man," Raleigh *Times*, July 19, 1964, Sec. III, p. 5.
       Descriptive review.

A BIBLIOGRAPHY OF WRITINGS BY AND ABOUT LOUIS AUCHINCLOSS

WORKS ABOUT

B826   CORBETT, EDWARD P. J. *America,* CIX (August 8, 1964), 140-141.
        Descriptive review.

B827   [CORMIER, ROBERT]. "The Sentinel Bookman," Fitchburg (Mass.)
        Sentinel, August 7, 1964, p. 6.
            Dr. Prescott is "living proof of the author's mastery of
        fiction and characterization--because the rector is a vital
        human being" and Auchincloss is "probably the most civilized
        writer of the day with a style that is a cool oasis in the
        desert of self-conscious, strident and sex-obsessed modern
        fiction."

B828   COURNOS, JOHN. "Puritans' Nest," Philadelphia *Evening Bulle-
        tin,* July 18, 1964, p. 6.
            "Here is a novel as novels used to be written, with a
        beginning, middle and an end, its drawing of details as
        meticulously precise as in the work of the Old Masters."

B829   CULLIGAN, GLENDY. "Capital Reading--Peabody Would Have Blown
        His Stack at This Vulgarity," Washington (D.C.) *Post,*
        July 14, 1964, p. A4.
            "All of the characters speak and write in a bland, un-
        differentiated style, homogenized for easier digestion by
        the masses. Worse, the novel is gratuitously enlivened by
        a series of self-conscious sexual scenes and even more awk-
        ward innuendoes...which although well within the limits of
        the legally permissible, function primarily as concessions
        to the market place."

B830   DERLETH, AUGUST. "Books of the Times--The Best Living American
        Novelist," *Capital Times* (Madison, Wis.), July 23, 1964,
        p. 15.
            Auchincloss's use of the journal form is "telling and
        effective" and this is "so good a novel that it would be a
        pity to overlook it as too much of Auchincloss' works have
        been thus far in his career."

B831   De WEESE, ALICE. "Headmaster's Portrait," Memphis *Commercial
        Appeal,* July 19, 1964, Sec. 5, p. 10.
            Descriptive favorable review: "a compelling profile of
        a man who might well become a classic in biographical fic-
        tion."

B832   DICK, KAY. "Mainstream," *The Spectator,* No. 7127
        (January 29, 1965), 143.
            Brief review. "It is a real pleasure to read a truly
        educated and cultured novel such as Mr. Auchincloss's *The
        Rector of Justin,* which belongs to the traditional stream
        of classical fiction."

138

B833   DINNAN, JAMES A. *Best Sellers*, XXIV (August 15, 1964), 189.
        Descriptive review. "Excellently written, *The Rector of
        Justin* struck this reviewer as much too long."

B834   DOLBIER, MAURICE. "Daily Book Review--Auchincloss' Best Nov-
        el," New York *Herald Tribune*, July 13, 1964, p. 23. Also
        Houston *Post*, August 30, 1964; Buffalo *Evening News*,
        July 25, 1964.
        This "is not only the best novel that Louis Auchincloss
        has written, but will assuredly have a place among the best
        American novels written in the 1960s."

B835   DRURY, ROGER W. "Vivid Portrait of An Academic Autocrat,"
        Berkshire Eagle (Pittsfield, Mass.), August 1, 1964,
        Sec. 2, p. 14.
        This "is a book for the reader whose ears are awake to
        the well-cut phrase and who is glad to be addressed as an
        equal by a writer of depth, cultivation and wit. The
        doubts and sympathies aroused in these pages go on debating
        one another long after the story ends."

B836   EDEL, LEON. "Grand Old Man--Not What He Seems to Be," *Life*,
        LVII (July 17, 1964), 11, 18.
        With this book, Auchincloss "must be reckoned in the
        front rank of mid-century American novelists." He "writes
        with high professional flair, the competence of a born
        storyteller, and a wit and suavity that are in marked con-
        trast to many recent heavy-handed novelists who rely for
        appeal on an obsessive pursuit of the varieties of sexual
        experience."

B837   FENSTERMAKER, VESLE. "Novel Regains Stature in 'Rector of
        Justin,'" Indianapolis *News*, August 8, 1964, p. 2.
        This "has the scope, the substance, the solid quality of
        the classic novels that shaped the form. Should it be
        widely read in this day when almost any string of words
        presumes to call itself a novel, it will do much to restore
        the novel to its stature as a serious art form that simulta-
        neously entertains, informs and lifts the spirit."

B838   FREEDLEY, GEORGE. "Of Books and Men--Auchincloss' New Novel
        Fascinating," New York *Morning Telegraph*, July 29, 1964,
        p. 2.
        "It is a serious novel which is fascinating to read and
        is a great addition to American novels of significance."

WORKS ABOUT

B839   FULLER, EDMUND. "Reading for Pleasure--Auchincloss' Finest,"
        Wall Street Journal, July 16, 1964, p. 10.
            This and Knowles' *A Separate Peace* are "the best Ameri-
        can novels with school backgrounds" and *Rector* is Auchin-
        closs's "finest accomplishment to date," "a distinguished
        performance, an achievement of substance and lasting val-
        ues."

B840   GAMMACK, GORDON. "Headmaster Is Portrayed Through Many Memo-
        ries," Des Moines *Sunday Register*, July 19, 1964, p. 5-F.
            "It's likely that 'The Rector of Justin' will be one of
        the most important novels of the year and with considerable
        justification, despite the fact it doesn't measure up to
        its early promise."

B841   GERMAIN, C. A. "Fall Comes Early in This Book Year," Green
        Bay (Wis.) *Press-Gazette*, July 26, 1964, p. 22.
            This is "a beautifully written, outstanding book."

B842   GEVERS, CARL M. "The Character of a Headmaster," Chattanooga
        Sunday Times, August 9, 1964, p. 18.
            Brief favorable descriptive review: "a splendid charac-
        ter study."

B843   GRAY, JOHN. *Books and Bookmen* (London), X (March 1965), 26.
            This novel "is admittedly well written, in a kind of up-
        dated Henry James-ese, but the multiple narration seems
        rather clumsily handled--and Auchincloss has chosen some
        strange protagonists to tell the story...." The book is
        "far too 'civilised' and ladies'-libraryish."

B844   HAMILTON, IAIN. "Recent Fiction--Auchincloss's American Arn-
        old," London *Daily Telegraph and Morning Post*,
        February 11, 1965, p. 21.
            "As a moral cartographer of Beacon Hill and its hinter-
        land, Mr. Auchincloss uses a fine pen and is sparing with
        his flourishes. The craftsmanship of 'The Rector of Justin'
        is as pleasurable as its dry ironies."

B845   HERR, DAN. "Books--The Books 'Everybody' Is Reading," *The
        Sign*, XLIV (July 1965), 59-60 [59].
            Favorable brief review. This novel is written in "a
        literary style more reminiscent of the leisurely past than
        the turbulent present."

B846   HICKS, GRANVILLE. "Literary Horizons--Headmaster For Hero,"
        Saturday Review, XLVII (July 11, 1964), 27-28. Reprinted in
        Hicks, *Literary Horizons*.(B3).
            "I am not sure that James would have approved of the way

(HICKS, GRANVILLE)
the book is put together, with the none too plausible introduction of various documents; but he could not have said,
as he did say about many writers, that the author had failed
to make the most of his *donnée*. For the method does work,
and we do come to feel the reality, the complicated reality,
of Francis Prescott."

B847   HIGBY, JIM. "Novelist Writes One of His Best," Buffalo *Courier-Express*, August 16, 1964, p. D-28.
"One of America's most gifted novelists has written what
well may be the best novel of the year. It is a story told
with skill and authority."

B848   HILL, BOB. "Looking at Books," Spokane *Daily Chronicle*,
July 16, 1964, p. 10.
"To read 'The Rector of Justin' is to learn much about
the perversity and deception of a man's motivations--and to
meet, in Dr. Francis Prescott, one of the most fascinating
and enigmatic characterizations of contemporary American
letters."

B849   HOLLAND, HENRIETTA FORT. "Book of the Week--A Distinguished
Novel of a Headmaster's Life," Chicago *Daily News*,
July 11, 1964, Panorama Section, p. 7.
"Beautifully written though this book is, sometimes its
author shows through, seems to be speaking instead of one
of his characters, who become inappropriately erudite."

B850   HONE, RALPH E. "'King Lear' Theme Updated in Novel," Los
Angeles *Times*, July 26, 1964, *Calendar* Magazine, p. 17.
Descriptive review. Auchincloss is "superb in skill and
taste."

B851   HOPKINS, FRATER RYAN, O.F.M. Cap. *Vision* (St. Fidelis Semi-
nary, Herman, Pa.), II (Winter 1965), 30.
The novel is "unpretentious but unmistakable value is
there for anyone willing to read it--the rewarding satis-
faction of experiencing the life, struggle, and devotion of
a man to his ideals."

B852   HOWE, MARJORIE. "New Books," Burlington (Vt.) *Free Press*,
July 15, 1964, p. 17.
"This is truly a magnificent and important novel; un-
doubtedly Louis Auchincloss' finest."

B853   HUGHES, RILEY. "Books in the Balance," *Columbia*, XLIV
(September 1964), 33, 36-37 [36].
This is a "richly executed, many levelled novel." "Its

WORKS ABOUT

(HUGHES, RILEY)
celebration of subtlety and value places *The Rector of Justin* in the great tradition of character and meaning."

B854   HUSTON, McCREADY. "The Soft, Convincing Voice of a Top-Rank Novelist," San Francisco *Sunday Chronicle*, July 12, 1964, *This World* Magazine, p. 32.
"So adroit is Auchincloss with the hidden flashback and the supplementary point of view that every seeming digression has its own immediacy, making its own thrust at the emotions or subtle appeal to the intellect."

B855   "In His 13th Novel--Author Auchincloss Looks at World of Private School," Miami (Fla.) *Herald*, July 12, 1964, p. 7-D.
Descriptive review. "It is a tribute to Mr. Auchincloss' skill that he can portray a novel of ideas and make it as interesting as an adventure."

B856   JAY, IVOR. "A Man to Rank With Mr. Chips," Birmingham (England) *Evening Mail*, January 22, 1965, p. 8.
"Here is a book that genuinely enriches the reader. Indeed, makes you feel wiser after having read it."

B857   JOHNSON, LUCY. "Justin School Was a World, the Rector Lord and Maker," Milwaukee *Journal*, July 12, 1964, Part 5, p. 4.
Auchincloss "has finally found the exact aspect of his subject which calls upon all the talents of which he is master, while not needing those which he has less highly developed."

B858   JOHNSON, TOM. "Headmaster in Hero's Role," Riverside (Calif.) *Press-Enterprise*, July 19, 1964, p. C-15.
"The technique of presentation is interesting, the story that emerges is interesting, the study of the character is interesting, and the insight into those who knew the hero is interesting. In short, this is a rare and exciting book."

B859   JONES, VICTOR O. "Notes From the Back of an Envelope--Read Any Good Books Lately?" Boston *Globe*, September 29, 1964, p. 11.
Brief descriptive review.

B860   KAY, JANE H. *Christian Science Monitor*, July 23, 1964, p. 7.
Auchincloss "triumphs over a certain lack of credibility, and a certain familiarity of theme," doing so "through craft and sensibility."

A Bibliography of Writings By and About Louis Auchincloss

B861   KEITH, DON. "Auchincloss Novel Is Like Biography," New Orleans
        Times Picayune, September 13, 1964, Sec. 3, p. 12.
            "It must be conceded that this is, without doubt, the
        most significant of Louis Auchincloss' 12 novels, combining
        perception, strength and compassion into one of the finest
        fictional biographies to hit the stands in a long time."

B862   K[ENNEDY], [MONSIGNOR] J[OHN] S., [P.A.] "Our Best People--
        The Fortunate Few," *Catholic Transcript* (Hartford, Conn.),
        August 13, 1964, p. 5.
            "The truth about Prescott is not sufficiently important
        and significant to justify the extended, inching explora-
        tion." *Rector* is "a modest masterpiece at best, heavy rath-
        er than substantial, arch rather than subtle, with a few
        flashes of wit and a dreadful descent into embarrassing
        sensationalism in the case of Cordelia."

B863   KING, FRANCIS. "Awesome Head," London *Sunday Telegraph,*
        January 24, 1965, p. 17.
            Descriptive favorable review.

B864   *Kirkus,* XXXII (May 1, 1964), 466.
            Descriptive review.

B865   KITCHING, JESSIE. *Publishers' Weekly,* CLXXXV (May 18, 1964),
        61.
            Brief descriptive review.

B866   KOHEN, HELEN. "Book Review--This Is Best of Auchincloss,"
        Miami Beach *Daily Sun,* August 4, 1964, p. 4.
            "If we had to choose one qualifying adjective for this
        book, a good one would be excellent."

B867   LAMPORT, FELICIA. "Making a Meal of the Upper Crust," *Book
        Week* (New York *Herald Tribune,* San Francisco *Examiner,*
        Washington *Post*), July 12, 1964, p. 3.
            "Viewed through these multiple I's, the rector stands
        always in a reflected light, often brilliantly reflected,
        but not quite in focus. Many of his facets emerge superbly,
        but his core remains obscure. The whole seems somehow less
        than its parts."

B868   LeCLAIR, EDWARD E., JR. "Lawyer's Novel Fine Character Study,"
        Albany (N.Y.) *Sunday Times-Union,* July 26, 1964, p. H-9.
            "Although the book is irritatingly complex in the de-
        vices the author uses to tell his story, it is another fine
        job of writing, and a successful major character study as
        well."

143

A Bibliography of Writings By and About Louis Auchincloss

WORKS ABOUT

B869   LERNER, ARTHUR. *Books Abroad*, XXXIX (Winter 1965), 87.
        Descriptive favorable review.

B870   LESLIE, ANDREW. "Books of the Day--New Fiction--An Arnold in
        New England," Manchester (England) *Guardian*, p. 7.
            This is "the best Auchincloss I have read. The wit is
        tougher and is used not as a piece of amusing interior dec-
        oration but as a more penetrating way of saying something."

B871   LEVINE, PAUL. "Individualism and the Traditional Talent,"
        Hudson Review, XVII (Autumn 1964), 470-477 [476-477].
            Auchincloss's narrator is "impossible," but he "does a
        creditable job of projecting the moral conflict between the
        idealist and the pragmatist in Prescott's soul."

B872   LEVY, WILLIAM TURNER. "In a Solid Ring, Secrets," *The Living
        Church*, CL (January 24, 1965), 13.
            "The pace is fine, the interest we have is sustained and
        even heightened, but the protagonist remains bloodless. I
        was somehow cheated of the man I knew must be there."

B873   LISTER, RICHARD. "Inside a Snob School for Yankees," London
        Evening Standard, January 26, 1965, p. 10.
            "It all seems rather mild. Perhaps in its native land,
        where private schools are very exceptional, the picture
        might seem more daring. It doesn't seem that to us, whose
        fiction is familiar enough with grand old humbugs, con-
        scious or unconscious, in gowns and mortarboards."

B874   McALEER, JOHN J. "Wonderful in Adversity," *The Pilot* (Boston),
        CXXXV (August 8, 1964), 10.
            The novel "shows that the life of a man of sterling
        worth is still a theme which makes grueling demands on the
        creative resources of the author and a call no less strenu-
        ous on the spiritual resources of the reader. Auchincloss's
        handling of it adds luster to a reputation already distin-
        guished."

B875   McKEEN, SIDNEY B. "Portrait of a Great Life," Worcester *Sunday
        Telegram*, July 12, 1964, p. 12 E.
            "As a story of one man, his strength, his weakness, his
        rationale and his far-reaching image, it is unsurpassed in
        contemporary fiction.... As a novel, it seems destined for
        great success, both artistically and commercially."

B876   MARTIN, JEAN. "Nobody's Fauve," Chicago *Sun-Times*,
        July 19, 1964, Sec. 3, p. 2.
            "While he handles his shifting narration with great
        skill, Auchincloss never convinces the reader of the

(MARTIN, JEAN)
'greatness' of his subject." *Rector* is "a well-bred bit of writing rather like one of those fine English hunting prints which fit beautifully into a certain decor but which lack the flash of the cloven hoof that marks exciting new art."

B877   MOODY, MINNIE HITE. "Urbanity and Wit in New Auchincloss Novel," Columbus (Ohio) *Dispatch*, July 19, 1964, TAB Section, p. 12.
Descriptive review.

B878   MOSER, MARGARET. "Book Review," Beeville *Bee-Picayune*, November 12, 1964, Sec. A, p. 4.
This "is more than a story. Essentially it is a plea for your moral judgment."

B879   MURRAY, JAMES G. "The Art of Reading--New Season--A Progress Report," *Long Island Catholic* (Rockville Centre, N.Y.), October 15, 1964, p. 9.
This is "a brilliant achievement from the standpoints of believability, readability, and technical excellence. It is by far the best book to date of this much too neglected writer and clearly the best novel published this season."

B880   "Name-Dropper," *Newsweek*, LXIV (July 20, 1964), 83.
Auchincloss's "notions of education, social responsibility, psychotherapy, and sex are charming archaisms, almost Jeffersonian in their benevolence" and "there is not much stylistic distinction between" *Rector* and "the serializable sagas of Frances Parkinson Keyes." What sets Auchincloss apart is perhaps "his ability to flatter some readers" by making them feel how patrician, "educated, social and urbane" they are when they read him.

B881   "New Fiction," London *Times*, January 28, 1965, p. 15.
This is an "extremely well-written" and "excellent novel."

B882   NEWQUIST, ROY. "'Rector' Is Auchincloss' Best," Chicago's *American*, July 12, 1964, Sec. 4, p. 10. Much of this is reprinted in Newquist, *Counterpoint* (B5).
Interview-review, which is mostly an interview.

B883   NORDLING, KARL. "'The Rector of Justin'--In the Flowering of a Prep School, Intimate Insights Into the Well-Bred," *National Observer*, July 13, 1964, p. 20.
"The most perplexing aspect of the book...is the method Mr. Auchincloss uses to tell his story. Though creating a fictitious journal can provide excellent insight into a

A Bibliography of Writings By and About Louis Auchincloss

WORKS ABOUT

(NORDLING, KARL)
man's thoughts, both about himself and of the life around
him, the author has revised the method--and thereby hindered
it."

B884 PASLEY, VIRGINIA. "Portrait of a New England Headmaster,"
Newsday (Garden City, N.Y.), July 11, 1964, p. 18W.
The "peripheral characters" are "much more interesting
than Prescott himself. They have a reality he never
achieves." This is particularly true of Brian.

B885 PEARRE, HOWELL. "Two Interesting Novels of Manners," Nashville
Banner, July 31, 1964, p. 21.
Auchincloss, who "could never have written a word if it
hadn't been for James and Wharton," has here made "at once
his most ambitious foray into the novel and also his best,
lacking that rush of meaning that he usually tacks on during
the last few pages."

B886 PECKHAM, STANTON. "Who Follows in His Train?" Denver *Sunday
Post*, July 12, 1964, *Roundup* Magazine, p. 10.
This is "not only the most ambitious effort of lawyer
Louis Auchincloss as a novelist, it is his best. It
strengthens the claim that Auchincloss...is 'the best living
American novelist.'"

B887 P[ENDEXTER], F[AUNCE]. "'Rector of Justin' Is Fine Auchincloss
Novel," Lewiston (Me.) *Journal*, August 8, 1964, p. 11-A.
"This is a truly splendid novel for those who demand excellent writing, the setting of realistic scenes and the
portrayal of flesh and blood characters."

B888 PETERSON, VIRGILIA. "A Crucible Covered With Ivy," *New York
Times Book Review*, July 12, 1964, pp. 1, 20.
"This is not only a passionately interesting, but a spir-
itually important study of the American character of, and
for, our time."

B889 PICKREL, PAUL. "Manners of Mammon," *Harper's Magazine*, CCXXIX
(July 1964), 97-98.
This is "an extremely fine novel. It is almost certainly
the best work of fiction ever written about an American
preparatory school..., and it is among the best novels about
American education, because it deals with the subject at a
morally significant level. It also gives the fullest scope
of Auchincloss's talents of any book he has so far written."

B890   POLLOCK, VENETIA. "New Novels," *Punch* (London), CCXLVIII
        (February 24, 1965), 294.
            Auchincloss "has evaded all the pitfalls which so often
        mar fictional grand old men in this truly magnificent por-
        trait of a modern American Arnold of Rugby."

B891   POTTER, NANCY A. J. "A Novel and a Novelist," Providence
        Sunday Journal, July 12, 1964, p. W-18.
            "In Marquand and Cheever the reader can be positive of
        the satire and can be sure that the real world rages at the
        edge of the manicured lawn. Here one cannot be sure that
        it does."

B892   PRESCOTT, ORVILLE. "Books of The Times--In Loving Memory of a
        Noble Failure," New York *Times*, July 13, 1964, p. 27. Also
        Los Angeles *Herald-Examiner*, July 26, 1964; Minneapolis
        Tribune, July 26, 1964; Sacramento *Bee*, July 19, 1964,
        p. L17; Omaha *World-Herald*, July 26, 1964.
            This is Auchincloss's "finest" novel because "there is
        an emotional power and a psychological fascination in this
        impressive novel that is new in Mr. Auchincloss' work and
        rarely found in anybody's."

B893   RHODES, ROYAL W. *New Frontiers* (Fairfield, Conn.), X
        (Summer 1965), 75.
            Descriptive mixed review.

B894   R[OBINSON], O[LIVE] C. "Books and Authors: *The Rector of
        Justin*," Lewiston (Me.) *Daily Sun*, July 16, 1964, p. 4.
            With this novel, Auchincloss "proves himself a master of
        significant and accurate detail on a subject he views as an
        insider."

B895   ROWE, PERCY. "Well Devised Tale," Toronto *Telegram*,
        December 5, 1964, Magazine, p. 30.
            "Mr. Auchincloss is experienced. His best-seller is
        cohesive, intelligent, and worth reading."

B896   ROY, GREGOR. *Catholic World*, CC (November 1964), 124-127.
            "With lance-like precision and a surgeon's eye for bio-
        graphical minutiae," Auchincloss "lays bare his subject's
        foibles and idiosyncrasies in urbane, lucid prose which is
        a delight to read in a literary age suffering from chronic
        anti-style."

B897   S., M. A. "His Way of Life," Trenton (N.J.) *Sunday Times-Ad-
        vertiser*, August 16, 1964, Sec. 3, p. 12.
            In this novel, Auchincloss "has given us a memorable fig-
        ure in his hero. But he has done even more, with a

WORKS ABOUT

(S., M. A.)
brilliant, mind-challenging view of a whole way of life.
It is a book that stands far above the superficialities of
much modern fiction."

B898   SCARDINO, KATHERINE M. "Penetrating Portrait of Individual,"
Savannah *Morning News*, July 19, 1964, Magazine, p. 8. Also
Greenville (Miss.) *Delta Democrat-Times*, July 19, 1964.
"This is the best novel I have read in over a year."

B899   SMITH, RUTH. *"The Rector of Justin*--Was He a Saint or a Sinner?" Orlando (Fla.) *Sentinel*, September 6, 1964, *Florida*
Magazine, p. 11.
"The book is a fascinating study--and a particularly
good picture of a famous private school, and the man who
guided its destinies."

B900   SPEARMAN, WALTER. "'The Rector of Justin' Looms Above Sea-
son's Run of Fiction," Rocky Mount (N.C.) *Telegram*,
July 26, 1964, p. 5B.
Descriptive highly favorable review.

B901   SQUIRRU, RAFAEL. *Américas*, XVIII (January 1966), 39-41.
Rector is a more "mature" novel than Bellow's *Herzog* or
Vidal's *Julian*, the other two "best" novels of the past
year. The "most formidable part of the book" is "the struggle...between the renegade student and the headmaster in
their bids for spiritual power."

B902   SULLIVAN, RICHARD. "Auchincloss in Academe," *The Critic*,
XXIII (August-September 1964), 75-76.
Auchincloss is "one of the most admirable and consistently effective American fiction-writers currently practic-
ing." This is "a big, rich, sturdily structured book, all
alive."

B903   THOMAS, SIDNEY S. "Society Takes Its Licks In Auchincloss'
Best Effort," Atlanta *Journal-Constitution*, July 19, 1964,
p. 5-D.
With this novel, Auchincloss "leaves Edith Wharton far
behind. He has written a book that would forever have been
beyond her."

B904   THORNTON, EUGENIA. "School Is Canvas For Depth Portrait,"
Cleveland *Plain Dealer*, July 12, 1964, p. 6-H.
This is Auchincloss's best novel and "in many ways"
Auchincloss is "one of the most satisfying of American nov-
elists."

A Bibliography of Writings By and About Louis Auchincloss

B905 THORPE, DAY. "The Faith of a Headmaster Who Became a Messiah,"
Washington (D.C.) *Sunday Star*, July 12, 1964, p. B-5.
This is "one of the most subtle and deftly executed
books of recent American fiction." A "gratuitous addition"
to the novel is Auchincloss's "sly and charming contribution to the Shakespeare birthday festivities, in the form
of perhaps 40 allusions to, and quotations from, the plays,
casually unidentified."

B906 TREVOR, WILLIAM. "New Novels," *The Listener* (London), LXXIII
(January 21, 1965), 115.
This novel, "no less serious because it has been written
in part as a comedy, might as easily have come out of England or France as America: the pettiness and paranoia of
locked-up communities change little with time or place and
the excellence of Mr. Auchincloss's writing transcends ob-
vious idiom. There are few other contemporary novelists
who could have given us so elegantly this microcosm of human confusion."

B907 *Virginia Quarterly Review*, XL (Autumn 1964), cxliv.
Brief review. "Few other contemporary writers handle
their material with so much composure and grace as Mr. Auchincloss. His quiet authority in an age of literary hysteria
is both gratifying and heartening."

B908 W., J. "Books in Review," Auburn (N.Y.) *Citizen-Advertiser*,
August 1, 1964, Sec. 2, p. 4.
This is "a great novel" which "stands superbly above the
many novels about boys' schools and their headmasters, from
the Dickensian Dotheboys type through honey-bun Chips and
the acid contemporary exposés."

B909 W., J. "New Louis Auchincloss Novel Is the Best Book He's
Done," New Haven *Register*, July 12, 1964, Sec. 4, p. 7.
This novel is "better than good. It is haunting." It is
"in a way a very special interpretation of what might have
been, and seemed, by one who was part of it. In a larger
way it is a universal unfolding of what always has been, is,
and will be."

B910 "Wall Street Prep.," *Times Literary Supplement* (London),
January 28, 1965, p. 61.
"Mr. Auchincloss is a good story-teller, and the narrative technique of *The Rector of Justin* almost succeeds in
obscuring the faults. But not quite. Nothing can quite
conceal the unreality of the young narrator."

A Bibliography of Writings By and About Louis Auchincloss

WORKS ABOUT

B911 WALSH, GEORGE. "God and Dr. Prescott," *Cosmopolitan,* CLVII
(July 1964), 24-25.
"The novel possesses the compelling power that we feel
when we recognize truth, yet it keeps its special humility.
Like Dr. Prescott, it is righteous, but it is never self-
righteous."

B912 WARDLE, IRVING. "An American Dr. Arnold," *The Observer* (London), January 24, 1965, p. 26.
"Episodic story-telling usually dislocates the reader's
attention, but here each episode is prepared to arouse cu-
riosity and make the reader feel himself a spy...."

B913 WEEKS, EDWARD. "The Making of a Headmaster," *The Atlantic,*
CCXIV (July 1964), 132-133.
Auchincloss's "urbanity" and his portraits of the older
women deserve praise; but the "shift from writer to writer
is not contrived with enough individual divergence."

B914 WELLEJUS, ED. "Ed Wellejus' Bookshelf," Erie (Pa.) *Times-News,*
July 19, 1964, p. 7E.
"More and more, I'm becoming convinced that Louis Auchincloss is the most gifted living American writer." This is
"a masterful" book.

B915 WHATELY, ROSALEEN. "There's Nothing Shameful About Ideals,"
Liverpool (England) *Daily Post,* January 27, 1965, p. 9.
Descriptive favorable review. "The story is a rare one,
for there is no cheap debunking, and ideals are for the
main part preserved."

B916 W[HEILDON], L[EONARD]. "A Major Novel," Boston *Sunday Herald,*
July 19, 1964, Sec. 5, p. 2.
"'The Rector of Justin' shows Auchincloss' story-telling
art at its best and then pushes a little bit beyond to an
almost Jamesian quality of analysis and introspection.
This is a major novel despite its limited theme."

B917 WHITE, TERENCE de VERE. "Hi! Mr. Chips," *Irish Times* (Dublin),
January 23, 1965, p. 10.
"If I was disappointed it was because I expected a book
which was, perhaps, a *Roman à clef,* but for that reason very
close to life. This seemed to me to be the elegant construction of a man of letters, not a book that was conceived in
the heat of imagination. But it is blessedly civilised and
mercifully free from the contemporary cult of the sub-human."

A Bibliography of Writings By and About Louis Auchincloss

B918 WHITE, VICTOR. "Deft, Deep Headmaster," Dallas *Morning News,*
      July 12, 1964, Sec. 4, p. 5.
          This is "first-rate reading" and "a brilliantly con-
      structed novel." Auchincloss's "deftness reminds one of
      Marquand, though the greater depth of his character probing
      gives him a decided edge; somewhat more valid would be the
      comparison with Somerset Maugham, but the writer Mr. Auch-
      incloss periodically and happily brings to mind is Henry
      James."

B919 WHITMAN, DIGBY B. "Magnificent Tale of a Crusty Headmaster,"
      Chicago Tribune Books Today, July 12, 1964, p. 1.
          Auchincloss quietly turns out "what probably are the
      best, and certainly are the most consistently good, novels
      written in America today." This "is not just a great
      school story or even a great novel. It is a great book."

B920 WILLIAMS, RALPH M. "A Man of Character," Hartford *Courant,*
      July 26, 1964, Magazine, p. 13.
          "Readers of today may find it difficult to 'get into'
      this novel of Mr. Auchincloss's simply because of the unu-
      sual form. That he has used this form so successfully is
      a tribute to the great craftsmanship and versatility of
      this author."

B921 WILLIS, KATHERINE TAPPERT. *Library Journal,* LXXXIX
      (September 1, 1964), 3180, 3182.
          Brief favorable review. "These are uneven sketches, but
      they are tied together by the appealing hero's dramatic
      personality."

B922 WILSON, WILLIAM E. "Books in Review--An Intricately Construct-
      ed Novel," Baltimore *Evening Sun,* July 17, 1964, p. A20.
          "Although intricately constructed, 'The Rector of Justin'
      is without innovations in technique, and the style too is
      conventional, save for occasional flamboyant passages in
      dialogue." Auchincloss "sees life only from the right side
      of the tracks, but what he sees he sees clearly."

B923 YODER, EDWIN M., JR. "The Literary Scene--Rector of Justin:
      Are There Good Traits Without Flaws," Greensboro (N.C.)
      Daily News, August 2, 1964, p. C3.
          This novel is "not only an excellent technical accomplish-
      ment," but is also "an important assertion...of a supremely
      important truth": in judging great men, "we must ponder not
      only the beauty of power humanely disposed but its human
      cost" and that "the superlative traits of character and mind
      that elevate the great man above the crowd are rarely unac-
      companied by flaws equally remarkable."

A Bibliography of Writings By and About Louis Auchincloss

WORKS ABOUT

Ellen Glasgow

B924   *Choice*, I (February 1965), 552.
        The book "contributes little new information on Ellen
        Glasgow, but is of some value as an introduction to her
        work.... Auchincloss relies heavily upon Miss Glasgow's
        collected prefaces and autobiography as a background for
        his essay; these sources, while indispensable to any clear
        understanding of her life and work, must be used with a
        cautious judgment not manifested in this pamphlet."

B925   RUSSELL, H. K. *South Atlantic Quarterly*, LXIV (Summer 1965),
        431.
        Brief descriptive review. Auchincloss "discusses inter-
        estingly Miss Glasgow's choices of point of view."

B926   SHELTON, J. K. *Modern Language Review*, LXI (October 1966),
        697-698.
        Descriptive favorable review.

B927   *Virginia Quarterly Review*, XL (Autumn 1964), clii-cliii.
        Brief review. "As an introduction, the book is of some
        value, but Auchincloss confuses judgment and analysis and
        allows his perceptiveness to become lost in a careless dis-
        play of amateur criticism."

Pioneers and Caretakers

B928   "Affirmative Note Struck By Women," Allentown (Pa.) *Sunday
        Call-Chronicle*, June 6, 1965, p. F-5.
        Favorable review which praises Auchincloss's style.

B929   ALLEN, WALTER. "American Novels and the World," London *Daily
        Telegraph*, February 3, 1966, p. 20.
        "Mr. Auchincloss writes agreeably but without much fire.
        If you have read his authors, he will evoke pleasant memo-
        ries of their books; if you have not read them, it seems to
        me unlikely he will persuade you to do so."

B930   BOHNER, CHARLES H. "Notes on Criticism and Biography," *South-
        ern Review*, n.s. VI (Summer 1970), 875-883 [877-878].
        Auchincloss's book is "good natured in tone and generous
        in judgment." The essay on Edith Wharton "is the best in
        his book and probably the best anywhere."

B931   BUTCHER, FANNY. "Following the Literary Trails of Nine Women,"
        Chicago Tribune Books Today, June 13, 1965, p. 9. Also
        St. Louis *Globe Democrat*, July 10-11, 1965, p. 4F.
        The book "is neither profound or pedagogical. It could

(BUTCHER, FANNY)
be read, and profitably, even by any high school student with a real interest in American fiction...but it is meant for you and me, and I hope you find it as intriguing as I did."

B932 *Choice*, II (October 1965), 480.
"The essays are as uncentered and as unsubstantial as their own efforts, though perhaps a bit more glib and sophisticated."

B933 COGAN, MARC R. "From Sarah Jewett to Mary McCarthy: A Synoptic Survey of Woman Novelists," Chicago *Daily News*, June 5, 1965, Panorama Section, p. 22.
"While 'Pioneers and Caretakers' can exist as a rather uncritical 'Life and Works' of some neglected or not-so-neglected woman authors, at its best it is bland and repetitive, often adopting a supercilious attitude to its subjects and never getting close enough to their work to do them the justice their critical (or at least historical) positions deserve."

B934 D[IAS], E[ARL] J. "Novelist Auchincloss Shows He's Perceptive Critic, Too," New Bedford (Mass.) *Standard-Times*, June 13, 1965, p. 18.
Descriptive favorable review.

B935 F[LEISCHER], L[EONORE]. *Publishers' Weekly*, CXC (August 8, 1966), 62.
Brief favorable review.

B936 *Forum for Modern Language Studies*, II (July 1966), 287.
Brief descriptive review: a "useful and perceptive study."

B937 FOURNIER, NORMAN. "The Book Story--Miss Jewett Gets Warm Appraisal," Portland (Me.) *Sunday Telegram*, July 18, 1965, p. 4C.
Descriptive review, which deals exclusively with Auchincloss's section on Jewett.

B938 GAUVREAU, WINIFRED R. "Of Books, Writers, Publishers--A Readable Gallery of Feminine 'Rebels,'" *Nevada State Journal* (Reno), August 1, 1965, p. 4.
Although Auchincloss "is a skilled observer and his evaluations are discerning, he somehow fails to carry through his theme that all of these novelists have a common denominator...."

A Bibliography of Writings By and About Louis Auchincloss

WORKS ABOUT

B939   GRISCOM, ISOBEL. "Heritage Keepers," Chattanooga *Times*,
        September 12, 1965, p. 16.
            The book is "an admirable introduction of these authors
        for anyone not yet acquainted with them." Auchincloss's
        "comments, furthermore, are refreshing and often challeng-
        ing to one long acquainted with a work or the works of the
        Nine."

B940   HICKS, GRANVILLE. "Literary Horizons--The Feminine Literary
        Mystique," *Saturday Review*, XLVIII (June 5, 1965), 19-20.
        Reprinted in Hicks, *Literary Horizons* (B3).
            Auchincloss "is interested in each of his writers for her
        own sake, and he deals justly with all, including those
        whose work is strikingly different from his own. In his
        quiet, unself-assertive way he is one of the best of con-
        temporary critics."

B941   HOLZHAUER, JEAN. "The Distaff Side of Fiction," Milwaukee
        Journal, August 1, 1965, Part 5, p. 4.
            "Although it will add little to the knowledge of readers
        familiar with these subjects, 'Pioneers and Caretakers'
        does offer a useful reference guide and some questions for
        speculation."

B942   HOWE, MARJORIE. "New Books--Biography of Isabella Gardner
        Memorable Book," Burlington (Vt.) *Free Press*,
        September 16, 1965, p. 13.
            Descriptive review: the essays are "brilliant."

B943   H[OYT], E[LIZABETH] N. "Women Novelists," Cedar Rapids *Ga-
        zette*, October 3, 1965, p. 2C.
            Descriptive favorable review: the essays are "highly
        readable."

B944   KIRSCH, ROBERT R. "The Book Report--Role of Women Novelists
        Weighed in Essay Collection," Los Angeles *Times*,
        August 4, 1965, Part IV, p. 3.
            "It is not too much to say that this is the fairest
        assessment so far of the particular role of women novelists
        in American fiction."

B945   "Ladies Saved Our Culture?" Dallas *Morning News*,
        September 26, 1965, p. 8 F.
            "This is a perceptive study, notable for its insight and
        for its skillful corraling of such diverse talents between
        the same two covers."

154

Book Reviews–*Pioneers and Caretakers*

B946   LEWIS, R. W. B. "Silver Spoons and Golden Bowls," *Book Week*
        (New York *Herald Tribune,* Chicago *Sun-Times,* Washington
        Post), February 20, 1966, pp. 1, 8 [8].
            "As a critic, Auchincloss is observant and sensible; he
        never presses very hard, and he does not clutch after
        strange 'meanings,' thereby missing one or two of the same."

B947   MANN, ELIZABETH L. "From Louis Auchincloss, A Look at Women
        Writers," Greensboro (N.C.) *Daily News,* June 13, 1965,
        p. D3.
            "For a reader not familiar with these authors, Mr. Auch-
        incloss supplies intelligent and entertaining introduc-
        tions.... For readers who already know the authors, his
        comments will be stimulating, even if not strikingly new."

B948   MARGOLIES, EDWARD. *Library Journal,* XC (June 1, 1965), 2555.
            Brief review. "Mr. Auchincloss has probably exaggerated
        the merit of some of his subjects, but, by and large, the
        book is intelligent, well written, and interesting."

B949   MOERS, ELLEN. "The Creation of Women," *New York Times Book
        Review,* July 25, 1965, pp. 1; 26.
            Auchincloss "loves novels, to read as well as to write.
        He becomes involved with plot, takes a personal interest in
        character, indulges a curiosity (and displays an expertise)
        about the subject of manners.... His tone, even when criti-
        cal, oscillates between the admiring and the deferential."

B950   MURPHY, JOHN J. *Criticism,* IX (Spring 1967), 202-204.
            "While the theme of conserving is loose enough to enable
        Auchincloss to treat each novelist without distortion, one
        could hope for a better integrated study.... The book is
        worthy despite all this, however."

B951   "Nine Novelists," London *Times,* February 17, 1966, p. 15.
            Brief favorable review: "a most readable introduction
        to what can be for many a world of new reading."

B952   *Nineteenth-Century Fiction,* XX (December 1965), 305.
            Brief review: "a series of smoothly written, generally
        informative, and somewhat bland studies."

B953   PARSONS, J. E. *Western Humanities Review,* XX (Winter 1966),
        86-88.
            "Too clumsy (and too lifeless) to be enjoyable as appre-
        ciation, too uninformed to be functional as criticism, *Pio-
        neers and Caretakers* defies these traditional distinctions.
        It belongs, properly, neither in the conversation pit nor
        the study, but on the remainder shelf."

WORKS ABOUT

B954   PICKREL, PAUL. "Miss Jewett to Miss McCarthy," *Harper's Maga-*
        zine, CCXXXI (August 1965), 112-113.
            "If Mr. Auchincloss' theory fails to advance very far our
        understanding of American women novelists as a group, each
        of the individual essays does a good deal to advance our
        understanding of its subject."

B955   PORTE, JOEL. "The Slant in Women's Writing," *Christian Science*
        Monitor, August 19, 1965, p. 5.
            "The body of Mr. Auchincloss's book suggests that there
        is a paradox lurking in his thesis. As caretakers, these
        writers have been involved in preserving through a species
        of nostalgia a past irrevocably lost. As pioneers, they
        are striking forward bitterly and shrilly into a world which
        they would not have made if they could, and which they are
        trying their best to undo."

B956   PRESCOTT, ORVILLE. "Books of The Times--Nine Women Novelists,"
        New York *Times*, June 7, 1965, p. 35. Also Indianapolis
        News, June 12, 1965, p. 2; Omaha *Sunday World-Herald*,
        June 27, 1965, Magazine, p. 27.
            "These essays contain wisps of biography, lucid analyses,
        some firm disapproval of lesser works and much generous
        praise. Mr. Auchincloss is an urbane critic and, on the
        whole, a just one. His prose is suave, brightened by glints
        of quiet humor."

B957   PRYCE-JONES, ALAN. "Daily Book Review--9 Women Novelists of
        U.S.: An Admirable Appraisal," New York *Herald Tribune*,
        June 10, 1965, p. 19. Also Philadelphia *Inquirer*,
        July 11, 1965, Sec. 7, p. 7; Chicago *Sun-Times*,
        August 8, 1965, Sec. 3, p. 2; Toledo *Blade*, June 27, 1965,
        Sec. B, p. 5; San Francisco *Examiner*, July 5, 1965, p. 21.
            "Critics of a complexion which distrusts value-judgment
        and gives a prime place to linguistic analysis may find
        Louis Auchincloss indulgently urbane. But they should not
        prevent less austere souls finding a great deal of sense
        and pleasure in these pages."

B958   *Publishers' Weekly*, CLXXXVII (April 5, 1965), 44.
            Brief review: "a splendid book, well written, informa-
        tive and stimulating."

B959   ROUSE, BLAIR. *American Literature*, XXXVII (November 1965),
        340-341.
            Auchincloss "in the descriptive and critical comment in
        these essays is usually informative and often stimulating
        in his observations. His views on the five older novelists

(ROUSE, BLAIR)
are more conclusive; his treatments of the other four are somewhat tentative."

B960   SEARS, WILLIAM P. *Education*, LXXXVI (May 1966), 567.
Very brief review. "The essays are readable and incisive."

B961   SHERMAN, JOHN K. "Women Novelists Get Accolade—Nine American Writers Get Understanding Study," Minneapolis *Tribune*, Entertainment Section, p. 6.
This is "sympathetic yet penetrating critical writing, fostering new respect for and deeper acquaintance with our women authors and their built-in insights into the American epic and the human comedy."

B962   STILWELL, ROBERT L. *Books Abroad*, XL (Spring 1966), 205.
"There are no stabbing insights throughout these quiet, low-pressure, almost conversational essays; but they offer pleasant reading and can prove useful as preliminary introductions to the writers discussed."

B963   "This Week," *Christian Century*, LXXXII (June 9, 1965), 745.
Very brief descriptive review.

B964   TORKELSON, LUCILE. "Women Preserve the Past," Milwaukee *Sentinel*, June 18, 1965, Part 1, p. 6.
Descriptive review.

B965   *Virginia Quarterly Review*, XLI (Autumn 1965), cxxvi.
"It is not the application of [Auchincloss's] thesis to the individual essays which makes this collection so informative, interesting, and readable, but the inclusion of biographical details, succinct summaries of novels and stories, and appraisals of an author's work as a whole."

B966   WASHBURN, BEATRICE. "Lack of Interest in Fellow Men Shows in Book," Miami (Fla.) *Herald*, July 11, 1965, p. 6-C.
Descriptive review which disagrees with Auchincloss's high opinion of *Ship of Fools* and suggests that Elizabeth Madox Roberts could have been omitted from this book.

The Embezzler

B967   ANDERSON, H. T. *Best Sellers*, XXV (February 15, 1966), 425-426.
"It is a beautifully executed piece of fiction."

A Bibliography of Writings By and About Louis Auchincloss

WORKS ABOUT

B968   B., C. R. "Gems of Wisdom Make Worthy Book," Durham (N.C.)
        Morning Herald, April 10, 1966, p. 5D.
            "The thing that makes this work outstanding is the skill
        of the author who makes us feel pity, admiration, and dis-
        gust without wallowing around in a lot of needless nasti-
        ness, and to understand that while money can provide sur-
        face comfort and beauty, it cannot diminish the acute suf-
        fering experienced by the victims of other's selfishness."

B969   BANNERMAN, JAMES. "Bannerman on Books--Is Lavatory Scribbling
        Necessary?" *Maclean's,* LXXIX (May 14, 1966), 46-47 [46].
        Descriptive favorable review.

B970   BROWN, JOHN MASON. *"The Embezzler*--A New Novel By Louis Auch-
        incloss--The March Selection," *Book-of-the-Month Club News,*
        February 1966, pp. 1-3.
        Descriptive favorable review.

B971   BRUNDIGE, LENORE. "Swindler or Dupe?--The Golden Boy of Wall
        Street," Pittsburgh *Press,* February 13, 1966, Sec. 5, p. 14.
            Descriptive review: "a book that is written with preci-
        sion and logic."

B972   BUTCHER, FANNY. "Three Revealing Portraits of a Defrauder,"
        Chicago Tribune Books Today, February 6, 1966, p. 1. Also
        Orlando (Fla.) *Sentinel,* February 20, 1966, *Florida* Maga-
        zine, pp. 10-F, 11-F.
            "Auchincloss tells the intriguing story with skill, so-
        phistication, and sensitivity."

B973   CABLE, MARY. *The New Mexican* (Santa Fe), February 20, 1966
        Pasatiempo Magazine, p. 3.
            What is wrong with this book is that "the reader can
        never really care very much, because the author has ushered
        him to a godlike seat, rather too far above it all. From
        such a height, it is all too apparent that Guy, Rex, and
        Angelica are rather a dull lot. Perhaps there is something
        to be pitied in each, but they all have so much money and
        such nice clothes and such pleasant country estates that
        it's hard to get terribly worked up in their behalf."

B974   CARBON, CARMEN. *The Catholic Week* (Pensacola, Fla.),
        July 1, 1966, p. 7.
            Auchincloss raises "a pure soap opera plot" to "the level
        of competent fiction."

B975   CARMAN, BERNARD R. "Books--A Minority Opinion on a Latter-Day
        Trollope," *Berkshire Eagle* (Pittsfield, Mass.),
        April 23, 1966, Sec. 2, p. 16.

(CARMAN, BERNARD R.)
Why Auchincloss "enjoys such a devoted following remains somewhat baffling. He writes workmanlike prose, certainly, but he is no stylist. Nor is he much of a storyteller."

B976   *Choice,* III (September 1966), 516.
"A nicely done, neat book with few shocks but some fine writing and characterization. One could do worse than Auchincloss as the James-Wharton heir."

B977   CLOWES, JOHN. "Scandal in the Establishment," Louisville *Courier-Journal,* March 6, 1966, p. D6.
Although the three versions of the story "seem to pull apart rather than combine to develop the character of Guy Prime," this is, nevertheless, "a wonderful novel, absorbing from the very first page."

B978   CORDDRY, MARY. "Auchincloss Novel Equals His Best," Baltimore *Sunday Sun,* February 6, 1966, Sec. D, p. 5.
This novel "is engrossing from start to finish and provocative for long afterward." Its "real strength...is in the questions of human sympathy and guilt that the author never asks but arouses with force in the reader."

B979   DAVIS, PAXTON. "Auchincloss And His Newest Novel," Roanoke *Times,* March 6, 1966, p. C-6.
Auchincloss "has given me an extremely satisfying two evenings in a world I do not know, with people who interest and bother me, involved in a series of actions that, though I do not yet fully realize their import, fill me with wonder and pity. It is a lot more, to put it mildly, than I ever got from the likes of Saul Bellow or Norman Mailer."

B980   DERLETH, AUGUST. "Mr. Auchincloss Again," *Capital Times* (Madison, Wis.), February 17, 1966, p. 24.
Auchincloss is "actually closer to Mrs. Wharton in what he achieves" than he is to James. This is "a highly competent and satisfactory novel; it is one which many readers will find rewarding to read, but not one to which they are likely to be driven a second time."

B981   "Detachment on the Inside," *Time,* LVII (February 4, 1966), 107-108.
While neutrality worked as a novelistic technique in *Rector,* it does not here, "partly because these are not very interesting people, mainly because Auchincloss' total detachment invites the same reaction from the reader."

A Bibliography of Writings By and About Louis Auchincloss

WORKS ABOUT

B982   DOLBIER, MAURICE. "Daily Book Review--Not Near So Wicked As World Made Out," New York *Herald Tribune*, February 4, 1966, p. 19.
        Descriptive favorable review.

B983   EDEL, LEON. "I Fear the Crook When Quoting Greek," *Life*, LX (February 11, 1966), 10.
        "The form of *The Embezzler* is simply not suited to the subject; and Mr. Auchincloss contributes a further air of unreality by making the three apologias sound all alike and all of them embarrassingly literary.... Auchincloss's 'Old New York' stock company seems to have played its parts too often; the actors all have stopped putting feeling into their lines. Though it is readable and lively, I think of *The Embezzler* as an off-year Auchincloss."

B984   EDELSTEIN, ARTHUR. "Wide, Wide World of Books--In Auchincloss Novel, Who Is 'The Embezzler'?" *National Observer*, February 7, 1966, p. 23.
        "Serious in intent, hovering at the brink of moral experience, this novel never quite manages the plunge. What it gains through multiplicity of viewpoint it loses through paucity of rendition." The first section is better than the other two.

B985   EDWARDS, WILLIAM H. "A Fall From on High in Wall Street," Providence *Sunday Journal*, February 6, 1966, p. N-36.
        Although "the machinery of the book is a little bothersome," it is "an absorbing tale that holds the reader's interest in a tight clasp throughout.... the writing is clear and smooth and direct.... the narrative has a kind of intellectual fascination that is exhilarating for the reader."

B986   ELLIOTT, JOHN R. "The Book Scene--Auchincloss' New Novel, 'The Embezzler,' Contrasts 1936 Morals With Today's," Louisville *Times*, March 17, 1966, p. A 11.
        Descriptive review: a "well done" novel, "a fascinating tale, thrice told."

B987   "Fiction--Pinched," *Times Literary Supplement* (London), June 23, 1966, p. 549.
        "The prose lacks the cutting edge which satire demands and the characters have not been sufficiently created for us to care about their feelings and relationships. We end with a sense that the novel, though easy enough to read and entertaining in an undemanding way, lacks pressure; it feels as if it would have been just as easy for Mr. Auchincloss not to have written it."

A Bibliography of Writings By and About Louis Auchincloss

B988   FLEISCHER, LEONORE. *Publishers' Weekly*, CXC (December 26, 1966), 101.
        Brief descriptive review.

B989   FLETCHER, JANE. "Heralding the New Books--An Elegant, Stylish Novel," Monterey (Calif.) *Peninsula Herald*, March 12, 1966, p. 20.
        This is "an engrossing book, written with elegance and style," although its characters "never seem quite to have emerged from their cellophane wrappings."

B990   FOSTER, JAMES. "Financial Peg Stuck On Old Plot," *Rocky Mountain News* (Denver), February 13, 1966, p. 22A.
        "The author does a masterful job of putting it all down but who cares to read a book centered around a crashing stock market? No writer can sell to such a down market."

B991   FOURNIER, NORMAN. "Book Beat," Portland (Me.) *Sunday Telegram*, February 27, 1966, p. 4C.
        "'The Embezzler' comes close to duplicating Auchincloss's remarkable performance in 'Rector of Justin' and will rank as one of the year's better fiction offerings."

B992   FREIBERG, BERNARD S. "Literary Scene," *Bucks County Life*, VIII (June 1966), 14.
        This novel "is a further example of the author's development from an entertaining story teller to an absorbing artist of character."

B993   FULLER, EDMUND. "The Bookshelf--A Skilled, Fascinating Novel By Auchincloss," *Wall Street Journal*, February 9, 1966, p. 18.
        This novel is "excellent." Its "only technical flaw... is one which simply must be accepted within literary convention, though it might have been avoided. Rex's narrative, in style, subtlety and allusiveness, seems far beyond his believable ability of self-expression, though its basic point of view is convincing. The objection does not apply to either Guy or Angelica."

B994   GALLOWAY, DAVID. "Big Ideas," *The Spectator*, No. 7199 (June 17, 1966), 765.
        Auchincloss "never seems certain whether he is making more of Guy Prime than there really is, or decidedly less, or indeed, whether it matters after all." But the book has "moments of vintage Auchincloss," although it is "like slightly flat champagne; still, no one could mistake it for stale beer."

A Bibliography of Writings By and About Louis Auchincloss

WORKS ABOUT

B995   GAMMACK, GORDON. "Novel Deftly Lacerates Snobs and Pretend-
        ers," Des Moines *Sunday Register*, February 6, 1966, p. 17-G.
        "If Auchincloss is faulty (and this is a bit like tell-
        ing a wise priest what constitutes a good man), the weak-
        ness may be that he is too good, too learned; that what is
        plausible in Auchincloss is not entirely plausible in the
        men and women he creates." But such criticisms are "unim-
        portant, really, because 'The Embezzler' certainly will be
        one of the most significant, most talked about and best
        sold novels of 1966."

B996   GILLIAM, STANLEY. "Auchincloss Is At His Best in Triple View
        of an Embezzler," Sacramento *Bee*, February 6, 1966, p. L-25.
        "The author does an excellent job of shading his grays
        between very dark and very light without going to black and
        white extremes in developing his characters and he leaves
        the reader with very properly mixed emotions ranging from
        approbation to disapproval of each."

B997   GORDON, NOAH. "3 Faces of Swindler--Romance of Dishonesty,"
        Boston *Sunday Globe*, February 6, 1966, p. A-41.
        "Despite his usual faultless literary style, in 'The Em-
        bezzler' Auchincloss has created people who are cold, ugly
        of spirit but never sufficiently damned to be very interest-
        ing."

B998   GOVAN, GILBERT E. "Themes of Permanent Interest," Chattanooga
        Times, February 27, 1966, p. 12.
        Auchincloss's is "an interesting if not always a com-
        pletely successful technique. But the people carry convic-
        tion and the situation is one which should have general in-
        terest for American readers."

B999   GREENWOOD, WALTER B. "Three Interpretations of One Man's
        Crime Pose Ethical Question," Buffalo *Evening News*,
        February 19, 1966, p. B-14.
        "'The Embezzler' and Auchincloss himself brighten an
        otherwise drab fictional season."

B1000   H., V. P. "Spectacular Defrauder Who Fouled His Nest," Omaha
        Sunday World-Herald, March 13, 1966, Magazine, p. 28.
        "This is the stuff of hypnotically readable fiction and
        Auchincloss makes the most of it in a book that may be
        more exciting reading for some people than even his bril-
        liant 'Rector of Justin.'"

B1001   HALL, JOAN JOFFE. "Color Us Dull," Houston *Post*,
        February 6, 1966, *Spotlight* Magazine, p. 14.
        "The lives of the characters are neither pretty nor

Book Reviews-*The Embezzler*

(HALL, JOAN JOFFE)
spectacularly sordid. They are passably interesting as accounts of upper class New York life in the early 20th century, but they simply aren't lifted into a story that makes that life sufficiently meaningful."

B1002   HANSCOM, JAMES. "Auchincloss Scores Again--3-Way View of an Embezzler," Norfolk *Virginian-Pilot*, February 6, 1966, p. B-6.
"The wonder of Auchincloss' achievement is that he has not relied on plot, on whodunit, in the conventional sense. His plot is three human beings, who reveal themselves in turn. The exposition of their characters, shifting as we see them through shifting eyes, provides the suspense. And there is suspense a-plenty."

B1003   HICKEY, E. V. "Auchincloss Slips in New Novel," Boston *Sunday Herald*, February 6, 1966, *Show Guide* Magazine, p. 21.
"The problem for the reader is that it is not terribly easy to identify with any of these characters in a deeper sense and all through the book one is aware of the sense of manipulation of characters to weave a sufficient story to warrant a hard cover."

B1004   HICKS, GRANVILLE. "Literary Horizons--A Bad Legend in His Lifetime," *Saturday Review*, XLIX (February 5, 1966), 35-36. Reprinted in Hicks, *Literary Horizons* (B3).
"Try as he may, Auchincloss cannot persuade the reader to take these people at their own valuation. One has to be wary in stating this kind of judgment; certainly the plots of many of Henry James's novels can be described in such a way as to make them sound ridiculously trivial. But James had resources, both of insight and of stylistic subtlety, that Auchincloss cannot draw on."

B1005   HILL, WILLIAM B., [S.J.] *America*, CXIV (March 5, 1966), 333-334.
"What keeps the book from being more immediately tragic is its unrelenting realism: none of the characters is ultimately appealing, capable of winning a reader's complete sympathy. Despite this one limitation, in itself a testimony to artistic integrity, this sophisticated and stylistically excellent book is well worth knowing."

B1006   HOGAN, WILLIAM. "World of Books--Another Point of No Return," San Francisco *Chronicle*, February 7, 1966, p. 47.
"'The Embezzler' is a workmanlike excursion through the financial jungle of a generation ago and an introduction to

WORKS ABOUT

(HOGAN, WILLIAM)
some of its glossy denizens. It appears to be a standard
Auchincloss performance, and as such should have a built-
in audience waiting for it. I found it to be a fairly
empty book, however."

B1007   HOLDEN, THEODORE L. "Auchincloss Views 3 Sides," Hartford
Times, February 5, 1966, p. 20.
This novel, while not as good as *Rector*, is "still
good enough to reaffirm my conviction that Louis Auchincloss' writing shows strength and maturity equal to that of
any other American novelist today."

B1008   HOLT, MARJORIE. "Catching the 'Embezzler,'" *Cornell Daily
Sun* (Ithaca, N.Y.), February 16, 1966, p. 5.
"It is very rarely amusing, very rarely startling--al-
ways fine, steady, solidly-constructed fiction. Auchincloss seems to have chosen his place at the end of the
Jamesian line--without the depth and irony of James. It
would be interesting--but nevertheless unlikely--to see
how Auchincloss would start a line of his own."

B1009   HOWE, MARJORIE. "New Books--'Double Image' Masterful Tale of
Terror, Suspense," Burlington (Vt.) *Free Press*,
February 10, 1966, p. 22.
Brief favorable review: "a fascinating tale by one of
America's finest novelists."

B1010   HOYT, ELIZABETH N. "Finally, a Good Novel Appears," Cedar
Rapids *Gazette*, February 6, 1966, p. 2C.
This is "far and away the best piece of fiction that I
have read in a long time."

B1011   JAMES, BERTHA TEN EYCK. "A Man and His Money," Worcester *Sunday Telegram*, February 6, 1966, p. E7.
Descriptive review.

B1012   J[ORDAN], E[LOISE] M. "'The Embezzler' Latest Book By Louis
Auchincloss," Lewiston (Me.) *Evening Journal*,
February 12, 1966, p. 2-A.
"These are all characters of an age and a time, but in
themselves they are not important enough to command the
attention of a writer of Mr. Auchincloss' caliber. Their
values are all material, there is nothing spiritual to
elevate them above their fellow men."

A Bibliography of Writings By and About Louis Auchincloss

B1013 K., J. S. "The Thrice Told Tale," *Catholic Transcript,*
February 11, 1966, p. 5.
"This is a novel of considerable literary distinction and
of uncommon subtlety. But there is something wearing and
wearying in going over the same ground three several, successive times. Hence, whereas this reviewer believed for some
time that *The Embezzler* was possibly the author's best book,
enthusiasm waned as the second, then the third rehearsal pro-
ceeded."

B1014 KEITH, DON LEE. "Auchincloss Is Again Master of Retrospect,"
New Orleans *Times Picayune,* February 27, 1966, Sec. 2, p. 4.
"Each move, each piece of dialogue, is carefully constructed to reveal a dignity which is undauntable even in
failure or defeat. The scenes, even those of sordid atmosphere, still connote a sort of *creme de la creme* reaction to
ordinary and extraordinary events and it is in this technique that Auchincloss has carved his niche as a craftsman."

B1015 KENNEDY, WILLIAM. "Happiness Is a Warm Smashup," *The Episcopa-
lian,* CXXXI (July 1966), 36-37.
"In *The Embezzler,* Mr. Auchincloss has given us a brilliant American tragicomedy about our national article of
faith that everything is all right as long as we are well-
liked and successful."

B1016 *Kirkus,* XXXIII (December 15, 1965), 1233.
This novel "(stronger than many he has done in the past)
is a poised, proportioned entertainment...."

B1017 KIRSCH, ROBERT R. "The Book Report—Hard Times of High Society," Los Angeles *Times,* February 15, 1966, Part IV, p. 5.
All of the novel's characters "believe that the moral
tone of the country is lower now than it was then. I am
not suggesting that Auchincloss shares the view but I do
think that he takes that world far too seriously, even for
a novelist of manners."

B1018 KITCHING, JESSIE. *Publishers' Weekly,* CLXXXVIII (December 6,
1965), 58.
Brief review. "The story is an enthralling mixture of
big-time financial ploys, marital scandal, and society
gossip, seasoned with marvelously funny epigrams."

B1019 KNICKERBOCKER, CONRAD. "The Crooked and the Straight," *New
York Times Book Review,* February 6, 1966, pp. 1, 38.
Auchincloss "causes us to admit that life is perhaps not
as alienating as we sometimes like to think. Nor is the
novel as moribund and symptomatic as we like on occasion to
believe. 'The Embezzler,' century-old conventions and all,
sets standards and lives up to them. And in the end they
are good standards, not because they are old, but because
they are still true."

A Bibliography of Writings By and About Louis Auchincloss

WORKS ABOUT

B1020   LANE, MADGE M. "From the Bookcase--A Wall Street Manipulator:
         3 Viewpoints on His Life," Birmingham (Mich.) *Eccentric*,
         March 17, 1966, p. 7-C.
                "None of the characters is sympathetic, and there is a
         paper-doll superficiality about them that doesn't warm the
         cockles of the heart." Although the novel is "eminently
         readable," it "falls short in that Guy does not come through
         as a lovable scamp or a gleeful villain...."

B1021   LAWRENCE, WES. "Auchincloss Captures the Evil 30s," Cleveland
         Plain Dealer, February 6, 1966, p. 7-H.
                Auchincloss "is one of the best if not the best novelist
         writing in America today, and if he has not received general
         recognition as such it is because of an upside-down snob-
         bishness which considers the sort of people he writes about
         as too superficial for literary concern." This novel is "a
         worthy successor" to Auchincloss's earlier works.

B1022   LEBHERZ, RICHARD. "Inside the Arts," Frederick (Md.) *Post*,
         May 26, 1966, p. 2.
                This is "a fine novel" and "an entertaining one. And
         it's first rate writing from beginning to end."

B1023   LEHAN, RICHARD. "The American Novel--A Survey of 1966," *Wis-
         consin Studies in Contemporary Literature*, VIII
         (Summer 1967), 437-449 [442-444].
                This, in many ways, is "a Galsworthy novel written by
         Henry James, a novel of plot that also tortures cultural and
         moral questions." Auchincloss's achievement "is in his
         ability to create a twilight realm of decision and indecision
         where characters are homeless...and in search of moral abso-
         lutes...."

         LEWIS, R. W. B. "Silver Spoons and Golden Bowls," *Book Week* (Wash-
         ington *Post*, New York *Herald Tribune*, Chicago *Sun-Times*),
         February 20, 1966, pp. 1-8. *See* B946.
                This is Auchincloss's "most satisfying work. It is not
         nearly as ambitious as *The Rector of Justin*, and its osten-
         sible subject-matter is far less absorbing than the dilemmas
         of religious faith there explored. But it is, I think, a
         better wrought if slenderer book."

B1024   LYNCH, DONNA. "*The Embezzler*--Auchincloss Brings New Under-
         standing to Financial World," Baton Rouge *Sunday Advocate*,
         June 19, 1966, p. 2-E.
                Descriptive favorable review.

B1025   McCORMICK, JAY. "Aristocracy of Money With a Counterfeit Ring,"
         Detroit *News*, February 20, 1966, p. 3-H.
                "All in all it makes a readable but not a memorable book,
         well written, subtle and telling in its fashion, but never

(McCORMICK, JAY)
  attaining those true, winding overtones that Auchincloss
produced in 'The Rector of Justin.'"

B1026 McGRADY, MIKE. "A Novel of Manners and Mannerisms," *Newsday*
(Garden City, N.Y.), February 5, 1966, p. 15W.
  "Auchincloss has gone to considerable trouble to catalog
his characters--the ties all carry the proper labels. But,
unfortunately, the characters have no more dimension than
the mannequins pictured in any slick catalog."

B1027 "A Master's Touch," *Newsweek*, LXVII (February 14, 1966),
96D-98.
  "In the hands of Auchincloss, the result [of the novel's
tripartite structure] is a tantalizing psychological and
moral mystery of human motivation." This review also includes an interview with Auchincloss.

B1028 MOODY, MINNIE HITE. "Shrewd, Droll Novel of Human Frailties,"
Columbus (Ohio) *Dispatch*, February 6, 1966, TAB Section,
p. 18.
  Auchincloss is "a novelist who is at once shrewd and
droll, witty and heart-breaking, revealing and subtle....
Though his world on the surface seems but seldom the milieu
of the common man, go a bit deeper and you will notice that
he is not fooling himself or anybody."

B1029 MOONEY, HARRY J., JR. "Auchincloss' Latest Novel Disappoints,"
Pittsburgh *Catholic*, February 24, 1966, Fine Arts Supplement, p. 4.
  "The ultimate limitation of 'The Embezzler' lies in the
enclosed quality of the society it depicts, in the unsympa-
thetic, and finally uninteresting, characters it portrays."
It is, finally, "an uncompelling novel for the most relevant
reason of all: it merely reflects its characters."

B1030 MOORE, HARRY T. "Book of the Week--Browning's Touch in a Novel
of Manners," Chicago *Daily News*, February 5, 1966, Panorama
Section, p. 7.
  This is "amusing though not necessarily deep reading,"
although "those who go through this book will feel that perhaps Guy Prime should have told some of his prison experiences. But for a fine, brittle, surface look at American
manners, this story--as glossy-smooth as the author's name--
will provide unfailing entertainment."

B1031 MURRAY, JAMES G. "Books By White, Greene, Auchincloss--Of
Friendly Marbles, Seething Haiti, Dry Finance," *St. Louis
Review*, March 4, 1966, p. 18.
  Auchincloss "has written a nothing book--weak on plot,
conventional on character, idea-less, humor-less, grace-less."

167

A Bibliography of Writings By and About Louis Auchincloss

WORKS ABOUT

B1032   PEARRE, HOWELL. "Fine Commentary on Ways of the Rich," Nash-
        ville *Banner*, February 11, 1966, p. 25.
           This is Auchincloss's "most perfect work to date" and "a
        brilliant novel, flashing with the hardness and beauty of
        life, in addition to being a fine commentary on the ways of
        the rich. Mr. Auchincloss has created three memorable char-
        acters, complex in their interrelationships but bristling
        with the vigor and pettiness of all humanity."

B1033   PECKHAM, STANTON. "Story of Phony Trite But Enjoyable," Denver
        Sunday Post, January 30, 1966, *Roundup* Magazine, p. 9.
           Guy Prime "evolves into a strangely phony paradox of a
        man, frequently charming but often a bore.... Representa-
        tive though he may be, he is not good material for a lasting
        work of fiction. Yet 'The Embezzler' is an excellent novel.
        It is well-paced, intriguing, full of surprises."

B1034   PICKREL, PAUL. "The Double Vision of Society," *Harper's Maga-
        zine*, CCXXXII (March 1966), 148-149.
           "The tension that braces the novels of Louis Auchincloss
        is a kind of double vision of society: he is deeply drawn
        to the conviction that men at certain times and places had
        an idealism or a grandeur that they no longer have, but si-
        multaneously he has a strong suspicion that most men have al-
        ways been out to get all they could and the splendor with
        which they have sometimes been able to surround their persons
        and their motives has been largely a disguise." In this nov-
        el, there "is a question whether Guy Prime is quite worth
        such an elaborate deployment of literary forces." The nov-
        el's success lies "with the shifting views of the lesser
        characters, particularly Guy Prime's mother and father...."

B1035   POLLOCK, VENETIA. "New Novels," *Punch* (London), CCL
        (June 29, 1966), 965.
           "*The Embezzler* is exquisitely precise and poised, full of
        social satire and gentle laughter. Auchincloss has surpassed
        himself in this magnificent comedy of manners and to his usu-
        al light deliberate touch is added a new tangy crisper wit.
        Possessing all the social acumen of a Jane Austen, he is *the*
        post-Freud snobographer."

B1036   PRESCOTT, ORVILLE. "Books of The Times--The Decline and Fall
        of Guy Prime," New York *Times*, February 7, 1966, p. 27.
        Also Indianapolis *News*, February 20, 1966; Shreveport *Jour-
        nal*, February 18, 1966; Seattle *Post-Intelligencer*,
        March 27, 1966.
           "'The Embezzler' may leave too much room for doubt about
        the motivating force that destroyed Guy Prime.... Never-
        theless, the novel is full of insights and full of sharply ob-
        served reports on life among the very rich in New York City
        a generation and more ago....there isn't a dull page in 'The
        Embezzler.'"

168

Book Reviews-*The Embezzler*

B1037   PRESCOTT, PETER S.   "Books," *Women's Wear Daily*,
          February 4, 1966, p. 24.
              What is wrong with the novel is that "the second half is
          far duller than the first.   It expands our knowledge of Guy's
          life, but it does little to change or enlarge our view of
          him.... But the fascination of Prime's story and the liter-
          ate embellishment of what Rex and Angelica have to say assure
          this a place among the year's best novels."

B1038   PREYER, L. RICHARDSON.   "'Embezzler': Off-Year Auchincloss,"
          Greensboro (N.C.) *Daily News*, May 1, 1966, p. C3.
              "The hero strikes a tragic pose, but the reader thinks of
          him as something out of soap opera rather than Sophocles.
          Auchincloss writes so smoothly and well that we find the
          first half of the book lively and readable.... When [Guy's]
          uninteresting wife and his pompous best friend tell their
          version of the same story it is strictly Dragsville."

B1039   Q[UILL], G[YNTER].   "Crooked Stock Broker of the Depression
          Era," Waco (Texas) *Tribune-Herald*, February 6, 1966, p. D-5.
              "There is no writer I would rather read than Auchincloss,
          for none can create with such precision a character who
          walks right out of the pages into the living room."

B1040   RAPHAEL, FREDERIC.   "Fiction of the Week," London *Sunday Times*,
          June 12, 1966, p. 29.
              "You sometimes feel that Mr. Auchincloss's premises are
          deduced from his conclusions, but his novel is full of inci-
          dent, perception and the kind of inside information, which
          makes one feel that one has for once been inside the doors of
          the kind of club that would never dream of having one as a
          member."

B1041   READ, DAVID W.   "The New Auchincloss--A Stylist at His Best,"
          St. Louis *Post-Dispatch*, February 6, 1966, p. 4D.
              "Written in the great tradition of Hawthorne and Edith
          Wharton and Henry James, this slim novel, apparently lesser
          than 'The Rector of Justin' but in reality greater, merits
          high praise."

B1042   REID, MARGARET W.   "A Three-Sided Portrait of a New York Bro-
          ker," Wichita Falls (Texas) *Times*, February 6, 1966, Fea-
          tures Magazine, p. 4.
              Auchincloss's "wit and urbanity, understanding of human
          nature, and his pleasing prose make his book highly readable."

B1043   ROGERS, W. G.   "Books--Auchincloss Reveals a Social Corruption,"
          Grand Rapids *Press*, February 6, 1966, p. 49.   Also St. Peters-
          burg (Fla.) *Times*, February 6, 1966, Leisure and the Arts Sec-
          tion, p. 12; Tucson *Citizen*, May 14, 1966; Knoxville (Tenn.)
          News-Sentinel, February 6, 1966; Rochester (N.Y.) *Democrat &*

A Bibliography of Writings By and About Louis Auchincloss

WORKS ABOUT

(ROGERS, W. G.)
Chronicle, February 6, 1966; Toledo *Blade,* February 6, 1966;
Lewiston (Idaho) *Tribune,* February 6, 1966.
"This absorbing story will have you in puzzlement and
wondering, long after Auchincloss' last page."

B1044   SCHLUETER, PAUL. "Triple Exposure," *Christian Century,*
LXXXIII (March 2, 1966), 272-273.
"*The Embezzler* is a highly competent and skillfully
developed piece of fiction dealing with believable people
involved in moments of high ethical complexity as well as
in the everyday activities of the rich."

B1045   SCHMIDT, SANDRA. "A Novelist at His Acrobatics," *Christian
Science Monitor,* February 10, 1966, p. 7.
"'The Embezzler' is not, by any means, a bad book. The
prose has flavor, mood, a quality of intrigued bemusement
that interests the reader in the most convoluted reflection." But Auchincloss, "whatever his hardwon skill as a
writer, whatever his ambitions, is not yet a chronicler of
character. At his best, he is an articulate acrobat among
a number of points of view."

B1046   SCHWARTZ, JOSEPH. "'Our Finest Novelist of Manners' Offers a
Study in Honor, Disgrace," Milwaukee *Journal,*
February 6, 1966, Part 5, p. 4.
"Auchincloss is our finest contemporary novelist of
manners.... Yet, there is a major flaw in the novel: Guy
should never have been allowed to tell his own story.
His romantic readiness would have been more mysteriously
convincing had it been dramatized through the expository
narratives of others. But it is the kind of flaw which
only a major artist could have committed. It is a flaw in
experimentation, and in art there is only the trying."

B1047   SHAFER, CAROL. "World of Finance Opens in Tale of Tangled
Lives," Minneapolis *Tribune,* February 13, 1966, Entertainment and the Arts Section, p. 6.
Auchincloss "brings to fiction some of the aloofness and
judiciousness of the legal mind. Though this may contribute to superior insight it probably hampers portrayal of
passion." Nevertheless, this is "a fine book."

B1048   SHAW, RUSSELL. *The Sign,* XLV (March 1966), 57-58.
Auchincloss's theme is one "that might have brought out
the best in an analyst of moral ambiguity like Henry James
or Graham Greene"; but what it brings out here "is, for
the most part, pomposity and mediocre writing."

170

B1049   SMITH, M[ILES] A. "Auchincloss at Peak Form," Tulsa *Sunday World*, March 13, 1966, p. 18-E. Also Allentown (Pa.) *Sunday Call-Chronicle*, February 6, 1966; El Paso *Times*, February 20, 1966; Santa Barbara (Calif.) *News-Press*, February 13, 1966.

"Auchincloss is a master of both narrative and character, an author whose unobtrusive skill leaves you captured for days in contemplation of the world he created."

B1050   SOMERVILLE, COL. D. S. "The Fatal Flaw," Hartford *Courant*, February 6, 1966, Magazine, p. 13.

"If there is any implausibility in 'The Embezzler,'... it must be found in those not infrequent instances where his characters (sometimes barely out of their 'teens) hide deep emotion behind measured wit or philosophy instead of giving out now and then with 'good mouth-filling oaths.' They've been heard even in the drawing rooms that Auchincloss' people inhabit."

B1051   SQUIRRU, RAFAEL. *Américas*, XVIII (April 1966), 47-48.

The novel "has no negligible degree of worldly wisdom to offer the reader. A wisdom by no means to be scorned. But even then, and granting that we come out the wiser after having read it, we also feel the wish that at some point the characters might have loved themselves and each other more deeply and more truly. A very unfair statement no doubt about this particularly craftsmanlike piece of art."

B1052   STERN, JEROME H. "Absorbing, Crisp, Unsatisfactory...That's Auchincloss," Charlotte (N.C.) *Observer*, February 13, 1966, p. 6F.

The novel is "continually absorbing and continually unsatisfactory. Absorbing, because Auchincloss has a certain cleanliness of plot and style which keeps his story moving, his characters running about, his scenes making their points crisply." Disappointing, because "the characters see themselves as more unusual than they are."

B1053   SULLIVAN, RICHARD. "Prime's Past," *The Critic*, XXIV (April-May 1966), 61-62.

"In *The Embezzler* Auchincloss has written, deftly, a relatively superficial novel. Relatively so, because not only has he shown in other books that he can go deeper, but the superficiality I note here would in the work of some writers be considered profound delving."

A Bibliography of Writings By and About Louis Auchincloss

WORKS ABOUT

B1054   T., A. M. "World of Finance," Trenton (N.J.) *Sunday Times-Advertiser*, February 20, 1966, Magazine, p. 9.
        Brief favorable review: a "thoughtful and skillfully told story."

B1055   THOMAS, ALMA S. "Author's Dexterity Assures Popularity of Latest Novel," Savannah *Morning News*, February 6, 1966, Magazine, p. 8.
        Auchincloss's "smooth flowing prose, his well turned phrases, his objectivity about his well known subjects proclaim his dexterity. If he is praised here with a faint 'damn,' it is because with all that smoothness and uncanny relevance one expects glory. But what one gets is a glorified version of a tattlesheet. One feels interest, but never that over-worked word 'empathy.'"

B1056   THOMAS, LUCY. "Uses Technique From 'Rector of Justin'--Auchincloss Lets Reader Be Judge," Fort Smith (Ark.) *Southwest-Times Record*, February 20, 1966, p. 10-B.
        The novel is "artfully constructed and eminently readable. It will undoubtedly be classed as one of the better books of 1966."

B1057   THOMAS, SIDNEY S. "Attempt at Embezzling," Atlanta *Journal and Constitution*, February 6, 1966, p. 2-B.
        "Actually, such as is the nature of the present, it is difficult to take quite seriously the people and the way of life Mr. Auchincloss describes. They seem too remote and unreal, like characters and situations in an operetta set in some mythical kingdom. They don't strike one as of the least importance. And, as a matter of fact, neither does this novel."

B1058   THORPE, DAY. "Books: Auchincloss Novel Is Solid and Entertaining," Washington (D.C.) *Sunday Star*, February 6, 1966, p. G-2.
        "'The Embezzler' is succinct, aphoristic, witty and fast-moving. However greatly Guy, Rex and Angelica may differ in matters of life, love and morality, they all show one inescapable consanguinity. The literary styles of all three are distinguished and indistinguishable."

B1059   TINKLE, LON. "Reading and Writing--Auchincloss Poses Problem of Values," Dallas *Morning News*, February 6, 1966, p. 2 G.
        Descriptive favorable review. "'The Embezzler' may augment your confusion but it will also enlarge your understanding."

B1060   *Virginia Quarterly Review,* XLII (Summer 1966), lxxxviii.
        Brief review. The book is good, "despite the fact that
        while his principal character is memorably conceived the
        others fade into the mists of the genteel era they so ad-
        mirably represent."

B1061   WAGENKNECHT, EDWARD. "The Book Parade," *News-Tribune* (Wal-
        tham, Newton, Weston, Lincoln, Mass.), February 16, 1966,
        p. 7.
        "I think Auchincloss more successful with the wife than
        with either of the men; in fact, it is a rather exciting
        revisioning of her character that the reader must do when,
        having seen her from two outside vantage-points, he finally
        sees her, at the end, from the inside. But with the oth-
        ers I sometimes get an uncomfortable impression of virtuo-
        sity for virtuosity's sake."

B1062   WAGNER, CONSTANCE. *Books Abroad,* XL (Autumn 1966), 463.
        "*The Embezzler* is painstakingly built, without baroque
        ornament or dazzling innovation. It is not until the book
        is almost finished that one realizes the subtlety of its
        implications and the sureness of the creative hand."

B1063   WARD, FERDINAND J., C. M. "'The Embezzlers' [sic.]--Auchin-
        closs' Portrait of New York Society Entertaining, Light,"
        The New World (Chicago), February 18, 1966, p. 16.
        Descriptive favorable review: an "easily read" novel.

B1064   WARDLE, IRVING. "Auchincloss in Wall Street," *The Observer*
        (London), June 12, 1966, p. 26.
        Although "characterization is Auchincloss's weakness,"
        the book is "stylistically a great pleasure, and full of
        affectionate insight into the mercantile high society
        which Auchincloss once defined as 'Brownstone Medici.'"

B1065   WEEKS, EDWARD. "The Peripatetic Reviewer--After the Market
        Broke," *The Atlantic,* CCXVII (February 1966), 129.
        "The literary artifice in all this seems to me question-
        able, but the story is such a good one and the three points
        of view so entertaining in their contrast that I can for-
        give it.... The author never persuades me that his men are
        in love, which is a pity since Guy must have been quite
        good at it. Of the three narrators, Angelica is the most
        believable, more downright and with far less special plead-
        ing than either of her lovers."

B1066   WILLIS, KATHERINE TAPPERT. *Library Journal,* XCI
        (February 15, 1966), 960.

WORKS ABOUT

(WILLIS, KATHERINE TAPPERT)
   Brief review. Despite the fact that "there is no character that will be remembered with any affection--or much
interest," this novel is "well balanced and entertaining."

B1067   WILSON, W. EMERSON. "Books in the News--Downfall of a Wealthy Embezzler," Wilmington (Del.) *Morning News*,
February 4, 1966, p. 19.
   "An excellent novel, this one should prove even more
popular than...'Rector of Justin' although the characters
and milieu are radically different from that book."

B1068   YAEGER, SUSAN M. "The Imitation of Models: New Fiction,"
Chicago Literary Review, III (April-May 1966), 4, 10.
   Auchincloss's characters "are heavily drawn and empty
creatures" by comparison with James's. They are "too ob-
vious to seem vibrantly real. The eye of their observer
has seen only generalities of thought and action, failing
to capture the hidden gestures, the revealing idiosyncra-
sies which flaw a surface only to make it more perfect."

Tales of Manhattan

B1069   ALEXANDER, JAMES E. "Three Short Stories By Louis Auchin-
closs--'Tales' Interesting But Without Significance,"
Pittsburgh *Post-Gazette*, March 25, 1967, p. 17.
   "His characters are beautifully delineated. You have
no wish to know any of them, but you certainly know who
they are."

B1070   BADEN, RUTH. "An Imaginary Talk With Mr. A," Boston *Sunday
Herald Traveler*, August 13, 1967, *Show Guide* Magazine,
p. 18.
   Review in the form of an imaginary interview with Auchincloss. Not much critical judgment included.

B1071   BAIL, JAY. "The Bookshelf--Like Gotham Gothic," Quincy
(Mass.) *Patriot Ledger*, March 23, 1967, p. 40.
   "One or two good stories do not keep Auchincloss from
being an extremely bad writer. It is almost impossible to
believe people actually speak the words he puts into the
mouths of his characters. His stories are never well constructed, the action wandering too often to the irrelevant.
It is difficult to pry apart one of his characters from the
others. And since there are very few points at which he
cuts into the reader's feelings, these stories are largely
ineffective."

A Bibliography of Writings By and About Louis Auchincloss

B1072   BARKHAM, JOHN. "Civilized Tales of Urbane Sophisticates," Wichita Falls (Texas) *Times,* April 2, 1967, Features Magazine, p. 5.
Auchincloss is "indubitably the tidiest of our name writers." Each of his stories "is itself a well-made piece of fiction and, in all probability, part of a larger plan."

B1073   BERGAMO, RALPH. "City's Teeming Life Seen By An Artist," Atlanta *Journal,* March 26, 1967, p. 10-B.
"Probably closest in spirit to Henry James of any of our modern American writers, Auchincloss has the same power as the master to write out of what seems personal experience with a leisure and detachment that set his work apart as a classical triumph."

B1074   B[OESCHENSTEIN], C. K. "Art Dealers, Lawyers and Matrons," St. Louis *Globe-Democrat,* April 1-2, 1967, p. 5F.
Descriptive favorable review.

B1075   C., J. "Auchincloss X-Rays Society in 'Manhattan,'" Buffalo *Courier-Express,* April 30, 1967, p. D-36.
"Auchincloss' deft technique is exceeded only by his marvelous usage and handling of the English language as it should be handled."

B1076   "Character Witness," *Time,* LXXXIX (March 31, 1967), 99-100.
"Within his esthetic code, Auchincloss tells the truth and nothing but the truth. But he does not tell the whole truth, which can be dismissed as irrelevant, immaterial-- and harder to write."

B1077   CHRISTOPHER, MICHAEL. *U. S. Catholic,* XXXIII (July 1967), 49-50.
"Unfortunately, the stories fall far below the quality of Mr. Auchincloss's novels and, as a matter of fact, stop perilously close to the threshold of boredom. But if you are tired of television and not attracted by the new fiction, you will find that even inferior Auchincloss is still fairly enjoyable reading."

B1078   CLAY, MARY. "Facades and Realities of N.Y.'s Upper Class," Providence *Sunday Journal,* April 23, 1967, p. W-24.
Book is "as much a sociological document as it is fiction."

B1079   DAVIDSON, JOHN L., JR. "Between Book Ends--New York Social Life, Told With Authority," St. Louis *Post-Dispatch,* June 14, 1967, p. 2D.

A Bibliography of Writings By and About Louis Auchincloss

WORKS ABOUT

(DAVIDSON, JOHN L., JR.)
"Unwisely, Auchincloss sometimes tries to write the thoughts of a woman." When he does, he "fails to convey the sense of complete knowledge which so strengthens most of his work."

B1080 DEGNAN, JAMES. "The Novelist as Gentleman," *The Critic*, XXV (June-July 1967), 86-88.
Auchincloss "is one of the few genuinely civilized, mature, and interesting storytellers working in America today. He is a great original by virtue of his successful sublimation of the usual temptations to be original."

B1081 DICKENS, MONICA. "It's All Class," Boston *Globe*, April 2, 1967, p. 34-B.
"It's all a blessedly civilized relief from the spew of novels which say we are beastliness. Here, even lust is very well bred, and adultery comes cleanly chilled, with an olive."

B1082 DOLBIER, MAURICE. "World of Books--Two Worlds of Manhattan Co-exist In Stories of Scrupulous Detail," New York *World Journal Tribune*, March 24, 1967, p. 20.
Descriptive favorable review.

B1083 EDEL, LEON. "High Polish," *Book Week* (Washington *Post*, New York *World Journal Tribune*, Chicago *Sun-Times*), April 9, 1967, p. 14.
"To reduce these tales to a brief sentence or two... does not suggest their insights and their delicate subtleties. Nevertheless, with a writer of such gifts, we ask ourselves why Auchincloss' work gives an impression of a certain thinness, of being in two dimensions.... With Auchincloss we are rushed along, in a kind of restless creation; the narrative leaves the reader--and the characters--little time for reflection and the sense of being in time and in space; we do not get a chance to live through the experience; it is over before we attain full awareness of it."

B1084 FOURNIER, NORMAN. "Looking at Books--Today's Fiction's 'Mr. Clean' Does It Again," Portland (Me.) *Evening Express*, May 8, 1967, p. 13.
Auchincloss's works "are probably this generation's most underrated." The theme of this book is "that appearance is only the visible tip of the iceberg, and that it is seldom possible to make a clearcut chart of the ice that is lurking underwater."

B1085   GARDNER, MARILYN. "Auchincloss's New York," *Christian Science Monitor*, March 30, 1967, p. 11.
        Ironically, Auchincloss's matrons are more convincing than his lawyers; but "more memorable" are his "unexpected word pictures of Manhattan itself."

B1086   GATZ, JOAN. "Reviewer Discovers What She Has Missed," Omaha *World-Herald*, April 2, 1967, Sec. I, p. 38.
        "Auchincloss is a master of innuendo and nuance and a skillful surveyor of the human heart with its welter of confused and contradictory motives. His 'Tales of Manhattan' is a fine collection, superb at rendering intelligent people and their response to their society."

B1087   GAUVREAU, WINIFRED R. "'Tales of Manhattan' Reflect Glittery, Toughness of City," *Nevada State Journal* (Reno), April 9, 1967, p. 2.
        "As a book of short stories this volume has the semblance of a novel because of its common theme and the writing is as clever and sharp as the characters which come alive in its pages."

B1088   GEISLER, THOMAS. "A Novel View of the Law and Lawyers," *Harvard Law Record*, XLVI (April 25, 1968), 15, 19.
        "Almost without exception, the stories are excellently written and constructed and seem well-nigh to crackle with electricity."

B1089   GILLIAM, STANLEY. "Auchincloss' Stories Are Cut in Classic Style," Sacramento *Bee*, April 2, 1967, p. L-32.
        While Auchincloss's techniques "may be out of another age, still the over-all effect has relevance in this, for while techniques may change, human nature does not--and Auchincloss does know people."

B1090   GOOLRICK, ESTEN. "New York Seen From Within," Roanoke *Times*, August 13, 1967, p. C-5.
        Auchincloss "presents his characters whole and as they are. The result is a book of integrity and virtue in the Auchincloss meaning of that word."

B1091   H[ALL], B[ARBARA] H[ODGE]. "New York Families--A World Viewed By Auchincloss," Anniston (Ala.) *Star*, March 26, 1967, p. 8C.
        Descriptive review. Auchincloss's world is "luxurious, cultured, long wealthy, slightly staid and a bit stuffy."

A Bibliography of Writings By and About Louis Auchincloss

WORKS ABOUT

B1092   HATCH, ROBERT. "A Cruel Note," *Harper's Magazine,* CCXXXIV
(April 1967), 110.
        "Mr. Auchincloss is deft at putting on his makeup, and
his act is light and fast and full of evocative detail.
In the end, though, it is trivial; time-wasting with an
aftertaste."

B1093   HICKS, GRANVILLE. "Literary Horizons--Perspective on Pros-
perity," *Saturday Review,* L (April 8, 1967), 39. Reprinted in Hicks, *Literary Horizons* (B3).
        Descriptive review. Auchincloss's vision is "not so
large" as one would wish.

B1094   HILL, WILLIAM B., S.J. *America,* CXVI (May 6, 1967), 701.
        Brief review. "The Marquand-like world of these tales
seems a bit remote, but Louis Auchincloss tells his tales
gracefully and infuses life into his characters."

B1095   _____. *Best Sellers,* XXVII (April 1, 1967), 2.
        "These are quiet narratives; the undercurrent of passion
is deep, evident, but not emphatic. The reader should not
expect too much, but anyone who enjoys a skilfully told
story about people of real character will enjoy this book."

B1096   HOYT, ELIZABETH N. "New Books--All That Glitters...," Cedar
Rapids *Gazette,* April 30, 1967, p. 2C.
        Auchincloss "writes highly readable prose polished to
perfection. Just as New York's brownstones are giving way
to structures of glass reaching heavenward, so are the
people who inhabited those brownstones giving way to a
faster, less dignified existence."

B1097   HUSTON, McCREADY. "Side Glances of New York," San Francisco
Examiner and Chronicle, April 2, 1967, *This World* Magazine,
p. 37.
        "As much for the author's stance as for the story inter-
est, these tales should be welcomed by the middle-aged and
elderly who find themselves lonely, even a little scared,
in the jungle of contemporary fiction."

B1098   J[OHNSON], D[ONALD] B. "Human Folly His Concern," Worcester
Sunday Telegram, April 16, 1967, p. 12E.
        "Auchincloss tells a story well. But there is more than
just story-telling in these well designed pieces. He is in
a sense a psychologist of human folly. He has studied the
ruling classes, and exposed its skeletons in some wise and
wonderful portraits."

B1099   JOHNSON, LUCY. "Neat--Never Gaudy--Louis Auchincloss Conducts a Tour of His Special Manhattan in New Set of Stories," Milwaukee *Journal*, March 26, 1967, Part 5, p. 4.
Auchincloss's stories "are full of plot and atmosphere and people with strongly marked characteristics"; but "they are short on passion, and even the characters are neat, not gaudy." As a result, the stories are "amusing entertainments of little depth or importance."

B1100   KENNEDY, WILLIAM. "Wide, Wide World of Books--Auchincloss Still Finds a Place For the Novel of Manners," *National Observer*, April 3, 1967, p. 23.
More an interview with Auchincloss and review of his career than review of this book.

B1101   *Kirkus*, XXXV (January 15, 1967), 74.
"For older readers," these stories "will be reassuring--certainly nothing ever changes here; but when does blue blood become tired, or *'declasse' demode?*"

B1102   KITCHING, JESSIE. *Publishers' Weekly*, CXCI (January 16, 1967), 75-76.
"Sardonic, psychologically fascinating, elegantly written with just a slight touch of purple, these stories are good Auchincloss and engrossing reading."

B1103   KNOX, GEORGE. "Manhattan Manners and Morals," Riverside (Calif.) *Press-Enterprise*, April 2, 1967, p. C-14.
Descriptive favorable review.

B1104   LA FLECHE, DUANE. "Books & Authors--An Aristocrat's Patrician Tales," Albany (N.Y.) *Knickerbocker News*, August 12, 1967, p. B4.
"Mr. Auchincloss is the writer John O'Hara could be if Mr. O'Hara didn't find it necessary to put people to bed or into the bushes every hour on the hour, if Mr. O'Hara was less in awe of the people he creates. Mr. Auchincloss is an aristocrat. Mr. O'Hara merely writes about them."

B1105   LAWLESS, JAMES T. "The Bookshelf--New Book Attains 'Delicate Balance,'" Flint (Mich.) *Journal*, April 9, 1967, p. 49.
"It is a narrow, confined world, but Auchincloss has that miracle quality of being able to bring his characters to life. If that were his only gift, it would be enough."

B1106   LAWRENCE, WES. "Auchincloss 'Oils' Skids For Critics," Cleveland *Plain Dealer*, April 16, 1967, p. 8-F.
"The 13 stories, like Auchincloss's novels, are the work of a genuine craftsman."

A Bibliography of Writings By and About Louis Auchincloss

WORKS ABOUT

B1107   M., D. "Double Standard Social Life and Nostalgia of Manhattan," Charleston (S.C.) *Evening Post*, July 7, 1967, p. 8-C.
"While this Manhattan is now as defunct as the dodo,
Auchincloss has provided a periscope into its inmost pretensions which will intrigue most readers."

B1108   McCLEARY, DOROTHY. *Book-of-the-Month Club News*, April 1967,
p. 9.
Descriptive review.

B1109   McKENZIE, ALICE. "The Bookshelf," Clearwater (Fla.) *Sun*,
May 28, 1967, p. 1-F.
"This is excellent reading and will give you a quiet
chuckle long after you have read it and presumably forgotten it in the spate of new books being published."

B1110   McMURTRY, LARRY. "The Fiction Wheels," Houston *Post*,
March 19, 1967, *Spotlight* Magazine, p. 13.
"Mr. Auchincloss is so competent, so prolific, and,
sadly, so monotonous that it is hardly necessary any longer to review his books: Announcing them is sufficient."
In this collection, "the stories are precise, observant,
serenely authoritative, unintense."

B1111   M[ALKIN], M[ARY] A[NN] [O'BRIAN]. *Antiquarian Bookman*, XXXIX
(April 10, 1967), 1501.
Very brief descriptive review.

B1112   MOORE, HARRY T. "In Edith Wharton's Footsteps," Chicago
Daily News, April 8, 1967, Panorama Section, p. 7.
"Altogether, the book presents a fascinating gallery of
Americans. They form a minority group--what used to be
the famous 400--of which Louis Auchincloss is notably
fitted to be the fictional historian. Once again he has
discharged his duties well and provided abundant, if somewhat rueful, amusement for his readers."

B1113   NEWQUIST, ROY. "In Review: Tales By an Insider," Chicago's
American, March 26, 1967, Sec. 3, p. 10. Also Chicago
Heights *Star*, March 26, 1967, Sec. 1A, p. 12.
"Tight little plots, characters who contain more than
nuggets of truth, and clean, precise writing, make this
one of Auchincloss's most satisfactory books."

B1114   OBERBECK, S. K. "Needlepoint," *Newsweek*, LXIX
(March 27, 1967), 106.
"The needle-pointed aphorisms and genteel clubman tradi-
tion go down easily enough in these deftly drawn stories,

A Bibliography of Writings By and About Louis Auchincloss

Book Reviews-*Tales of Manhattan*

(OBERBECK, S. K.)
> but an aura of armchair diversion lingers in the end, the yawning sensation of having been charmingly entertained."

B1115 PERLEY, MAIE E. "The Book Scene--Auchincloss' Short Stories Have Quality of a Novel," Louisville *Times*, April 5, 1967, p. A11.
> "Auchincloss is a master of cryptic comment who, without benefit of sentiment, exposes the frailties and frustrations that eat at the heart of rich and poor alike."

B1116 PHILLIPS, MARGARET R. "World of Books," Shreveport *Journal*, May 19, 1967, p. 6B.
> Auchincloss, "who is a member of the society about which he writes, not only knows it well, but being an unusually fine writer and storyteller, tells of it well."

B1117 POORE, CHARLES. "Books of The Times--Pavanes For an Age of Innocence," New York *Times*, March 23, 1967, p. 33.
> Descriptive review.

B1118 PORTER, DONALD. "Upper Class Populates Short Tales," New Orleans *Times Picayune*, April 30, 1967, Sec. 2, p. 8.
> Although the stories "are above the merely competent," one wonders why Auchincloss "hasn't penetrated deeper into his characters. As if for fear of losing his superfine control, his prose is held back from plunging into the morass of his characters' lives, a plunge that would give a better understanding of the motives that really create the moral universe Mr. Auchincloss knows and feels so well."

B1119 PRESCOTT, PETER S. "Books," *Women's Wear Daily*, March 24, 1967, p. 28.
> In his novels, Auchincloss "can engage the reader's interest in the complexity of a character and the points of view which adumbrate it. But the characters in his short stories are so uninteresting one can't believe that Auchincloss cares for them either."

B1120 ROSOFSKY, H. L. *Library Journal*, XCII (April 1, 1967), 1509.
> Brief review. Auchincloss writes "with wit, urbanity, and inherent good taste.... This book is worth reading."

B1121 S., D. H. Sioux Falls (S. Dak.) *Argus-Leader*, April 30, 1967, Sec. C, p. 17.
> Auchincloss's stories "reflect a penetrating perception of the quirks and foibles of humanity."

A Bibliography of Writings By and About Louis Auchincloss

WORKS ABOUT

B1122 S., W. "Auchincloss a Master of Short Story, Too," Columbus (Ohio) *Dispatch*, April 23, 1967, TAB Section, p. 31.
"The writing is of the very best and the insights given are timeless."

*B1123 SAYRE, NORA. "Lampshades," *The Reporter*, XXXVII (July 13, 1967), 60-61.
"By depicting an age of infinite tassels, social prejudice, and little else, Auchincloss has done the past a disservice. In fact, he has preserved the lampshade without the bulb. His characters have none of the violence and few of the valid dilemmas bestowed by Edith Wharton and Henry James."

B1124 SCHOTT, WEBSTER. "Beneath the Smooth Surface," *New York Times Book Review*, March 19, 1967, p. 5.
Auchincloss "has everything necessary to create essential art except what is absolutely vital, passion.... Buried in its own riches, his world exists like Shangri-La, lost to inhabitation. Yet his characters cannot escape it to make contact with the present, except through remembering. Deep within, Louis Auchincloss is a Tory--a reluctant and ambivalent one, which makes him disarming. But his heart belongs to economic royalty. And that devalues his talent."

B1125 SEYMOUR, WHITNEY NORTH, JR. "The Lawyer's Bookshelf," *New York Law Journal*, July 14, 1967, p. 4.
Auchincloss's "great genius is his clear-eyed ability to recognize the weaknesses and faults in those who wrap themselves in mantles of respectability and false values. He is, above all, a great leveler."

B1126 SHANNON, OPAL. "Fiction--Auchincloss Returns With Short Stories," *The New Mexican* (Santa Fe), April 16, 1967, p. D2.
"In this age when everybody seems to be trying to 'discover' his identity, as if it were a separate discoverable entity, it's nice to read a book which leaves you with a feeling that identities are built of a series of try-out self images and not so mysterious after all."

B1127 SIEGEL, GERALD W. "Stories By Auchincloss," Washington (D.C.) *Post*, March 28, 1967, p. A18.
"The tales of Manhattan will not qualify for classification with the stories of Balzac or Maugham, but they are written with great competence, do not pale by such comparison and are great fun to read, even for one who only visits Manhattan."

B1128   SOMERVILLE, COL. D. S. "Study in Characters," Hartford *Cour-ant*, March 19, 1967, Magazine, p. 15.
        Auchincloss is a "master of his trade" with "a special talent for fresh and graphic metaphor. But don't expect much hard riding or blood-letting in these hills."

B1129   STASIO, MARILYN. "The Portable Manhattan--A Reader's Guide to Books About Town," *Cue*, XXXVI (July 22, 1967), 10.
        Brief favorable review: "altogether, a most urbane coup for Manhattan's mannered Auchincloss."

B1130   STYRON, N. DEVEREUX. "Tales in Manner of James," Raleigh *News and Observer*, April 9, 1967, Sec. III, p. 3.
        "'Tales of Manhattan' is good substantial fare. I kept hoping Auchincloss would show a little more heart but you can't have everything."

B1131   SUDLER, BARBARA. "Blueblood Manners and Morals," Denver *Sunday Post*, April 2, 1967, *Roundup* Magazine, p. 19.
        Descriptive review.

B1132   SULLIVAN, RICHARD. "A World of Values and Standards," *Chicago Sunday Tribune Magazine of Books*, March 26, 1967, p. 5.
        "They are beautifully structured stories, all witty and alive. Each one does, with deceptive ease, precisely what it sets out to do. And taken all together they assume a kind of collective power, much closer to that of a fine novel than to the scattered hits of a succession of random pieces." Auchincloss "will be remembered with pride long after most of his more sensational American contemporaries will justly have been forgotten."

B1133   THEMAL, HARRY F. "Books in the News--Stories of New York Society," Wilmington (Del.) *Morning News*, April 4, 1967, p. 23.
        This "is another distinguished work by a man America can proudly claim as one of its finest writers."

B1134   THOMAS, PHIL. "Theme Variations By Auchincloss Prove Fascinating," Birmingham (Ala.) *News*, April 16, 1967, Sec. E, p. 7. Also El Paso *Times*, April 23, 1967.
        Descriptive favorable review.

B1135   THORPE, DAY. "New Auchincloss Stories," Washington (D.C.) *Sunday Star*, March 26, 1967, p. C-2.
        Descriptive review.

A Bibliography of Writings By and About Louis Auchincloss

WORKS ABOUT

B1136   TUCKER, MARTIN. *Commonweal*, LXXXVI (June 16, 1967), 372-373.
         "The passion of Auchincloss' people does not carry much
         urgency, and their convictions all seem part of a crafty
         puppeteer show." The book is characterized by a "dehuman-
         izing" "academic tone" which is "a pity" because "all the
         virtues of Auchincloss--precision, elegance, wit of style--
         are not allowed to add up to more than decoration."

B1137   VANSITTART, PETER. "New Novels--Gaudy and Grey," *The Specta-
         tor*, CCXIX (September 29, 1967), 367-369 [369].
         Brief review. The stories are "inquests on luminous
         careers, with no credit to coroner or witnesses." Auchin-
         closs's writing "is the banal style of the professional
         reconteur."

B1138   VON BLON, JOANNE. "Tell It Like It Was in Brownstone Age,"
         Minneapolis *Tribune*, April 2, 1967, p. 8E.
         "While the author's nostalgic evocations and his wit at
         the expense of his characters have appeal, the stories do
         not satisfy. Because he cannot make these lives seem im-
         portant, the Auchincloss relevance quotient again approach-
         es zero."

B1139   WAGENKNECHT, EDWARD. "The Book Parade," *News-Tribune* (Wal-
         tham, Newton, Weston, Lincoln, Mass.), March 28, 1967,
         p. 7.
         "Mr. Auchincloss's special interest is in the character
         and personality of his characters rather than the work
         they do, but it is his special gift that he is able to re-
         veal character and personality through professional activ-
         ity."

B1140   WALL, STEPHEN. "Cosmopolitan Close-ups," *The Observer* (Lon-
         don), November 26, 1967, p. 27.
         "Too many of his pieces are loose, baggy affairs that
         give the impression of being collapsed novels: inert and
         under-dramatised (even though one story is written as a
         play), their excessively summary nature prevails over all
         Mr. Auchincloss's considerable resources of urbanity and
         poise."

B1141   WEEKS, EDWARD. "The Sheen of Society," *The Atlantic*, CCXIX
         (May 1967), 126-127.
         Descriptive review which sees "The Matrons" as the best
         section of the book and "Sabina and the Herd" as the best
         story.

B1142   WELLS, SALLY.   "Auchincloss' New York Tales 'Intellectual's
        Resort Spot,'" Chattanooga *News-Free Press*, June 18, 1967,
        Weekend Magazine, p. 7.
            Descriptive review.   "This is deliciously exhaustive
        reading."

B1143   WERLE, PATRICIA.   "A Particular Segment of American Society,"
        Lexington (Ky.) *Herald-Leader*, April 16, 1967, p. 76.
            The "impersonal tone" of the stories "suggests the pos-
        sibility that interesting plot developments have been de-
        liberately bypassed rather than overlooked (in any event
        there aren't any), in order to fit the style of writing to
        the characters.   An interesting technique if true.   How-
        ever, it doesn't make for very interesting reading in a
        good number of the stories."

B1144   WHITE, EDWARD M.   "Tales of Fashionable New York Society,"
        Los Angeles *Times*, April 2, 1967, *Calendar* Magazine, p. 35.
            "It is artificiality of style, plot and genre that pre-
        dominates in 'Tales of Manhattan.'   Only a few of the sto-
        ries have enough vitality to seem relevant, and the limita-
        tions of vision and wit are more reminiscent of silver fork
        fiction than the intended brilliance of a Jane Austen or
        Henry James."

B1145   WILLIAMS, ELMER J.   "Private Lives in Gotham," Detroit *News*,
        March 19, 1967, p. 3-E.
            "Since creative prose began to flourish in America there
        have been critics who predicted its demise.   But at all
        times there have been a handful of such writers who could
        endure.   Auchincloss is one of these."   He "should be
        ranked high among our most talented writers."

A World of Profit

B1146   ALFORD, HAROLD J.   "Auchincloss Again Probes Affluent--Crafts-
        man Tells Story Well," Minneapolis *Tribune*,
        December 22, 1968, Sec. E, p. 11.
            "Auchincloss writes of elemental things relevant to
        every generation."   He "doesn't ask us to like any of his
        characters or what they do.   But reflected opaquely in the
        scum of Flushing Bay, the face we see may be our own."

B1147   *Antioch Review*, XXIX (Summer 1969), 261.
            This novel, "for all its style and its fascinating
        treatment of unfamiliar undercurrents of New York life,"
        is "not quite in the brittle sophisticated class" of Auch-
        incloss's earlier works; because "its controlled and

WORKS ABOUT

(*Antioch Review*)
understated yet savage criticism of contemporary business activity is finally vitiated by a pervasive sense of placidity."

B1148   [BANNON, BARBARA A.] *Publishers' Weekly*, CXCIV (September 23, 1968), 92.
Brief favorable review. The book is "intelligent and well-written" and "sophisticated and literate."

B1149   BEAM, ALVIN. "Just Not Quite Up to Snuff," Cleveland *Plain Dealer*, December 15, 1968, p. 9-G.
"The chief failure in this book, unusual for [Auchincloss], is that none of his characters ever quite becomes the fully rounded, believable person one is hoping for." Nevertheless, "for the most part the book is absorbing reading."

B1150   BIGGS, BARTON M. "Barron's on Books--*A World of Profit*-- Vintage Auchincloss," *Barron's*, XLIX (February 24, 1969), 30-31.
Admitting that he is an Auchincloss "aficionado," the reviewer sees this novel as below *Rector* in quality but "in a class with two of his best, *Powers of Attorney* and *The Embezzler*."

B1151   BLICKSILVER, EDITH. "Ibsen Did It Better," Atlanta *Journal and Constitution*, January 12, 1969, p. 13-D.
Comparison is made with Ibsen's "Rosmersholm." In this "disappointing" novel, Auchincloss "overwhelms us with too many one-dimensional puppets whose destinies and disasters move us not."

B1152   B[ROWN], J. A[DGER]. "Auchincloss Produces Soap Opera," *The State*-Columbia (S.C.) *Record*, December 8, 1968, p. 15-F.
"What might have been an intriguing story of conflict between older, aristocratic values and the rapacious vulgarity of the nouveau riche is...reduced to a sudsy level which would scarcely have merited the talents of the late Grace Metalious."

B1153   BUSH, M. "Book Review--Greed Is Motivation In 'World of Profit,'" Asbury Park (N.J.) *Evening Press*, December 12, 1968, p. 6.
"Auchincloss, a master in the presentation of character analysis, has achieved a remarkable cohesiveness in this work that depicts greed and all of its ramifications."

B1154   COLLIER, CARMEN P. *Best Sellers*, XXVIII (January 1, 1969),
         401–402.
            "Mr. Auchincloss is an important writer. He brings to
         the contemporary scene a compassionate yet ruthless prob-
         ing of the past. His characterization is superb and the
         world in which his men and women move is created with re-
         markable keenness of understanding."

B1155   CROW, DIANE. "Faithless in World of Profit," Los Angeles
         Times, December 1, 1968, *Calendar* Magazine, p. 59.
            "The Auchincloss novel is devoid of dimensions. It is
         a well-worded, fast-reading, historical case-history. The
         characters are sterile stereotypes vampirized by their
         world. We cannot care or weep for them."

B1156   CUNNINGHAM, MILES. "Up and Up, Dragging Men Down," Philadel-
         phia *Bulletin*, December 15, 1968, Sec. 2, p. 3.
            "Auchincloss' craftsmanship saves the book from a kind
         of soap-opera quality, but he gets perilously close."

B1157   DAVIDSON, JOHN L. "Auchincloss Once Again Good, But Not
         Great," St. Louis *Post-Dispatch*, December 1, 1968, p. 4C.
            "Auchincloss's story is entertaining, but neither in
         character development nor in writing does he demonstrate
         the talent that has made him one of America's great writ-
         ers." Jay Livingston is compared to Jay Gatsby.

B1158   D[IEHL], S[UZANNE]. "Auchincloss Novel Improbable," San An-
         tonio *Express and News*, December 29, 1968, p. 8-H.
            The novel "reads like a potboiler, written with a weary
         contempt of possible readers. And if it manages to bring
         any pot at all to a boil, it'll have to be a very small
         one."

B1159   DUHAMEL, P. ALBERT. "Four Novels By Established Writers,"
         Boston *Sunday Herald Traveler*, December 1, 1968, *Show Guide*
         Magazine, p. 8.
            Descriptive review.

B1160   EDWARDS, WILLIAM H. "The Promoter Pushed Too Far," Providence
         Sunday Journal, February 2, 1969, p. W-24.
            Descriptive favorable review which suggests that Auchin-
         closs should simplify his plots.

B1161   ETHRIDGE, MARK, JR. "The Dreams of a Dying Family," Detroit
         Free Press, December 22, 1968, Sec. B, p. 5.
            This novel "is not original, and Auchincloss is not
         quite himself. His newest book is somehow the artistic

A Bibliography of Writings By and About Louis Auchincloss

WORKS ABOUT

(ETHRIDGE, MARK, JR.)
offspring of Budd Shulberg and Anton Chekhov. Unlikely as
it might sound, "A World of Profit" is Sammy Glick against
the background of 'The Cherry Orchard.'"

B1162 F., P. C. "Auchincloss Misses Target," Sacramento *Bee*,
December 29, 1968, p. P-9.
The "fundamental flaw" in the novel "seems to be one of
attitude--the author decided to use his characters as elements in 'a spirit of New York' rather than as people."

B1163 FENTON, JAMES. "High Society," *New Statesman*, LXXVII
(May 30, 1969), 777.
"The problem...is to determine whether the weakness of
the social structure as depicted by Mr. Auchincloss is
merely a reflection of the times or whether it stems from
the author's inability to handle his material convincingly."

B1164 FRANKEL, HASKEL. "Mr. Auchincloss' Novel Affords No Chance
For Cheers," *National Observer*, December 30, 1968, p. 16.
"Granted that there are dodos such as the Shallcrosses
still alive and operative, and that there still are climb-
ers like Jay Livingston about. But they are no longer
suitable for consideration in serious fiction. Taken
seriously, as Mr. Auchincloss takes them, the people of
A World of Profit seem ludicrously *passé*, almost camp."

B1165 FRENCH, WARREN. "Auchincloss Only Reflects an Image of His
America," Kansas City *Star*, December 22, 1968, p. 3D.
Although this is "unmistakably a serious book" which
treats "a matter of current significance with dignity and
thoughtfulness," its "principal weakness is that Auchin-
closs--like many competent writers--is an excellent reporter but a mediocre creator.... His characters are images
in a fashionable mirror rather than people who live in
their own right. He has all the qualities of a fine novelist but intensity; he remains too fastidious to overcome
his distaste for the things he must talk about."

B1166 FULLER, EDMUND. "The Bookshelf: Auchincloss in Business,"
Wall Street Journal, December 4, 1968, p. 18.
"Before Auchincloss has finished his absorbing tale all
the complacently imagined distinctions of manners and moral
values have been blurred and the reader has been forced not
so much to a reversal as to a chastened suspension of judgment."

A Bibliography of Writings By and About Louis Auchincloss

B1167   GAMMACK, GORDON. "From Plutocrat to Pitiable--The People of These Novels," Des Moines *Register*, December 8, 1968, p. 13-T.
        "On the plus side of this new novel...are Mr. Auchincloss' magnificent command of English (few, if any, living writers surpass him); his great skill in developing characters; and his understanding of New York City's upper crust, the genuine and the pretenders. On the minus side: where is the action midst all the exquisite prose?" One suspects that Auchincloss's material "is wearing a trifle thin."

B1168   GOLLIN, JAMES. "A Fable For the Fair Sex," *Catholic World*, CCVIII (February 1969), 240.
        "Even if we swallow whole the plot of *A World of Profit*, the rhetoric Mr. Auchincloss stuffs into the mouth of his figures kills their credibility--and his--right in its tracks."

B1169   GREENLEAF, RICHARD. "The Underworld of Landlord Profits," *Daily World* (New York, N.Y.), January 23, 1969, p. 8.
        "One thing is certain: there is nowhere in this novel any fundamental protest against a system which permits real estate operators to gamble with the roofs over people's heads and render whole neighborhoods homeless when they decide to go for broke. How sad, says our author, but then--what can you do?"

B1170   GREENYA, JOHN. "The Wrong Kind of Rich," Milwaukee *Journal*, December 1, 1968, Part 5, p. 7.
        "Although not up to the level of 'The Indifferent Children' or 'The Rector of Justin,' Auchincloss' latest novel is quite readable--and most salable."

B1171   GROWALD, RICHARD H. "The Book Beat: 3 Novels of Upper Crust," San Francisco *Examiner*, January 29, 1969, p. 37. Also Montreal *Gazette*, January 25, 1969.
        Descriptive mixed review.

B1172   HALL, BARBARA HODGE. "'A World of Profit' Rings True," Anniston (Ala.) *Star*, December 15, 1968, p. 2D.
        "Auchincloss' understanding, unfailing pen catches movingly all of the love and pride and greed involved in this tragically doomed pouring together of social oils and waters."

B1173   HALL, JOAN J. "No Profit," Houston *Post*, November 24, 1968, *Spotlight* Magazine, p. 14.
        Brief sarcastically unfavorable review.

A Bibliography of Writings By and About Louis Auchincloss

WORKS ABOUT

B1174 HILL, WILLIAM B., S.J. *America*, CXX (May 3, 1969), 539.
       Brief review. "The plot is good, the style superb; but
       strangely enough, the author, literate himself and writing
       for a literate audience, thinks that the trivial activi-
       ties of the rich are important."

B1175 HOWE, MARJORIE. "New Books--'Sarah's Cottage' Appealing Se-
       quel to Novel 'Sarah Morris Remembers'," Burlington (Vt.)
       Free Press, December 27, 1968, p. 12.
       Brief favorable descriptive review.

B1176 HOYT, ELIZABETH N. "Interloper," Cedar Rapids *Gazette*,
       January 5, 1969, p. 2C.
       "Although 'A World of Profit' is well constructed and
       has some pertinent things to say about the encroachment
       of the new upon the old, it does not rate as one of Mr.
       Auchincloss' better works."

B1177 HUMBER, TOM. "*A World of Profit* By Louis Auchincloss," *Lit-
       erary Guild Magazine*, January 1969, pp. 3-5.
       Descriptive favorable review. Auchincloss "will cer-
       tainly be this decade's chronicler of the faces, facades
       and foibles of New York upper class life. But the joy of
       Auchincloss is that we don't have to wait until the future
       to appreciate him, we can do it just as easily and enjoy-
       ably now."

B1178 HUSTON, McCREADY. "A Magnetic Opportunist," San Francisco
       Chronicle, December 22, 1968, *This World* Magazine, p. 38.
       Parts of the novel "prove the Auchincloss title to a
       high place on the list of writers upon whom the American
       novel at present seems to depend."

B1179 HUTCHENS, JOHN K. *Book-of-the-Month Club News*, January 1969,
       p. 12.
       "For all his high polish as a stylist and social his-
       torian, Mr. Auchincloss is not one to neglect drama or
       even melodrama.... In this newest of his novels,... that
       dramatic gift is well displayed, and, as always, he writes
       with admirable authority of money, manners, and social
       change."

B1180 JACKSON, KATHERINE GAUSS. *Harper's Magazine*, CCXXXVIII
       (January 1969), 104.
       "It is an interesting concept; the author's New York is
       always interesting and convincing; but the people are card-
       board whose conversation often seems embarrassingly con-
       trived."

A Bibliography of Writings By and About Louis Auchincloss

B1181   KENNEDY, JOHN S. "Intricate Patterns of Failure," *Catholic Transcript* (Hartford, Conn.), January 3, 1969, p. 5.
"As an exercise in sociology, [Auchincloss's] book has interest. But where it is wanting is in the vital area of character. Despite some dialogue which is exactly right, these figures do not come alive as people, but remain types maneuvered by the author to suit his purpose."

B1182   KNIGHT, ANDREW. "Mores in New York," Washington (D.C.) *Post*, December 31, 1968, p. A10.
"Auchincloss is at his best when in the thick of a conversation, or midstream in the bruised consciousness of one of his characters. Only his prose is banal.... Perhaps Auchincloss writes too much too easily."

B1183   LADNER, MILDRED. "An Upstart Starts Up," Tulsa *Sunday World*, January 19, 1969, *Your World* Magazine, p. 12.
"Observers of the rapidly changing financial world will find this latest Auchincloss novel fascinating. This reader felt only disappointment at the sketchiness of detail concerning Jay's financial maneuverings as against the plethora of detail about the snobbish world of the Shallcrosses."

B1184   LISTER, RICHARD. "Why Sophie Said No," London *Evening Standard*, June 3, 1969, p. 13.
"Mr. Auchincloss is a thoroughly professional novelist, but I find this book somewhat schematic--built to prove his theme. It doesn't seem to belong really to the modern America we read of: it doesn't for me have the real throb of life in it. It is elegantly written, competently composed, but only half alive."

B1185   MADDOCKS, MELVIN. "George Apley, Get Back in That Mummy Case," *Life*, LXV (December 6, 1968), 10.
"No one is better at his specialty than Auchincloss. After about half an hour of artificial respiration and a session with the makeup kit, he can get the Genteel Tradition on its feet and tottering down those dangerous brownstone stoops. What he can no longer do is make the old gentleman seem relevant to what's going on in the street."

B1186   MAURER, ROBERT. "To the Manor Not Born," *Saturday Review*, LI (November 30, 1968), 43, 55.
"Novels about the rich may not be passé, but if Elly and Sophie are really going to encounter our century, they will have to do it not in the language of Henry James and Edith Wharton but in some other, newer tones. Resurrecting

191

A Bibliography of Writings By and About Louis Auchincloss

WORKS ABOUT

(MAURER, ROBERT)
antique modes to try to deal with 'the future' is like at-
tributing our present situation to the decline of Emily
Post as a social force."

B1187 MAYER, B. *Oregon Journal* (Portland), December 28, 1968,
p. 6J.
"One would never suggest that the author is running out
of steam and that there is just so much one (even the ob-
vious insider) can repeatedly weave into stories concerning the *beau monde*, but must admit that Auchincloss hit
the top with his 'Rector of Justin'...and has been gradual-
ly side-slipping ever since."

B1188 MEIER, T. K. *National Review*, XXI (May 6, 1969), 453.
"In this book, Auchincloss has allowed his characters
more complex personalities and therefore more opportunities
for experiencing believable stress and anguish, and he has
at last made convincing use of his legal background in describing the proxy fight and divorce suits which are the
climax of the novel."

B1189 M[OODY], M[INNIE] H[ITE]. "Empathy For a Rogue In Auchincloss Novel," Columbus (Ohio) *Dispatch*, December 8, 1968,
Entertainment Section, p. 17.
If Auchincloss "expects the reader to side with the old
aristocracy instead of with Jay, he has goofed, for it is
Jay who has all of the appeal. This reviewer is one who
does not believe Mr. Auchincloss capable of any such goof."
The theme of the novel is: "The past is a lost cause;
tomorrow is opportunity."

B1190 MORRISON, THEODORE. "'A World of Profit'--Traditional Novel
From Auchincloss," Boston *Sunday Globe*, November 24, 1968,
p. 81.
"Auchincloss tells his story readably, intelligently,
clearly. Sophisticated literary tastes on the hunt for
aesthetic novelties of form or method will not find much
to reward them here."

B1191 MURRAY, ISOBEL. "A House and Its Heritage," *Financial Times*
(London), May 29, 1969, p. 8.
In Jay Livingston, Auchincloss "has created a splendid
and believable character whose rise and fall raise this
book above the common run, for his stature, like his spirit, is great."

B1192   NELSON, BARBARA S. *Library Journal*, XCIII (November 1, 1968),
         4162, 4164.
              Brief review. "Mr. Auchincloss has written another ur-
         bane and absorbing commentary on the minority group he
         knows so well."

B1193   NEWQUIST, ROY. "In Review: A Triumph By Auchincloss," Chi-
         cago Heights *Star*, December 25, 1968, Sec. I, p. 12.
         Also Chicago's *American*, December 22, 1968.
              "'A World of Profit' is the best novel Auchincloss has
         turned out--more finely textured than 'Rector of Justin,'
         more incisive than 'Power of Attorney.' The prime reason
         for its brilliance is the depth of character explored
         throughout; each principal is fully exposed by both bold
         and subtle means, with the result that there seems to be
         nothing withheld from our fund of knowledge, no outside
         manipulation to distort the destiny of the various Shall-
         crosses and the intense but likeable Jay Livingston."

B1194   OATES, JOYCE CAROL. "Louis Auchincloss' Theme--Everything
         Has Its Price, Even a Man's Soul," Detroit *News*,
         December 22, 1968, p. 3-E.
              "'Profit' is clearly Auchincloss' great theme--the
         things people will do for profit, selling their own souls
         and those of loved ones. But he does not really treat
         this tragic phenomenon with profundity; it is all rather
         sketchy, like an outline for a very long, plodding, rich
         novel by Edith Wharton or Henry James."

B1195   PASLEY, VIRGINIA. "Cracks in the Upper Crust," *Newsday*
         (Garden City, N.Y.), November 30, 1968, p. 23W.
              "To this reviewer it is much the best book Auchincloss
         has ever written; one suspects even that there are a few
         characters he has some fondness for."

B1196   PECKHAM, STANTON. "Louis Auchincloss Sounds Social Protest
         In Novel Concerning New York Family," Denver *Sunday Post*,
         December 8, 1968, *Roundup* Magazine, p. 54.
              This is the "most bitter" novel Auchincloss has written.
         It fails "for the simple reason that he has depicted a crew
         of characters for whom he obviously his little sympathy,
         and the reader has none."

B1197   POORE, CHARLES. "Books of The Times--Veins of Irony," New
         York *Times*, December 5, 1968, p. 45.
              Descriptive review.

A Bibliography of Writings By and About Louis Auchincloss

WORKS ABOUT

B1198   QUILL, GYNTER. "Reading and Reviewing--Honor, Loyalty Haven't
Gone Out of Style, Yet," Waco (Texas) *Tribune-Herald*,
December 4, 1968, p. B-4.
Descriptive favorable review.

B1199   REID, MARGARET W. "Social Climbing--Proxy Fights," Wichita
Falls (Texas) *Times*, December 29, 1968, Magazine, p. 4.
Descriptive favorable review.

B1200   RHODES, RICHARD. "He Left His Heart at Prep School," *Book
World* (Washington *Post*, Chicago *Tribune*), December 29, 1968,
p. 7.
"If I were the Rector of Justin, and young Louis Auchincloss were my pupil, I think I would hand his manuscript
back to him and ask for something with a little more heft,
a little more respect for God, who did not put us on this
earth to be full-time fools, or at least a little more respect for the grace of fiction, the rules of which I had
thought were well-known."

B1201   RODRIGUEZ, MARY. "Society Gossip," Monterey (Calif.) *Peninsula Herald*, February 15, 1969, p. 16.
"Though his dialogue seems stilted and unrealistic, the
author is an acknowledged master of captivating narration
and is extremely capable of putting acute character analysis on paper."

B1202   [ROGERS, W. G.] "Auchincloss Pits Tough Financier Against
'Society,'" Grand Rapids *Press*, December 8, 1968, p. 78.
Also Toledo *Blade*, December 8, 1968, Sec. H, p. 5.
"Auchincloss never fails to be Auchincloss, and if a
novel utterly free of faults is a perfect novel, this is
a perfect novel."

B1203   SACHS, MARTHA. "Delightful Soap Opera," Worcester *Sunday
Telegram*, December 15, 1968, p. 22 F.
Descriptive favorable review.

B1204   SCHLESINGER, TOM. "Auchincloss' 'A World of Profit'--A Thin-
ning Lode," Norfolk *Virginian-Pilot*, December 8, 1968,
p. C-10.
Not that Auchincloss's "mocking nostalgia for things
past isn't still appealing or that aspects of fading duty,
manners and affluence aren't still good hooks for plot
hanging. But familiarity should breed greater contempt
and the aimlessness of his current indictment of a world
of profit without honor indicates a certain point of no
return. It's a bit like lunching on yesterday's leftovers."

B1205　SMITH, MILES A.　"Selfishness and Snobbery Theme of Auchin-
closs Tale," Jackson (Tenn.) *Sun*, December 29, 1968,
p. 8-C.　Also Durham (N.C.) *Morning Herald*,
February 9, 1969; El Paso *Times*, January 19, 1969.
　　　Auchincloss's approach was "effective" in *Rector* and
The Embezzler; but "in this volume the effect is muddled."

B1206　SOURIAN, PETER.　*New York Times Book Review*,
November 24, 1968, p. 5.
　　　This is a "sometimes psychologically acute and ultimately depressing novel of manners--mannered with the very manners that it purports to find disgusting."　Though themat-
ically similar to *Gatsby*, there is no drama in Auchincloss's novel, "much less the tragedy that Fitzgerald
evolved."

B1207　SULLIVAN, RICHARD.　"Louis Auchincloss' Latest--Good, Sound
Prose--But Slight and Familiar," *Chicago Sunday Sun-Times
Book Week*, December 1, 1968, p. 10.
　　　"As a technician, Auchincloss is almost faultless.
But he spends his time revealing a sad little dreary
world.　If a good writer had never before shown us how
meanly ingrown and dismayingly selfish people could be,
this would be an illuminating book.　But it has all been
done before, in countless ways."

B1208　THORNTON, SISTER MARY MADELENA.　"Aristocrats vs. Profiteers:
One World Meets Another," *The New World* (Chicago),
February 14, 1969, p. 13.
　　　This novel is not as good as *Rector*; but "it throws a
bright light on several 'real worlds' corrupted by the
mores of the world of profit.　And it is free of both cyn-
icism and sentimentality about those worlds and their inhabitants."

B1209　THORPE, DAY.　"Auchincloss and His 'World,'" Washington (D.C.)
Sunday Star, December 1, 1968, p. E-2.
　　　"Mr. Auchincloss's literary style is clear, sober and
precise.　He can use the words 'albeit' and 'osculations'
seriously and get away with it--with the skin of his teeth
but without question.　Is there any other living writer who
can turn the trick?"

B1210　TUOHY, FRANK.　"Quintessential Wasp," London *Times*,
May 31, 1969, p. 20.
　　　"*A World of Profit* is written by an insider.　It lacks
the edge of rancour and also the intensity of such eminent
non-Wasps as Scott Fitzgerald or John O'Hara."　Auchincloss

A Bibliography of Writings By and About Louis Auchincloss

WORKS ABOUT

(TUOHY, FRANK)
has "all the advantages of the novelist as professional
man, with the concomitant disadvantage, that he seems to
deal with his characters instead of creating them."

B1211   *Virginia Quarterly Review*, XLV (Spring 1969), xlviii.
Brief descriptive review.

B1212   WALKER, ROBERT. "Money, Metaphysics and Old-Fashioned Story
Telling," Houston *Chronicle*, December 8, 1968, Magazine,
p. 23.
Descriptive review.

B1213   WALL, STEPHEN. "Novels--Highland Growing Pains," *The Observer* (London), June 1, 1969, p. 28.
Descriptive favorable review.

B1214   WEEKS, EDWARD. *The Atlantic*, CCXXII (December 1968), 136.
Some of Auchincloss's characters, like Mrs. Shallcross
and Alverta, are "one dimensional"; but Hilary Knowles is
"beautifully drawn" and "Jay Livingston in his eager un-
scrupulous way is the Great Gatsby of the 1960s."

B1215   WILSON, HELENA PERIN. "*A World of Profit*--Latest Auchincloss
Novel Should Join List of Top Sellers," Baton Rouge *Sunday
Advocate*, January 26, 1969, p. 2-E.
"The characterization and philosophy portrayed in this
novel are intensely interesting...."

B1216   WILSON, W. EMERSON. "Books in the News--Old Family Threatened By Outsider," Wilmington (Del.) *Morning News*,
December 2, 1968, p. 9.
Auchincloss "has a lucid, smooth style of writing that
holds the interest of the reader and keeps events moving
swiftly."

B1217   WORDSWORTH, CHRISTOPHER. "Showing the Cracks in the Masonry,"
Manchester (England) *Guardian*, May 29, 1969, p. 9.
"Engrossing as *A World of Profit* is, the all-important
Jay is blurred. The author has confessedly used him to
epitomise the incorrigible, unsnubbable, unsinkable spirit
of New York and he founders under too many attributes."

B1218   YODER, EDWIN M., JR. "Charting the Rising Wages of Greed,"
Greensboro (N.C.) *Daily News*, December 15, 1968, p. C3.
"This is the kind of story--of character and code beset
by pressures equal to their strength--at which Louis Auchincloss excels. Here he maintains his standard with

A Bibliography of Writings By and About Louis Auchincloss

(YODER, EDWIN M., JR.)
richness; and allowing for the necessary contemporary
wrinkles, it is the great tradition of Henry James and
Edith Wharton he is preserving."

B1219 YORK, JUDY CARMACK. "Recent Book--Lawyer Auchincloss Considers 'World of Profit,'" *Harvard Law Record*, XLVIII
(February 6, 1969), 13.
Auchincloss is "able to describe new money versus old
line with finesse. The style is polished and literate;
no-nonsense prose. Only the dialogue tickles the reader's
credibility."

Motiveless Malignity

B1220 ADAMS, PHOEBE. *The Atlantic*, CCXXIV (September 1969), 126,
128.
Brief review. Auchincloss's "observations are gracefully put and largely unpretentious, and while there is
not a surprise in the package, there is not a stupidity to
be found there, either."

B1221 [ANDERSON, DOUG]. "Critic Eyes Motives in Shakespeare," Wichita *Eagle and Beacon*, September 28, 1969, p. 2D. Also
Lexington (Ky.) *Herald-Leader*, October 26, 1969.
"Some scholars will find [Auchincloss's] interpretations
unacceptable, but they are uniformly interesting and certainly arguable."

B1222 BEAM, ALVIN. "Shakespeare Performs For Auchincloss," Cleveland *Plain Dealer*, August 10, 1969, p. 8F.
Readers of this book will be "moved to go back to the
plays themselves."

B1223 *Best Sellers*, XXIX (September 1, 1969), 204.
Brief descriptive review.

B1224 BROWN, IVOR. "Shakespeare and Consistency," *Drama*, No. 70
(Autumn 1970), 67-68.
"Mr. Auchincloss is excellent in his fresh approach to
his subjects, but he is sometimes looking for consistency
in the work of a man and of a period in which consistency
was absent because it was not wanted."

B1225 *Choice*, VI (January 1970), 1568-1569.
The book "has its value not as a work of methodical
criticism or profound scholarship, but as the genial and
intelligent responses of a man of letters to his favorite
Shakespearean plays."

A Bibliography of Writings By and About Louis Auchincloss

WORKS ABOUT

B1226   DORENKAMP, J. H. "An Insight Into Bard," Worcester *Sunday Telegram*, August 17, 1969, p. 19 F.
    This book "raises more questions than it answers. But ...that is the elusiveness of Shakespeare. We have to catch him ourselves. Auchincloss' book will help."

B1227   F[OLEY], B[ERNICE] W[ILLIAMS]. "The Bard Is Analyzed By a Modern Novelist," Columbus (Ohio) *Dispatch*, September 7, 1969, TAB Section, p. 14.
    "As an additional evaluation of the Bard of Avon, this slim volume, dropped into the ocean of Shakespearean comment, creates stimulating and perceptive ripples."

B1228   FRIEND, JAMES. "Mr. Auchincloss Wrestles With the Bard," Chicago *Daily News*, September 6-7, 1969, Panorama Section, p. 7.
    "Certainly not profound, it is nonetheless a highly readable and relevant account not only of many of Shakespeare's plays and sonnets, but of our own contemporary understanding of them as well."

B1229   GEWIRTZ, ARTHUR. "Trudging Through Sterile Paths," *New Leader*, LII (October 13, 1969), 19-20.
    The book "emerges as a tedious affair offering some fine individual insights." The chapter on *Coriolanus* is an example of the latter.

B1230   GRANT, LOUIS T. "Doing Shakespeare an Injustice," Washington (D.C.) *Post*, September 3, 1969, p. B7.
    "You might think *Motiveless Malignity* was some fond reminiscence of a teacher Auchincloss had studied under at Yale or of a novelist chum. Nowhere in these essays does one find the respect and excitement of a vivid imagination encountering the most powerful poetic intelligence in English literature. Instead, there is a reductionist approach."

B1231   GREBANIER, BERNARD. *Saturday Review*, LII (October 11, 1969), 59-60.
    "Mr. Auchincloss is a well-known novelist, but it is as the practicing lawyer that he also is that he cross-examines the characters he writes about with an eye to discrediting to a degree the reputations they have borne. Always interesting, the results are, as in skillful cross-questioning, sometimes a little startling, sometimes much to the point."

A Bibliography of Writings By and About Louis Auchincloss

B1232 JONES, D. A. N. "Taking Sides," *The Listener* (London),
LXXXIV (August 20, 1970), 249-250.
Auchincloss is called "an elderly American novelist and
lawyer" and the book, "meditations based on a long experience of life," is "worth reading."

B1233 KELNE, MIKE. "Author Discusses Shakespeare's Works," Columbia *Missourian*, January 11, 1970, Sec. C, p. 8.
Descriptive review.

B1234 KERMODE, FRANK. "A New Era in Shakespeare Criticism?" *New
York Review of Books*, XV (November 5, 1970), 33-38 [35-36].
"It may seem extraordinary that this highly professional
writer should, in the limited context of Shakespearian
studies, lend himself so abjectly to the proposition that
the one thing worse than professional musing is amateur
musing."

B1235 LASK, THOMAS. "Books of The Times--The Spring of Action,"
New York *Times*, September 13, 1969, p. 25.
"Even if we do not buy all the author's theories, we
can still read the essays with profit."

B1236 LEWIS, ALLAN. "A Novelist Illuminates the Bard's Works," *New
York Times Book Review*, September 14, 1969, p. 8.
Auchincloss "offers refreshingly provocative and personal insights into the plays and sonnets." He is an "urbane,
witty, knowledgeable student of Shakespeare."

B1237 LEWIS, NAOMI. "Shakespeare and the Readers," *New Statesman*,
LXXX (December 25, 1970), 870-871 [870].
"These are shrewd, agreeable, gossipy pages, diverting
enough in the off-course points but generally hit-or-miss
in the main idea."

B1238 LINTON, CALVIN D. *Shakespeare Quarterly*, XXII (Winter 1971),
70-71.
"The fact of primary importance about this volume...is
that it provides on almost every page sensitive and perceptive insights, expressed in prose of rare precision and
economy."

B1239 LOWER, CHARLES B. *Georgia Review*, XXIV (Fall 1970), 382-385.
"Auchincloss' judgment is usually discerning; and his
manner is refreshing and, in consequence of its forthright-
ness, illuminating of dramaturgical achievement. *Motiveless Malignity* can be heartily endorsed for the general

A Bibliography of Writings By and About Louis Auchincloss

WORKS ABOUT

(LOWER, CHARLES B.)
reader because it is so blatantly non-academic, lacking
the threatening stultification of documentation, scholarly
quibbling, the passive construction, and the colorless ad-
jective."

B1240   McDOWELL, J. R.   Chattanooga *Times*, October 26, 1969, p. B 2.
"Criticism of the bard is fair game, and Auchincloss
ranks with the best. His points are sensible and uncompli-
cated.... The reader may feel he is fully appreciating a
few of these familiar characters for the first time."

B1241   MacNEIL, ALAN.   "On the Bookshelf," *Connecticut Valley Times
Reporter* (Bellows Falls, Springfield, Vt.),
August 11, 1969, p. 4.
"It is fascinating to read of the plays from so astutely
observant a point of view."

B1242   MARDER, LOUIS.   "Shakespeare: A Learned Medley," *CEA Critic*,
XXXIII (May 1971), 37-41 [39].
"The case is well set forth, but it leads to a lame and
impotent conclusion: the evidence is not substantial
enough. Yet the book is interesting and even important because Auchincloss sets forth novel positions in a straightforward manner."

B1243   MEADOWCROFT, DORIS.   "Auchincloss' Concept of Shakespeare,"
Charleston (S.C.) *Evening Post*, October 31, 1969, p. 7-C.
Auchincloss "gives us a fresh and stimulating concept
of some major characters in Shakespeare's plays."

B1244   OGBURN, CHARLTON, JR.   "Books: Probing the Problems of
Shakespeare," Washington (D.C.) *Sunday Star*,
August 17, 1969, p. D-2.
The "all-but-fatal weakness" of the book is that "it
treats Shakespeare's plays as if they were written in a
vacuum by a largely disembodied spirit"; but "its saving
grace" is that, "thanks to its author's conscience and despite him, Shakespeare does come through as a real person
and of the kind he must have been."

B1245   PHILLIPS, JAMES A.   *Library Journal*, XCIV (September 15, 1969),
3064-3065.
Brief review. The book "should be popular with general
readers of Shakespeare yet might be considered too cursory
and personally conjectural for Shakespearean scholars."

A Bibliography of Writings By and About Louis Auchincloss

Book Reviews-*Motiveless Malignity*

B1246   PRYCE-JONES, ALAN. "Shakespeare Notebook--Novelist Assesses
        Bard's Characters," Toledo *Blade,* August 31, 1969, Sec. C,
        p. 5.
            This is "a most readable and luminous little book, re-
        freshingly free of the crankiness and the empty theorizing
        that mar much of contemporary Shakespeare criticism."

B1247   *Publishers' Weekly,* CXCV (June 16, 1969), 74.
            "Readers should know that Auchincloss as critic, fasci-
        nating as he is for his very personal insights, is a far
        cry from Auchincloss the novelist."

B1248   SCOTT, WINFIELD P. "Shakespeare and the Irrational," Provi-
        dence *Sunday Journal,* September 7, 1969, p. W-28.
            The book gives "not a new view of Shakespeare's plays,
        but a view of Auchincloss" and Auchincloss "presents this
        slim volume as homage to the master from the craftsman,
        passing thoughts in continuing the celebration of Shake-
        speare."

B1249   SEYMOUR-SMITH, MARTIN. "Whose Shakespeare?" *Encounter,*
        XXXIV (June 1970), 56-58, 60-61, 63 [61, 63].
            Auchincloss "writes in the worst tradition of the un-
        scholarly amateur." His discussions "are on the level of
        chit-chat: very pleasant, wholly commonplace."

B1250   SMITH, MILES A. San Francisco *Examiner,* August 19, 1969,
        p. 35. Also Durham (N.C.) *Morning Herald,* August 17, 1969;
        St. Petersburg *Times,* August 17, 1969; Allentown (Pa.)
        Call-Chronicle, September 7, 1969.
            Auchincloss "has developed some very cogent ideas on
        the interpretation of Shakespeare's plays."

B1251   WAGENKNECHT, EDWARD. "The Book Parade," *News-Tribune* (Wal-
        tham, Newton, Weston, Lincoln, Mass.), August 26, 1969,
        p. 10.
            "I think Mr. Auchincloss is often at his best when he
        seems most disposed to forget his thesis. I find him
        quite convincing in demolishing theories previously formu-
        lated to explain the sonnets, but less so when he expounds
        his own 'thousandth theory' as he calls it."

B1252   WEST, PAUL. "Shakespeare's 'Monster Manunkind,'" *Book World*
        (Washington *Post,* Chicago *Tribune*), August 31, 1969, p. 5.
            "Auchincloss has done his best by Shakespeare...and one
        cannot read his book of essays without finding several
        things worth saying that he is the first to say."

201

A Bibliography of Writings By and About Louis Auchincloss

WORKS ABOUT

B1253   YODER, EDWIN M., JR. "William Shakespeare at the St. Regis,"
         Greensboro (N.C.) *Daily News*, September 14, 1969, p. B3.
              Auchincloss's essays are "seldom distinguished by sub-
         tlety or deepened by learning" and he "has reduced the new
         criticism to its ultimate absurdity by viewing Shakespeare
         as a comfortable contemporary who confides his design to a
         fellow writer, merely by virtue of their shared interest
         in character and plot."

B1254   YU, ANTHONY C. "Uncanny Insight," *Christian Century*, LXXXVII
         (May 6, 1970), 569.
              Because Auchincloss brings to Shakespeare's *personae*
         and to their situations "an artist's uncanny insight into
         human nature, a lawyer's attention to details and a nov-
         elist's skill with language, the essays contained in this
         book are often accurate, occasionally surprising, always
         provocative."

Second Chance--Tales of Two Generations

B1255   ABBEY, EDWARD. *New York Times Book Review*, August 30, 1970,
         p. 32.
              Auchincloss "writes in a plain and simple style, grace-
         ful and direct, about a special American breed--the WASPS
         of Long Island, Park and Fifth Avenue...."

B1256   ATKINSON, MARY LOU. "People Are Real in These Tales," New
         Orleans *Times Picayune*, September 20, 1970, Sec. 2, p. 4.
              "One can really savor this collection of tales only if
         he, or she, treats it like a pound of chocolate creams,
         and takes just one at a sitting."

B1257   BARKHAM, JOHN. "The Literary Scene," New York *Post*,
         August 26, 1970, p. 52.
              "And so it goes all through the book--the intriguing
         plots, the smooth characterization, the suave prose and
         the provocative resolution to top it off. Yet somehow--
         except for 'Double Gap'--it all sounds like faraway and
         long ago. Can it be that Auchincloss is still saluting a
         parade that has passed him by?"

B1258   BARRETT, BETTY. "Two Generations," Hartford *Courant*,
         August 16, 1970, Magazine, p. 21.
              "An enjoyable book, as we read one short story after
         another, we can generally find a character in our own en-
         virons that fits the identity and gives us a rare chuckle,
         with its fine delineation."

A Bibliography of Writings By and About Louis Auchincloss

B1259   BEAM, ALVIN. "The World of Auchincloss," Cleveland *Plain Dealer*, September 13, 1970, p. 15-G.
        "Auchincloss is a master at the kind of story he writes--and that kind, come to think of it, is different now and especially refreshing."

B1260   BENNETT, ALICE KIZER. "Auchincloss Now Gathers Short Tales," Dallas *Morning News*, August 30, 1970, p. 36 A.
        "Each story has gem-like clarity and brilliance but not much warmth. Perhaps Mr. Auchincloss is warning himself of all the pitfalls to be avoided as one gets older. As always he writes with skill and charm."

B1261   BERTHELSEN, JOHN. "Cry Havoc and Have at Them," Sacramento *Bee*, October 25, 1970, p. L-22.
        "These are not stories of poverty or blood and death, or even of hatred and passion. They are stories just as filled with terror, however--the terror of men who may lose their social status or the terror of women who see age overwhelming them."

B1262   BOSTON, RICHARD. "Proper Stations," *The Observer* (London), August 29, 1971, p. 23.
        Descriptive favorable review.

B1263   BRADY, SISTER MARY WILLIAM. *Best Sellers*, XXX (October 1, 1970, p. 23.
        Brief descriptive review.

B1264   BRUNK, CHARLOTTE. "Short Stories," Des Moines *Sunday Register*, September 20, 1970, p. 15-T.
        Brief descriptive review: an "excellent" collection.

B1265   BUTCHER, FANNY. "Books Today--Short Stories of Quality," Chicago *Tribune*, October 12, 1970, Sec. 1, p. 18.
        "All the stories are involved with today, but they echo yesterday, which makes them differ from many of the short stories now being written. His [Auchincloss's] are novels in embryo, not recitals of a dramatic incident." The "best story in the book" is "Double Gap."

B1266   FELTON, KEITH S. "An Ungapping of Generations," Los Angeles *Times*, September 27, 1970, *Calendar*, Magazine Section, p. 49.
        Descriptive review.

B1267   FREEDMAN, RICHARD. "More Tales From the Homer of Wall Street," Washington (D.C.) *Post*, September 20, 1970, *Book World*, p. 4.
        "This collection...is like a twelve-course dinner in a

A Bibliography of Writings By and About Louis Auchincloss

(FREEDMAN, RICHARD)
Chinese restaurant. Each story is delicious as it slithers down, but an hour later you're hungry again for some Chekhov or James." Auchincloss's characters, "though temporarily arresting," are "really paper thin, often nothing more than one-dimensional 'humors.'"

B1268 FRIEND, JAMES. "Tales of a Mannered Life-Style," Chicago *Daily News,* August 29-30, 1970, Panorama Section, p. 8. Also Toledo *Blade,* September 6, 1970, Sec. C, p. 5.
This book is "the finest expression of Mr. Auchincloss' theme since 'The Rector of Justin' and certainly the best collection of short stories he has written thus far."

B1269 HALL, JOAN J. "Starting Over," Houston *Post,* August 23, 1970, *Spotlight* Magazine, p. 13.
The final story, "The Sacrifice," is "liberating not because of its 'happy' ending but because it recognizes the sense of possibility beyond the ropes of the familiarly grey and uptight Auchincloss world; it tells us something we don't already know."

B1270 JELLINEK, ROGER. "Books of The Times--A Ride and a Drive," New York *Times,* August 26, 1970, p. 39.
In this collection, one gets the sense that he is "reading reports about stories."

B1271 KEATES, JONATHAN. "Mannerists," *New Statesman,* LXXXI (May 21, 1971), 711.
Brief review. "Only the last of these New York stories, 'The Sacrifice,' effectively redeems their author from grave charges of time-serving and pomposity."

B1272 *Kirkus,* XXXVIII (June 15, 1970), 651.
"This collection is...much less trivial and more incisive than...*Tales of Manhattan*...."

B1273 LADNER, MILDRED. "'Relevant' Short Tales," Tulsa *Sunday World,* November 1, 1970, *Your World* Magazine, p. 12.
Descriptive favorable review.

B1274 MINNICK, MIRIAM SHARP. *Library Journal,* XCV (August 1970), 2711-2712.
Brief review. "The reader will understand and sympathize intellectually with the characters, and he will admire and appreciate the author's art and skill. But he will not be moved emotionally."

Book Reviews-*Second Chance--Tales of Two Generations*

B1275   MINTZ, EDWARD N. "Celebrity Spotlight," *Travel*, CXXXV
         (March 1971), 14, 16 [14].
              Very brief favorable review.

B1276   MOODY, MINNIE HITE. "Auchincloss Stories Limn By-Passed
         Folk," Columbus (Ohio) *Dispatch*, September 20, 1970, TAB
         Section, p. 16.
              Auchincloss "writes with power, very sure of himself and
         what he is going to say." But he cannot "sympathize" with
         his characters: "What masks as compassion is more often an
         exquisitely phrased form of irony."

B1277   N., K. *Oregon Journal* (Portland), October 24, 1970, p. J11.
              Brief favorable review: a "delightful collection."

B1278   NEAR, GEORGE. "Dozen Stories in 'Second Chance,'" Abilene
         (Texas) *Reporter-News*, September 27, 1970, p. 5-B.
              The book is "rich in variety of characters and settings
         yet has underlying unity rare in any such collection."

B1279   O'HARA, MARY. "Tackles Current Issues--'2nd Chance' Cracks
         Short-Story Woes," Pittsburgh *Press*, August 30, 1970,
         Sec. 8, p. 7.
              "The collection of tales is not uniformly perfect (what
         collection is?) but it's one of the most readable to appear
         in a long time, particularly if you enjoy the milieu of
         today's urban civilization."

B1280   O'LEARY, THEODORE M. "In What a Variety Human Beings Do
         Fall," Kansas City *Star*, August 23, 1970, p. 6D.
              Descriptive review.

B1281   *Publishers' Weekly*, CXCVII (June 15, 1970), 59.
              Brief descriptive review: "a dozen polished and urbane
         short stories that display Mr. Auchincloss's talent for
         irony and his considerable insight into the human heart."

B1282   REEVES, CAMPBELL. "Good Wine and Good Writing Age Well--Auch-
         incloss' 'Second Chance,'" Raleigh *News and Observer*,
         October 11, 1970, Sec. IV, p. 6.
              Descriptive favorable review: a "marvellously varied
         and often amusing collection."

B1283   RUFFIN, CAROLYN F. "Correctness Is Not Enough--Conscience
         Lurking," *Christian Science Monitor*, August 20, 1970,
         p. 13.
              Auchincloss "has done a fascinating study of the various
         ways people react when the moving finger is put on them.
         Some of the stories are a little too neat and precise. And

A Bibliography of Writings By and About Louis Auchincloss

WORKS ABOUT

(RUFFIN, CAROLYN F.)
unless the plot is thoroughly thickened, his even-tempered,
gentlemanly prose gets a little transparent and unconvinc-
ing." But the "saving grace" of the book is that "Puritans
from whatever era make good drama." And Auchincloss's
Puritans "grapple with those hard to get at sins--prejudice
and neglect of others."

B1284   SHARP, SALLIE. "Auchincloss Work Timely Reading," Galveston
Daily News, November 16, 1970, p. 10.
Descriptive favorable review.

B1285   [SMITH, MILES A.] "Folk Lore, Tall Tales, Humor Conscience
of Silent Majority," Lexington (Ky.) *Sunday Herald-Leader,*
August 23, 1970, p. 77. Also San Diego *Union,*
August 23, 1970; Allentown (Pa.) *Call-Chronicle,*
August 30, 1970; Trenton (N.J.) *Sunday Times-Advertiser,*
August 30, 1970.
"A couple of these items...do not come off at all; they
seem too sketchily done and implausible. Yet at his best
Auchincloss is a deft chronicler of the vagaries, self-
delusions and vulnerable weaknesses of the fading remnants
of an older establishment."

B1286   STIX, FREDERICK. "Two Generations," Cincinnati *Enquirer,*
February 25, 1971, p. 9.
Brief favorable review: "all have substance, and none
is shoddy or shabby."

B1287   THORPE, DAY. "Books: Shop Talk of a High Order," Washington
(D.C.) *Sunday Star,* August 9, 1970, p. C-2.
"The stories suffer from a certain glib contrivance and
considerable stiff dialogue. Their strength lies in their
unflagging pace, the color of New York which Auchincloss
knows so well, and the fluency of their narrative style."

B1288   TURNILL, OSCAR. "Short Stories," London *Sunday Times,*
July 25, 1971, p. 26.
Brief favorable descriptive review.

B1289   *Virginia Quarterly Review,* XLVII (Winter 1971), xiv.
Brief review. "What must surely win the admiration of
many readers is the skill with which Mr. Auchincloss tells
each story."

B1290   WAGENKNECHT, EDWARD. "The Book Parade," *News-Tribune* (Waltham, Newton, Weston, Lincoln, Mass.), August 26, 1970,
p. 10.
Auchincloss's characters are "always interesting...and

A Bibliography of Writings By and About Louis Auchincloss

(WAGENKNECHT, EDWARD)
the situations presented hold the reader if only for the skill with which they are presented and the charm of the author's style." Auchincloss should be chided for "the occasional vulgarities" with which he "seems to think it necessary to regale us."

B1291 WASHBURN, BEATRICE. "The Sidewalks of New York Fail to Come Through Here," Miami (Fla.) *Herald*, September 3, 1970, p. 19H.
"Actually the problems that his characters meet are not very interesting; in fact, the people themselves cease to exist when you set the book down."

B1292 WEBER, BROM. *Saturday Review*, LIII (August 29, 1970), 24–25.
"Auchincloss's authority is such that one hesitates to reject his conclusion. He probably has good sociological support for it. Nevertheless, not having plumbed the regenerative powers of his characters sufficiently in these stories, he has not established his conclusion's validity artistically."

B1293 WEEKS, EDWARD. *The Atlantic*, CCXXVI (September 1970), 124.
"One may not like Mr. Auchincloss' collection of selfish people, but one must admire the skill with which he characterizes them in the messes they create."

B1294 WENDT, ROBERT L. "Skillfully Done Short Stories That Call For Some Reflection," Winston-Salem (N.C.) *Journal & Sentinel*, September 20, 1970, Sec. D, p. 8.
Descriptive favorable review.

B1295 YARDLEY, JONATHAN. "About Books," Greensboro (N.C.) *Daily News*, September 6, 1970, p. B-3.
"The collection reveals Mr. Auchincloss more often in ordinariness than brilliance. Too many of the stories are mere offhand exercises in which the reader will derive little more than a certain academic pleasure in watching a skilled craftsman at work."

Henry Adams

B1296 ASSELINEAU, ROGER. *Études Anglaises*, XXIV (juillet-septembre 1971), 350.
In French. Auchincloss is criticized for dwelling on biographical trivialities rather than focussing on the works.

WORKS ABOUT

Edith Wharton--A Woman in Her Time

B1297   *American Literature,* XLIV (March 1972), 177.
        Very brief descriptive review.

B1298   BRYER, JACKSON R. "Pictures Better Than Words," Baltimore
        Sunday Sun, January 9, 1972, p. D 5.
        "As a piece of writing," the book "is gracefully exe-
        cuted; as literary criticism and biography, it is super-
        ficial and sketchy; but as a depiction of the life and
        times about which Edith Wharton wrote and in which she
        lived, it is excellent."

B1299   *Choice,* IX (May 1972), 364.
        The photographs "give us a fairly vivid sense of Edith
        Wharton's energy and interests"; but Auchincloss's text is
        "sketchy at best, occasionally trivial, and often beside
        the point."

B1300   CONNOLLY, CYRIL. "Genius Observed," London *Sunday Times,*
        April 2, 1972, p. 31.
        Descriptive review.

B1301   FREEDMAN, RICHARD. *Saturday Review,* LIV (December 4, 1971),
        64.
        This is "a charming picture book...which amounts to
        little more than a coffee-table valentine." The "woman
        within...ultimately eludes" Auchincloss and, in the criti-
        cal passages, he has "liberally plagiarized from his own
        ten-year-old essay on Mrs. Wharton in *Pioneers and Care-
        takers,* sometimes quoting entire sentences verbatim from
        the earlier work."

B1302   HARDWICK, ELIZABETH. "Edith Wharton--Grandeur and Strength
        Out of the Ordinary," *Vogue,* CLVIII (September 15, 1971),
        90-91.
        "No doubt the assemblage of the 'pictorials' is valu-
        able, but the glossy text is retrogade.... it is not con-
        cerned to be anything new or fresh or really additional."
        It also suffers "from a mood too familiar; its accents be-
        come testimonial, like those reserved for memoirs about
        the head of the family."

B1303   HARTLEY, LODWICK. "New Study of Edith Wharton--'A Biography
        of Extraordinary Charm,'" Raleigh *News and Observer,*
        November 21, 1971, Sec. IV, p. 6.
        Auchincloss has written "an intimate biographical essay
        of extraordinary charm and interest.... For its pictorial

Book Reviews-*Edith Wharton--A Woman in Her Time*

(HARTLEY, LODWICK)
and its critical contributions the book provides within its short compass as good a brief introduction to Mrs. Wharton, her work and her era, as one will likely find anywhere."

B1304   HILL, WILLIAM B., S.J. *Best Sellers*, XXXI (January 1, 1972), 440.
Very brief favorable review. "Nobody could be better situated than Louis Auchincloss to do the Viking Studio Book on Edith Wharton."

B1305   HUTSON, JOAN. "Writers of Old New York," *Northern Echo* (England), May 5, 1972, p. 6.
"The book is perhaps over-decorative but it draws attention to an important writer...."

B1306   KIRSCH, ROBERT. "The Book Report--Profile of Edith Wharton," Los Angeles *Times*, October 14, 1971, Part IV, p. 14.
"This is a rich and fair book...but most of all it is an evocation of the whole woman, done with the same understanding, rational and lucid, which illuminates her own work. One cannot ask much more from a biography...."

B1307   MARTINE, JAMES. "In the Best of Her Work, She Was Magnificent," Philadelphia *Sunday Bulletin*, December 19, 1971, Sec. 2, p. 3.
Auchincloss "is capable of real insight but rarely supports his points with details" and he has said all of what he says here in earlier essays. But "the photos alone are worth the price of the book."

B1308   MERCIER, VIVIAN. "Whose Edith?" *The Nation*, CCXIV (January 3, 1972), 21-22.
Auchincloss's "text is...far above the usual level of writing to be found in picture books, while the illustrations he has chosen are either beautiful or interesting or both at once." But a number of Auchincloss's readings of Wharton's novels are open to dispute.

B1309   "No Lost Lady," *Times Literary Supplement* (London), May 5, 1972, p. 510.
This book on Wharton "is the best concise appraisal of her, her life, and her major novels that we have yet seen."

B1310   "Old New York," *The Economist* (London), CCXLIII (May 13, 1972), 80.
"This is a beautiful book."

A BIBLIOGRAPHY OF WRITINGS BY AND ABOUT LOUIS AUCHINCLOSS

WORKS ABOUT

B1311   THEROUX, PAUL. "The Yankee Jane Austen: Brilliant Eye, Good
         Heart," London *Times,* April 13, 1972, p. 16.
              Descriptive favorable review.

B1312   WASHBURN, BEATRICE. "Auchincloss on Wharton--Preoccupied With
         Edith," Miami (Fla.) *Herald,* November 28, 1971, p. 7-H.
              Descriptive review.

B1313   WEEKS, EDWARD. *The Atlantic,* CCXXVIII (December 1971), 134.
              The book is a "penetrating, well-judged, not unsympa-
         thetic characterization."

B1314   WHITE, TERENCE DE VERE. "Two Ladies," *Irish Times* (Dublin),
         April 8, 1972, p. 10.
              Auchincloss "has written a very sympathetic and compe-
         tent account."

B1315   WHITE, WILLIAM. *Library Journal,* XCVI (November 1, 1971),
         3600.
              Brief review. The book is "written with style and
         grace, knowledge and sympathy."

I Come as a Thief

B1316   A., H. "Man's Career Is Placed In Jeopardy," Buffalo *Courier
         Express,* June 17, 1973, Focus Section, p. 22.
              Auchincloss is "more interested in character develop-
         ment than the circumstances that shape character."

B1317   ACKROYD, PETER. "Symbols on His Sleeve," *The Spectator,*
         No. 7579 (September 29, 1973), 406-407 [407].
              "We are informed that there are 'two Tonys,' and his
         past is dragged in as exculpation, but we never learn who
         or what or why. Tony remains an enigma, and the whole nov-
         el behaves like the proverbial sibyl."

B1318   BEAM, ALVIN. "Auchincloss Elegance," Cleveland *Plain Dealer,*
         August 13, 1972, p. 7-G.
              Although moments in the novel stand out, "somehow the
         novel as a whole fails to convince, or mean very much."

B1319   BEARDSLEY, CHARLES. "Surface Glitter and Inner Experience,"
         Peninsula Living (Redwood City, Calif.), February 24, 1973,
         p. 33.
              "In this slim novel Auchincloss writes, as always, with
         the immense assurance of a man intimately acquainted with
         upper power brackets and social prestige, but he is never
         impressed with these superficialities except to hang upon
         them subtle moral judgments."

A Bibliography of Writings By and About Louis Auchincloss

B1320   BENEDICTUS, DAVID. "Recent Fiction," London *Daily Telegraph*, September 20, 1973, p. 11.
     Brief review. "The writing is fundamentally inept, at times embarrassingly so."

B1321   BITKER, MARJORIE M. "The Collapse of Charisma: Crime Can Wear Gloves," Milwaukee *Journal*, August 20, 1972, Part 5, p. 4.
     "As always with Auchincloss, the style is restrained, but the substance is there. These are all people worth knowing, perhaps even people we know." The book is a "morality play in modern dress skillfully presented."

B1322   BOGER, MARY SNEAD. "Book Browsing," Charlotte (N.C.) *Observer*, September 24, 1972, p. 4F.
     This novel explores "the author's familiar territory of upper class New Yorkers, but this time there is more depth, less concern with manners and more of fundamental truths."

B1323   BOOTH, SONYA. "Books In Brief," Orlando (Fla.) *Sentinel*, September 3, 1972, *Florida* Magazine, p. 11.
     Auchincloss "has written a rather slick, but interesting novel; nothing in 'I Come as a Thief' is especially profound, but it's entertaining, anyway."

B1324   BRADY, CHARLES A. "Auchincloss, Keneally Add to Their Laurels," Buffalo *Evening News*, September 2, 1972, p. B-8.
     "Auchincloss is after bigger game this time than just the gratifying psychological and social comedy one has come to expect in his suave entertainments. A sharp metaphysical point pierces the moral center of his book."

B1325   BRESLIN, JOHN B. *America*, CXXVII (September 2, 1972), 130–131.
     "Mr. Auchincloss has made an unfortunate blending; in choosing a contemporary setting, he has surrendered the richness of the past without gaining the sharp tang of the present. Somehow, life has slipped away from his characters. They are too glib, too facile, too predictable. One can only hope that *I Come as a Thief* does not signal a serious diminishment of the author's powers. The pleasures of Auchincloss are too good to lose."

B1326   BREWER, NORMAN. "He Understands the Upper Crust," Des Moines *Register*, August 20, 1972, p. 11-C.
     Brief review. Auchincloss's "sophisticated style...captures the pressure on newcomers to 'put it all together,' and the trauma of the old elite whose position is eroding."

A Bibliography of Writings By and About Louis Auchincloss

WORKS ABOUT

B1327   BRUNSDALE, MITZI M. "Auchincloss' Latest Is Not His Best,"
         Houston *Post*, September 10, 1972, *Spotlight* Magazine,
         p. 31.
             The tension in the novel dissipates "through dialogue
         that runs a banal gamut from stilted cliché to stuffy and
         overripe religious experience. Surprisingly, too, for a
         writer of Auchincloss' experience, the book is rife with
         extraneous shifts of point of view hardly called for in
         its limited scope.... *I Come as a Thief* shows an author of
         seemingly spent energies."

B1328   BURNHAM, SCOTT. "Auchincloss Probes the Soul of a Lawyer,"
         The Commentator (New York University Law School),
         November 21, 1972, p. 7.
             "Auchincloss' characters are not of sufficient complexi-
         ty to contain the ironies which would give them lives in-
         dependent of their roles in the morality play. The moral
         dilemmas and the levels of meaning finally come to seem
         merely compensation for the lack of compelling human activi-
         ty."

B1329   BURTON, HAL. "Books--Lacks the Old Bite," *Newsday* (Garden
         City, N.Y.), August 29, 1972, p. 8A.
             The novel, "which has the potential of power, never
         really achieves it, either as tragedy or as social tragi-
         comedy. The theme, perhaps, is one of the most promising
         undertaken by Auchincloss, but the promise is not ful-
         filled."

B1330   CANTRELL, BILL H. "Link to Mafia Creates Puzzle," Spring-
         field (Mo.) *Sunday News & Leader*, October 22, 1972, p. C24.
             "This is a moving, honest story of deep and complex re-
         lationships. Auchincloss treats with brilliant clarity
         the intermesh of friends, lovers, family, in-laws, chil-
         dren, and husband-wife. His characters become living,
         breathing people."

B1331   *Choice*, IX (December 1972), 1288.
             Auchincloss is "one of the most perceptive observers of
         dilemmic man in metropolitan America" and this novel is
         "his finest achievement.... The scene where the full reve-
         lation of Tony's act is presented to him is one of Auchin-
         closs' most discerning efforts."

B1332   CHURCHILL, R. C. "New Fiction," Birmingham (England) *Post*,
         September 29, 1973, Saturday Magazine, p. 2.
             This is "a novel of guilt and attempted expiation, well
         up to the high standard Mr. Auchincloss has set for him-
         self."

212

A Bibliography of Writings By and About Louis Auchincloss

B1333   DAVIS, L. J. "A Moral Drama From the Age of Eisenhower,"
         Washington (D.C.) *Post*, August 20, 1972, *Book World*,
         pp. 3, 9.
             "It simply beggars the imagination to think that a suc-
         cessful lawyer--much less a serious novelist--could possess
         so little knowledge of human affairs, so little cynicism
         coupled with so little insight. Anyone reading this book
         will realize at once that Louis Auchincloss is not really
         the novelist of the rich, but their attorney, trying to
         sway a jury made up of the rest of us, and his rhetoric has
         grown thin."

B1334   DAY, CHRISTIAN C. "New Novel From Louis Auchincloss: An
         Anachronism," *The Retainer* (Philadelphia Bar Association),
         I (December 6, 1972), 11.
             This "is not Auchincloss' best novel. It lacks a uni-
         form tautness. The reader must be willing to accept a
         seemingly incredible break with character. However, the
         portrait that emerges of a man twisting his way through the
         wreckage of his career toward a salvation proves to be
         worth it."

B1335   DEVANEY, SALLY G. "He Loved Too Well," Hartford *Courant*,
         December 17, 1972, p. 5F.
             "Mr. Auchincloss's latest book won't number as one of
         the landmarks of modern literature but it is worth read-
         ing for its sensitive portrayal of the grays of human foi-
         bles that lay between the white of good and the black of
         evil." Thus, the novel "is almost fascinating but falls
         short of being memorable."

B1336   DONAHUGH, ROBERT H. *Library Journal*, XCVII (August 1972),
         2638.
             Very brief review. "As usual, the author's meticulous
         prose and familiarity with the very and the nearly rich
         are evident throughout this very enjoyable novel."

B1337   DUHAMEL, P. ALBERT. "'I Come as a Thief,'" Boston *Sunday
         Herald Traveler and Sunday Advertiser*, August 20, 1972,
         Sec. 6, p. 28.
             This book "is not very different in plot, and less in
         personalities, from earlier Auchincloss efforts." If
         Auchincloss "wants to win the big ones, he will have to
         abandon his sentimental attachment to his familiar charac-
         ters and tell the whole truth."

B1338   EDWARDS, THOMAS R. "News From Elsewhere," *New York Review of
         Books*, XIX (October 5, 1972), 21-23 [22-23].
             Auchincloss "(however unfairly) has going against him
         our odd insistence in thinking that plain folk are more

A Bibliography of Writings By and About Louis Auchincloss

WORKS ABOUT

(EDWARDS, THOMAS R.)
credible, in novels if not generally, than people like Tony Lowder and his crowd.... I wish someone would write the novel Auchincloss wants to, someone with an equally re-fined concern for ethical nuance and a somewhat better ear, but I doubt that it can be done in times like these."

B1339   FRAZER, JAN. "Book Review," Naples (Fla.) *Star*, November 16, 1972, Sec. A, p. 4.
Descriptive favorable review.

B1340   FREEDMAN, RICHARD. "Epiphanies of a Limousine Liberal," *Life*, LXXIII (August 25, 1972), 22.
"The excellence of this novel is that despite what may seem like Boy Scout homiletics, it is a tautly written, fast-paced, and above all believable examination of the religious foundation for our code of public ethics."

B1341   FRYE, BURTON. "*I Come as a Thief*...Exposé of a Man," Myrtle Beach (S.C.) *Sun-News*, November 4, 1972, Sec. B, p. 2.
"Readers may approve of the juxtaposition of discoveries in the field of psychology with the word of the man from Galilee but the critic must remark that it is always nec-essary to know just where psycho-analysis is applicable and where the power of religion is more so." In spite of this "flaw," however, "it is a giant step in the right di-rection."

B1342   FULLER, EDMUND. "The Bookshelf," *Wall Street Journal*, August 22, 1972, p. 18.
"The seeds of the development are all planted, but per-haps with too mechanical a perfection. Yet in the end the novel comes out impressively, disturbingly, provocatively."

B1343   GARDNER, MARILYN. "Temptation in Nice Circles," *Christian Science Monitor*, November 15, 1972, p. 19.
Auchincloss "will probably never write the Great Ameri-can Novel. Here once again, however, he gives us a Good American Story. For all its imperfections, 'Thief' re-mains a pleasant divertissement--carefully wrought, mostly credible, and not without point."

B1344   GILLIAM, STANLEY. "Nourishing But Unexciting," Sacramento *Bee*, September 10, 1972, p. L-13.
"Good reading? Well, good enough. But a literary home run? Hardly. This is more of a soft line drive that fails to get past the infield."

A Bibliography of Writings By and About Louis Auchincloss

B1345   GILLOTT, JACKY. London *Times*, September 20, 1973, p. 16.
        Tony is a character "of peculiar interest," made "all
        the more interesting in that there's a strong sense of the
        novelist himself not quite knowing what to make of the
        character he's spawned."

B1346   GOLD, CHARLES H. "Guilt Without Blood," St. Louis *Post-Dis-
        patch*, November 26, 1972, p. 4B.
        "The novel is a moral tale, but the action is slow, the
        characters wooden. One is far more interested in the phil-
        osophic implications than in the action, a fatal flaw, I
        think, for a work of fiction."

B1347   GREACEN, ROBERT. *Books and Bookmen* (London), XXI
        (October 1974), 63.
        "*I Come As a Thief* has a strong narrative line even
        though Mr. Auchincloss is aiming at something bigger than
        good entertainment. This is a novel about moral choice
        and the flaw in character that can wreck a seemingly in-
        tegrated man. It involves the reader and forces him to
        take sides. Strongly recommended."

*B1348 HICKS, GRANVILLE.. *New York Times Book Review*, September 3,
        1972, p. 6.
        "My recurrent quarrel with Auchincloss is that the lit-
        tle world in his novels usually seems to me to be detached
        from the real world.... 'I Come as a Thief' has a differ-
        ent quality because it portrays a man who escapes from *his*
        little world not by changing his social class but by moving
        into a realm of absolutes. In literature, one does not
        have to believe in the validity of a vision but merely that
        the visionary believes in it." Auchincloss "is the only
        writer of our time who has done something interesting with
        something like the novel of manners."

B1349   J., D. "New Novels--Big Mouth and the Mafia," London *Evening
        News*, September 22, 1973, p. 6.
        Brief review: a "striking story."

B1350   J., L. M. Chattanooga *News-Free Press*, October 1, 1972, *Week-
        end* Magazine, p. 6.
        Descriptive favorable review: "an absorbing story, told
        in the quiet Auchincloss way."

B1351   KANAVY, MARGARITA B. El Paso *Times*, November 5, 1972, p. 27.
        "Although the reader is not inundated with sex and vio-
        lence, he is well impressed by that which today appears to
        represent affluent Suburbia."

A Bibliography of Writings By and About Louis Auchincloss

WORKS ABOUT

B1352   KANON, JOSEPH. *Saturday Review*, LV (August 26, 1972), 60-61.
        "Does it matter, after all this, that the book is re-
        lentlessly superficial or that the characters have no more
        life than a connect-the-dots puzzle or that the language
        has the elegance of an over-reaching governess?... Probab-
        ly not, for Mr. Auchincloss is no longer even writing the
        fantasies of the upper-middle class--he has taken on their
        soap operas, and such stuff works on a level beyond argu-
        ment."

B1353   KING, FRANCIS. "Fiction--Craving Defeat," London *Sunday Tele-
        graph*, September 30, 1973, p. 16.
        It is a novel "remarkable both for its sour ironies and
        for the moral certainty, so rare in fiction today, that
        permeates it."

B1354   *Kirkus*, XL (June 15, 1972), 689.
        "Once again during the course of the novel, Auchincloss
        deals with patterns of compromise, default and expiation
        and converts them into polished entertainment: more,
        there's the worldly perspicacity and suede-gloved crafts-
        manship which are the language of any Auchincloss novel.
        It will surely be bought, borrowed or stolen."

B1355   KNICKMEYER, STEVE. "Auchincloss Tries Too Hard to Be Novel-
        ist," Ada (Okla.) *Sunday News*, January 21, 1973, Sec. II,
        p. 11.
        "Auchincloss is trying so hard to write a NOVEL that
        his characters and plot have no semblance of reality."

B1356   KOON, WARREN. Natchez (Miss.) *Democrat*, October 30, 1972,
        p. 5.
        The "major disappointment" in the book is "a lofty view
        of what life really is all about." Auchincloss's prose
        "is stilted and his characters utter lines one can hardly
        imagine in these liberated days."

B1357   KOWALKE, DONNA. Sioux Falls (S. Dak.) *Argus-Leader*,
        September 10, 1972, Sec. C, p. 10.
        Descriptive review.

B1358   LADNER, MILDRED. "Tales Star Money Game," Tulsa *Sunday World*,
        October 15, 1972, *Your World* Magazine, p. 8.
        Auchincloss fails to make Tony's dilemma real and the
        character remains "lifeless." He is more successful in
        handling Jason Steele, where he works with his material
        "deftly and convincingly."

B1359   LASK, THOMAS. "Books of The Times--To Damnation and Back,"
        New York *Times*, September 25, 1972, p. 35. Also Seattle
        Post-Intelligencer, October 8, 1972, Arts and Book World
        Section, p. 18; Monterey (Calif.) *Peninsula Herald*,
        October 7, 1972, p. 24.
            "The virtues of Louis Auchincloss as a writer of prose
        and as a writer of fiction are confirmed in...'I Come as
        a Thief.' There are the same clear, effortless sentences,
        a rhythmic pulse in the prose that never falters, a smooth
        bright way with dialogue that make his verbal exchanges an
        epigrammatic delight, a sense of form that knows exactly
        where to cut the passage before it becomes tedious or repe-
        titious. The writing is transparent, the story line order-
        ly, the world of his characters glittering. He must be,
        with John Updike, the most readable writer in America.
        And he is always knowledgeable."

B1360   LOTTMAN, EILEEN. "Checks, Mates, and a Hollow Knight," Provi-
        dence *Sunday Journal*, August 27, 1972, p. H-17.
            "The novel is a bland picture of life on a bland plane--
        the medium-high social WASP level where it's okay to cheat
        providing you get away with it. But the people never come
        to life, their actions stem from the plans of the author
        and not from situation or character. Too much is unex-
        plained; all of it is superficial."

B1361   LOUKIDES, PAUL. "Turning Point in One Man's Life," Detroit
        Sunday News, September 17, 1972, Sec. E, p. 5.
            Descriptive review. "If books could have sentimental
        violins playing as the action fades, this book would have
        hundreds."

B1362   McMAHAN, ALLAN. "Agonies of One Who Came As a Thief Good
        Reading," Fort Wayne *Journal-Gazette*, August 27, 1972,
        p. 5E.
            Descriptive favorable review: "story telling at its
        best."

B1363   MANNING, MARGARET. "Book of the Day--An Evil World and Its
        Lessons," Boston *Globe*, August 21, 1972, p. 19.
            "The process of damnation is an old-fashioned fictional
        theme, perhaps, but Louis Auchincloss has handled it with
        clarity, depth and even an occasional smile."

B1364   MASSARI, ALFRED F. *Wall Street Review of Books*, I
        (March 1973), 82-84.
            This novel "amply confirms" that Auchincloss is "a lit-
        erate and knowledgeable novelist, an unobtrusively skillful
        craftsman, a gifted storyteller. Yet, he is plagued by

A Bibliography of Writings By and About Louis Auchincloss

WORKS ABOUT

(MASSARI, ALFRED F.)
infuriating stylistic devices.... Because this novel concentrates on the internal reactions of his protagonists to crisis, the characters are given to musing, reflecting, questioning, wondering, and soul-searching. Privately and publicly, they remove their masks, shed their customary roles, and indulge in interminable, interrogatory forays."

B1365 MOODY, MINNIE HITE. "Auchincloss Reaches Peak in Newest Novel," Columbus (Ohio) *Dispatch*, August 27, 1972, TAB Section, p. 16.
"Structure, suspense, suave sophistication, and best of all, substance, combine to distinguish *I Come as a Thief* and make it" the best of Auchincloss's work to date.

B1366 MORGAN, JAMES. "The Thief That We Call Conscience," Kansas City *Star*, September 3, 1972, p. 3E.
Descriptive review. Auchincloss is "one of contemporary fiction's most relentless explorers of the human soul."

B1367 MORSMAN, JULIA. "'Thief' Unworthy as Character or Book," *The Metro* (Waterloo, Neb.), November 29, 1972, p. 2.
"In truth, this book leaves me so cold that I turned it into the library for collection, thereby leaving both me and the thief equally cool and collected."

B1368 NEAR, GEORGE. "Auchincloss Not Up to Standards," Abilene (Texas) *Reporter-News*, October 29, 1972, p. 13-D.
"What starts out to be a moral investigation of modern man ends up as an exercise in manipulated plotting. The author touches on the spiritual problems, but scarcely explores them."

B1369 *New Yorker*, XLVIII (August 26, 1972), 78-79.
Brief review. "We can comprehend Tony's impulse toward evil and his conversion to good, but they seem thin and unreal. The intricate family politics that surround Tony's acts are fully worked out, but in a blandly impartial manner. It seems as though Mr. Auchincloss's tact and decorum, which are so helpful in capturing a wide range of personal mannerisms, hold him back from entering very deeply into his characters."

B1370 NYE, ROBERT. "Reviewer's Rapture," Manchester (England) *Guardian*, September 20, 1973, p. 16.
"Mr. Auchincloss is brilliant at describing furniture, and this aspect of his work always impresses: it could be said in criticism that some of his moral insights partake

(NYE, ROBERT)
of this nature of interior decoration, but then admirers of this kind of novel would be disappointed if anything more penetrating were offered."

B1371   "On the Slippery Slope," *Times Literary Supplement* (London), September 28, 1973, p. 1100.
"The novel ends with a line intended to clinch matters: 'But monsters could still be men'--a confusing affirmation, which hardly enables the reader to know whether or not Mr. Auchincloss agrees with the view that Tony has no business wrestling with his conscience, let alone succumbing to it."

B1372   OPPENHEIM, JANE E. and RICHARD. *Best Sellers*, XXXII (September 15, 1972), 275-276.
Descriptive review. The novel "brilliantly explores the inner core of a man besieged by temporal temptations."

B1373   ORR, L. ANDERSON. "Testing the Powerful," Norfolk *Virginian-Pilot*, September 10, 1972, p. C6.
"Credible characterization might have given life to this novel.... It is a pity that Auchincloss's reputation and his book's fashionable topics...spiced with some un-focussed religiosity might lead many to fork over the $6.95 for a copy--extending further, perhaps, the title's signif-icance."

B1374   OSTERMANN, ROBERT. "'I Come As a Thief'--When Auchincloss Totes Up the Bill, Everyone Pays for Moral Defections," *National Observer*, September 2, 1972, p. 17.
"With all due respect to the author's ethical purposes, as a novel *Thief* doesn't make it. Its passions are anti-septic; its emotions are synthetic; characters talk like they're reading their lines off a Teleprompter; the social scene is realized with a shallowness and triviality that are shocking in a writer with more than a dozen books of fiction behind him."

B1375   *Publishers' Weekly*, CCI (June 19, 1972), 58.
Brief descriptive review.

B1376   QUIGLEY, ISABEL. "Fiction--Cool Millions," *Financial Times* (London), September 27, 1973, p. 14.
"Like all Auchincloss's books it makes literate, pleas-ant reading; but much more than most of them it makes mor-al demands and asks unanswerable questions."

A Bibliography of Writings By and About Louis Auchincloss

WORKS ABOUT

B1377   QUILL, GYNTER. "Reading and Reviewing--Trying to Become Rich, Man Tempted By Mafia," Waco (Texas) *Tribune-Herald*, August 20, 1972, p. 13.
Descriptive favorable review. "It's an intriguing story, and it isn't told without some of Auchincloss' familiar jibes at the society these people represent."

B1378   REEVES, CAMPBELL. "Slick Novel Recognized As Truthful," Raleigh *News and Observer*, September 17, 1972, Sec. IV, p. 6.
Auchincloss and Graham Greene "both consistently hammer upon the theme of man and his spiritual salvation in a decaying civilization, in a world where the old values are changing too rapidly to be contained." Although this novel has its "faults," "it has a distinction which is happily inconsistent with the limitations of its pasted-up characters. It rings constantly off-key, but with a jangling accuracy which proves again that Auchincloss is a master craftsman in the contemporary American scene."

B1379   ROGERS, W. G. "The Literary Scene," New York *Post*, August 23, 1972, p. 30. Also *Army Times*, September 6, 1972, p. 30; Wichita Falls (Texas) *Times*, August 27, 1972.
"This is written in the faultless, clean, limpid prose that we associate with Auchincloss' two literary loves, Henry James and Edith Wharton."

B1380   ROSE, JEANNE. "Conscience of the Upper Crust," Baltimore *Sun*, August 20, 1972, p. D5.
"One closes the book somewhat relieved, but with no feeling of catharsis. How can one care too much about the future of Tony Lowther, a loved but wholly unlovable man?"

B1381   ROWLEY, PETER. "Examiner Book Forum--Corruption of a Lawyer," San Francisco *Examiner*, September 11, 1972, p. 37. Also Chicago *Sun-Times*, August 20, 1972, *Showcase* Magazine, p. 18; Cleveland *Press*, September 8, 1972, *Showtime* Magazine, p. 20.
"Auchincloss is to be congratulated for trying to depict the clash between old-family Americans and more recent immigrants such as Tony and Max Leonard. But he does not seem to understand Irish-Americans, limiting himself to banal observations on conviviality and Catholicism."

B1382   S[MITH], M[ILES] A. "A Story of Slipping Morality," Dallas *Times Herald*, August 27, 1972, p. H-8. Also Allentown (Pa.) *Sunday Call-Chronicle*, August 13, 1972, p. F-7.
"Somehow this does not seem to be the best of Auchincloss's chronicles of people with position and money. It

Book Reviews-*I Come as a Thief*

(S[MITH], M[ILES] A.)
has the theme of moral principles, and it develops the
theme well. Yet the writing is not up to the author's
high standards."

B1383   SCHERMAN, BERNARDINE. *Book-of-the-Month Club News*,
October 1972, p. 6.
Descriptive favorable review.

B1384   S[HACKELFORD], A[RN]. "First-rate Auchincloss--Morality and
Armageddon," Grand Rapids *Press*, August 27, 1972, p. 2-H.
"'Thief' is Auchincloss at his best, baring the loyal-
ties of men and society, proclaiming that we must all live
together--alone."

B1385   SKOW, JOHN. "Downfall and Upfall," *Time*, C (September 18,
1972), 100.
"There is no logical point at which to begin an analysis
of what went wrong with *I Come as a Thief*. The reader is
left with the vivid impression that Auchincloss forgot why
he called his characters together in the first place, and
was too embarrassed to ask them to disband."

B1386   SKWIRE, DAVID. "Miss Oates, Mr. Auchincloss, the Kitchen
Sink," *Cleveland Magazine*, I (October 1972), 82-84.
Although the novel is "excellent," it "should have been
longer, for the issues are too rich and complex to be done
full justice in 200-odd pages. The author probably should
have made a bigger production number of Tony's lunchtime
vision; the reader believes it, but it's nowhere near as
vivid as everything else in the book."

B1387   SMOOT, JESSIE M. "Author Takes Hack Story; Produces Enjoyable
Novel," Goldsboro (N.C.) *News-Argus*, August 20, 1972,
p. 4C.
"The author's shining ability to take a hack story with
plastic characters and produce an entertaining novel is
proven."

B1388   SOLMSSEN, ARTHUR R. G. "The Godfather Got to Him," Philadelphia *Sunday Bulletin*, August 20, 1972, Sec. 5, p. 7.
Although "the characters spend too much time explaining
their moral positions to themselves and to each other,"
the novel is "witty, thoughtful and thoroughly entertaining."

B1389   SUESS, KARL. "Louis Auchincloss Examines the New Babylon of
Our Time," Chicago *Daily News*, August 19-20, 1972, Panorama Section, p. 7.

A Bibliography of Writings By and About Louis Auchincloss

WORKS ABOUT

(SUESS, KARL)
"Auchincloss has somehow created a convincing Christian, which is not a mean accomplishment in our time, when Christianity is exploited by some and out of fashion with others."

B1390   THWAITE, ANTHONY. "Living and Partly Living," *The Observer* (London), September 23, 1973, p. 36.
"This is American melodrama of a decent, old-fashioned, ramrod-backed kind"; and Auchincloss "gives the impression of knowing his Fifth Avenue, even if the flavour is 1913 rather than 1973."

B1391   WEEKS, EDWARD. *The Atlantic*, CCXXX (September 1972), 107-108.
Descriptive favorable review. "It is a novel principle, which is rare in any season."

B1392   WHITMAN, DIGBY. "A Convincing Tale of Moral Seduction, Told By a Master," *Chicago Tribune Book World*, August 27, 1972, p. 1.
Except for *Rector*, this is Auchincloss's best book.

B1393   WILSON, W. EMERSON. "Novel's Story Hinges on Mafia Deal," Wilmington (Del.) *Morning News*, August 21, 1972, p. 33.
Although this is "not the best" of Auchincloss's books, "it still has many virtues and should have wide appeal."

B1394   WOESSNER, BOB. "Auchincloss Adds Twist," Green Bay (Wis.) *Press-Gazette*, August 27, 1972, Close Up Section, p. 7.
"The writing is slick, the story generally hangs together. No great shakes, and not the usual Auchincloss epic, but an enjoyable evening's read if you have nothing else on your mind."

B1395   WOODBURY, DR. GEORGE. "A Really Good Novel," *New Hampshire Sunday News* (Manchester), August 20, 1972, p. 35.
"This really first-rate novel is a welcome change and a real contribution to our own understanding of the society in which we live."

*B1396 YARDLEY, JONATHAN. "About Books," Greensboro (N.C.) *Daily News*, August 27, 1972, p. E3.
Auchincloss is "a remarkably old-fashioned novelist, yet he is not an anachronism. The principles of faith, honor and humility with which he is preoccupied are in no way diminished because he explores them in a world of pinstriped suits, city clubs and Long Island mansions.... Even at his less-than-best, which is where *I Come as a Thief* must be placed, he remains true to his novelist's

222

(YARDLEY, JONATHAN)
creed and demands respectful attention." With O'Hara and Marquand, Auchincloss is "America's most prominent novelist of manners."

*B1397 _____. "A Refreshing Conservatism," *New Republic*, CLXVII (September 16, 1972), 30.
"The story is cluttered with awkward melodrama; much of the dialogue is pregnant with wordy philosophizing; and Lowder, in the central moment when he discovers his obligation to God and his own conscience, comes across less as a man of religious conviction than as a self-righteous prig." But, nonetheless, Auchincloss's theme holds up: "*I Come as a Thief* is concerned not only with how much freedom a person has in his society but also with how much freedom he has been granted by God. The answer, to which Auchincloss returns in novel after novel, is that if he has the freedom to sin he also has the obligation of expiation. Auchincloss is, for all his wit and sophistication, a stern Christian who demands that the people in his world pay for their transgressions."

Richelieu

B1398 BECKER, MARVIN B. *History--Reviews of New Books* (Washington, D.C.), I (April 1973), 129.
Auchincloss's "laudable aim of popularizing could have been more amply confirmed through a broader familiarity with the monographic literature on France of the 16th and 17th centuries."

B1399 "Briefly Noted," Washington (D.C.) *Post*, December 24, 1972, *Book World*, p. 15.
Very brief descriptive review.

B1400 "The Cardinal in Charge," *Times Literary Supplement* (London), July 27, 1973, p. 878.
Auchincloss's portrait is "brash, lively and essentially unhistorical" and "there is a good deal of sense in his approach to the personalties of Richelieu and Louis XIII,... as an exercise in popular history the book is far from despicable."

B1401 CARNEY, ROBERT. "Cardinal Richelieu--He Identified Himself With France," Sacramento *Union*, February 4, 1973, p. E6.
Descriptive favorable review. Auchincloss "makes a valiant effort" to make Richelieu seem human.

A Bibliography of Writings By and About Louis Auchincloss

WORKS ABOUT

B1402   CHRONIS, PETER G. "Richelieu Sinister in Auchincloss Work,"
Rocky Mountain News (Denver), March 25, 1973, *Startime*
Magazine, p. 16.
Descriptive favorable review.

B1403   COOGAN, DANIEL. *America,* CXXVIII (February 17, 1973),
147–148.
"Richelieu, the man, emerges rather more clearly than
Richelieu the statesman, but there is so much of interest
in the man that one can forego the exegesis of history."

B1404   DOLBIER, MAURICE. "History and Some of the Men Who Made It,"
Providence *Sunday Journal,* January 28, 1973, p. H37.
Descriptive favorable review.

B1405   GIFFORD, EDWARD S. "Machiavelli's Creed Aided Richelieu,"
Philadelphia *Sunday Bulletin,* February 4, 1973, Sec. 5,
p. 9.
Auchincloss presents his story "with scant detail, little analysis, and a confusing disregard for chronology."
But the illustrations "are almost worth the price of the
book."

B1406   "Gift Books in Profile," Portland *Sunday Oregonian,*
December 31, 1972, Family, Features, Fashion, Entertainment
Section, p. 7.
Very brief descriptive review.

B1407   [HOENIG], N[AT]. "Today's Books," Long Beach (Calif.) *Inde-
pendent-Press Telegram,* January 16, 1973, Sec. B, p. 3.
Brief favorable review.

B1408   HOFFMAN, RICHARD C. *Library Journal,* XCVIII (March 15, 1973),
862.
Brief review. "Small libraries may find this a useful
popular study of an important figure."

B1409   JOHNSON, DOUGLAS. "Architect of France," Birmingham (England)
Post, April 14, 1973, Saturday Magazine, p. 2.
Auchincloss's account is "neat and skilful."

B1410   JONES, HOWARD MUMFORD. "A Studio Book," *Michigan Quarterly
Review,* XIII (Winter 1974), 76–78.
"Because his prose is graceful and intelligent and
Mr. Auchincloss nowhere tries to force an interpretative
note, the general reader may get a good deal out of his
chapters, which are in the best tradition of *la haute vul-
garisation.* Unfortunately the author fails to indicate on

(JONES, HOWARD MUMFORD)
what sources he draws, so that it is sometimes a little difficult to be sure about the basis of his judgments."

B1411   KALTENBORN, RUTH. "Book Review--Think Things Bad Now? Read Auchincloss' Newest Book," Palm Beach (Fla.) *Daily News,* January 28, 1973, p. 14.
Descriptive favorable review.

B1412   KINIERY, PAUL. *Best Sellers,* XXXII (February 15, 1973), 506.
Descriptive review.

B1413   LEVI, HONOR. "Prince in Red," *The Month* (London), CCXXXIV (September 1973), 317-318.
Mixed review which criticizes Auchincloss's lack of bibliographical references and his habit of reporting contemporary gossip as fact.

B1414   *The Living Church,* CLXVI (February 4, 1973), 14.
Brief favorable review. "*Richelieu* is the kind of book you want to return to, either to re-read, or to look at the pictures again, or both."

B1415   PARSONS, A. W. "Cardinal Sin...The Man Who Couldn't Handle Women," London *Daily Mail,* April 12, 1973, p. 7.
Descriptive review.

B1416   PLOWDEN, ALISON. *Books and Bookmen* (London), XVIII (July 1973), 119-120.
Descriptive favorable review: a "sane and sensible biography"; "an honest appraisal"; "a beautifully produced and lavishly illustrated book."

B1417   "Quick Guide," London *Times,* May 3, 1973, p. 11.
Auchincloss "adopts a ponderous style, studded with innumerable rhetorical questions, quite unlike that of his novels, with depressing results."

B1418   SMITH, MILES A. "Deft Picture of Richelieu," Tulsa *Sunday World,* May 13, 1973, *Your World* Magazine, p. 5. Also Savannah *Sunday News-Press,* April 1, 1973, p. 5F.
"Auchincloss, an accomplished novelist, has a great advantage as a storyteller. Far from being a dry academic, he recounts the historic tale in prose that stirs the lay reader with its insight, crisp phrasing and on-the-mark characterization."

A Bibliography of Writings By and About Louis Auchincloss

WORKS ABOUT

B1419   TUCKER, PAT. *Smithsonian*, III (March 1973), 90-91.
        "Despite its magnificent cover, large size, lavish il-
        lustrations and high price, the book shows a great many
        evidences of hasty production, both textually and visually.
        The writing is not up to Auchincloss' standard. One gets
        the feeling that he grew bored with the work."

B1420   *Virginia Quarterly Review*, XLIX (Summer 1973), cxx.
        Brief review. "The book should be of some interest not
        only to the lay reader but to knowledgeable students of
        the period, because the author examines the cardinal's
        character and his personal relationships with a novelist's
        practiced eye."

B1421   WAGENKNECHT, EDWARD. "Inside the Red Robe," *News-Tribune*
        (Waltham, Newton, Weston, Lincoln, Mass.),
        January 26, 1973, p. 7.
        Descriptive favorable review.

B1422   WELDON, JILL. "Books," *Vogue* (London), CXXX (April 15, 1973),
        29.
        Brief descriptive review: an "excellent biography."

The Partners

B1423   ACKROYD, PETER. "Fiction--Coming of Age in Fairyland," *The
        Spectator*, No. 7623 (August 3, 1974), 150-151 [150].
        "Auchincloss creates entertainments, sometimes verging
        upon the mask, in which character is perfectly congruent
        with story and story with that lack of conclusiveness which
        is Auchincloss's hallmark. *The Partners* is one of those
        occasions in which a dry and even dessicated social prose
        is able to rise to something higher than itself."

B1424   BARKHAM, JOHN. "Novelist of Manners," Wichita Falls (Texas)
        Times, February 17, 1974, Magazine, p. 5.
        Descriptive favorable review.

B1425   BAUER, MALCOLM. "Bauer on Books--French Journalist Zeroes In
        on American Media," Portland *Sunday Oregonian*,
        February 24, 1974, Family Features, Fashion, Entertainment
        Section, p. 16.
        "'The Partners' is..., in a way, fiction of escape, es-
        cape into a world neither so sordid nor so frenzied as that
        in most modern fiction and in many real lives. It is for a
        quiet evening before the fire, with the gas tank full in
        the garage."

A Bibliography of Writings By and About Louis Auchincloss

B1426   BEAM, ALVIN. "Books--Auchincloss: Law and Love," Cleveland
         Plain Dealer, March 3, 1974, p. 8-F.
             The book "is hardly the author's best but entertaining
         and often enough even fascinating."

B1427   BITKER, MARJORIE M. "The Law and the Profits," Milwaukee
         Journal, March 10, 1974, Part 5, p. 4.
             "Even lawyers are likely to find [the book] slow going.
         True it is; quietly entertaining it is; dynamic it isn't."

B1428   BLOOMINGDALE, TERESA. "Humor, Sorrow...and Compassion," *The
         Metro* (Omaha, Neb.), March 7, 1974, p. 2.
             "As always, Auchincloss has speckled his book with hu-
         mor, satire, and sorrow. But in 'The Partners' he has
         added a quality which I found missing in his previous nov-
         els...compassion. It is this component which makes 'The
         Partners' his finest novel."

B1429   BLYTHE, RONALD. "Lawyer in the House," London *Sunday Times,*
         August 4, 1974, p. 36.
             "Highly literate, these studies of clever people who
         throw their life's energies. into wealth retention, for
         themselves as well as for others, are enthralling."

B1430   BOARDMAN, KATHRYN G. "Rich Irish Families Are Different,"
         St. Paul *Sunday Pioneer Press,* February 17, 1974, *Focus*
         Section, p. 10.
             "This is a good, calming novel for readers who would
         like to escape from the crisis a minute present."

B1431   Burlington (Vt.) *Free Press,* March 28, 1974, p. 18.
             Brief review: "a masterful characterization of lawyers
         and of the people in whose service they gain riches and
         prestige."

B1432   CANTRELL, BILL H. "Own Profession Lawyer's Topic," Spring-
         field (Mo.) *News & Leader,* February 24, 1974, p. C5.
             Auchincloss's "latest effort may not be his greatest,
         but it is certainly no shallow shadow of earlier suc-
         cess.... It is not his best. His best may be yet to
         come."

B1433   CHAPPEL, DAVID. "Author Provides Insight Into How People
         Think," Tallahassee *Democrat,* August 18, 1974, p. 16E.
             "One wonders what Auchincloss could have produced if
         he'd struggled to develop a style to match his broad un-
         derstanding.... At any rate this writer's...intelligent,
         sensitive, and he has too much to say to be as completely
         ignored as he is."

A Bibliography of Writings By and About Louis Auchincloss

WORKS ABOUT

B1434   COHEN, H. RODGIN. "Manners and Morals on the Street," *Juris Doctor*, IV (May 1974), 10, 12.
         Descriptive favorable review.

B1435   CONN, PETER J. "Auchincloss Vignettes Occur in a Law Office," Philadelphia *Sunday Bulletin*, February 24, 1974, Sec. 2, p. 3.
         Despite the fact that Auchincloss raises fundamental ethical questions, "with a few exceptions, there is no particular reason for any of these stories to appear quite where it does. There is, furthermore, a disconcerting, stuttering rhythm in the telling of the tales, since some are fully shaped, while others have missing middles or endings."

B1436   CORRELI, RON. Springfield (Ill.) *State Journal-Register*, June 9, 1974, p. 20.
         Descriptive review.

B1437   CORRIGAN, ANNE L. "Auchincloss Pens Story About Lawyers," *Catholic Post* (Peoria, Ill.), July 7, 1974, p. 10.
         "As a straightforward piece of writing, set apart from many of the confused, surrealistic works that are being produced, I thoroughly enjoyed it."

B1438   COTTER, JOHN. "Auchincloss Introduces Some Starchy 'Partners,'" Raleigh *News and Observer*, February 10, 1974, p. 6-IV.
         "The separate stories do nothing to advance the plot, such as it is, and far too many of the principals are never heard from again.... there are no painstakingly built characterizations, and the conversations, the core of a novel of manners, fail miserably." Taken as a whole, "the novel fails."

B1439   CRAMER, DWIGHT. "Partners In Rhyme," *Harvard Crimson*, March 16, 1974, p. 2.
         Auchincloss fails to be a modern-day Edith Wharton for two reasons: "He does not hate his culture enough.... And the society itself has changed, disintegrated, lost its potency; it is no longer so hateable or loveable."

B1440   CUNNINGHAM, VALENTINE. "Unsmiling," *New Statesman*, LXXXVIII (August 2, 1974), 163.
         "So far...from attacking like a dose of salts, these vignettes from the law office are about as bland as a soft-sell, as paunchily social-critical as those late-night American telly serials intended to wash warmly down like cocoa."

A BIBLIOGRAPHY OF WRITINGS BY AND ABOUT LOUIS AUCHINCLOSS

B1441   DE MERS, JOHN. "By Louis Auchincloss--'Classy' Novel Provokes Thought and Admiration," Baton Rouge *Sunday Advocate,* February 17, 1974, p. 2-E.

        "The book's greatest asset is its immersion in the motions and motives that direct each human relationship, on the job or away from it." It is "the first truly classy novel of the new year, a work that provokes both thought and admiration."

B1442   "Disastrous Liaisons," *Times Literary Supplement* (London), August 9, 1974, p. 849.

        Auchincloss's "narratives are direct, old-fashioned and a bit solemn--and perhaps none the worse for that"; but the "quality in Mr. Auchincloss which makes him finally a rather dull writer is the fastidiousness that spreads from his scrutiny of the law to the characters he writes about, encouraging a high-toned blandness and too firm a belief in the possibility of solutions."

B1443   EMICK, DUDLEY J., JR. "A Law Firm Is Like a Family," Roanoke *Times,* July 14, 1974, p. H-4.

        "This is a well-written book. I recommend it for all members of the public, and were it in my power, I would order every lawyer who has ever been in a partnership or contemplating same to read the book for the insights one can obtain."

B1444   FORSHAW, THELMA. "The Monsters, The Heroes and the Victims of the Law," Sydney (Australia) *Morning Herald,* November 16, 1974, p. 16.

        "A novel about lawyers, you say? No, a novel about all of us, understood as we have not been for a long time--and forgiven without being diminished."

B1445   FRENCH, MARION FLOOD. "Bookmarks--A Worthy Successor," Bangor (Me.) *Daily News,* April 5, 1974, p. 11.

        "Probably not since Marquand have we had a writer so gifted in understanding and portraying a world we mostly only read about, but one which is real nevertheless and which has a valid contribution to make."

B1446   FRIEND, JAMES. "Auchincloss' Sprightly Manners," Chicago *Daily News,* February 23-24, 1974, Panorama Section, p. 8. Also Cleveland *Press,* March 22, 1974.

        "Yes, it is all mannered and highly urbane--but I don't think entirely irrelevant. Auchincloss is too good a writer, and our pursuit of nostalgia has proven that we are too fond of tradition to relegate either the novel or novelist of manners to the trash heap."

A Bibliography of Writings By and About Louis Auchincloss

WORKS ABOUT

B1447   FULLER, EDMUND. "Lawyers and Life's Grandstand," *Wall Street Journal*, March 11, 1974, p. 15.
    Auchincloss is compared with Balzac: *The Partners* is "deliberately Balzacian in its matter and frequently in its ironic manner." It contains "shrewd and engaging chapters in our continuing human comedy."

*B1448   GALBRAITH, J. K. "Novelist With a Sting," *Books and Bookmen* (London), XXI (January 1975), 24-25.
    "One-dimensional or otherwise, Auchincloss is a superior writer whose milieu is his own kind and he has risen wonderfully above the difficulties of his subject." Auchincloss "tells his stories with restraint, and in my judgement, vast skill."

B1449   GAMMACK, GORDON. "Series of Stories to Delight," Des Moines *Sunday Register*, March 3, 1974, p. 3B.
    "The magnificent use of language to describe the characters and the action makes the stories that Auchincloss tells of secondary importance."

B1450   GEESLIN, CAMPBELL. "Lawyer--Dry View," Houston *Post*, February 3, 1974, *Spotlight* Magazine, p. 16.
    Auchincloss "is not a graceful writer. He is lumpy and operatic. His descriptive passages are like heavy recitative between the arias of unconvincing dialogue...." His characters "are neither all black nor all white, they are every one both black AND white. Their goodness is responsible for awful things, and their evil turns out really to be quite an effective force for good. What we have here obviously has little or nothing to do with reality." Nonetheless, the book is "readable and, in its limited way, entertaining."

B1451   GLASSER, STEPHEN A. "Behind Scenes On Wall Street In Auchincloss's 'The Partners,'" *New York Law Journal*, March 25, 1974, pp. 40-41.
    Auchincloss "comes through as a keen observer of the Wall Street scene. Known as a novelist of manners or the last of the American WASP novelists, his days may be numbered, however, for just as the nature of Wall Street practice is changing, so are its personages."

B1452   HAGEMAN, ADELINE. Sioux Falls (S. Dak.) *Argus-Leader*, February 24, 1974, Sec. C, p. 5.
    Brief descriptive review: an "entertaining novel."

B1453   HAKIM, JOY. "Novels With Manners," Norfolk *Virginian-Pilot*, May 5, 1974, p. C5.

A Bibliography of Writings By and About Louis Auchincloss

Book Reviews-*The Partners*

(HAKIM, JOY)
"It's a pleasant book, often fascinating, consistently informative, typically Auchincloss. It's a fine gift book, if you know someone in the hospital for a hysterectomy."

B1454   HEINEMANN, KATHERINE A. El Paso *Times,* February 24, 1974, *Sundial* Magazine, p. 26.
When Auchincloss "comments that in an increasingly classless society the novel of manners cannot survive, he is right.... For better or for worse."

B1455   HILL, WILLIAM B., [S.J] *America,* CXXX (May 4, 1974), 350.
Brief review. "The book is episodic, the writing--as always with Mr. Auchincloss--is urbane, polished."

B1456   HOLZER, ERIKA. "The Lawyer's Bookshelf," *New York Law Journal,* October 25, 1974, p. 4.
"With its vignette approach in place of a plot, the book could have been half, or twice, as long without noticeable difference. One can, however, become absorbed with the problems of some of the characters."

B1457   *Kirkus,* XVI (December 1, 1973), 1320.
"Incidental Auchincloss but there's that *nihil obstat* readership for whom the sometimes amusing commentary, careful scene-setting and perfect haberdashery is enough."

B1458   KIRSCH, ROBERT. "The Book Report--Novel of Manners Reborn," Los Angeles *Times,* February 11, 1974, Part IV, p. 8.
Auchincloss "shakes up" the novel of manners form, "gives up the compulsion to remain firm in the old limits and decides to have some fun."

B1459   KOHN, MARTIN F. "A Novel About Wall Street Lawyers," Providence *Sunday Journal,* March 17, 1974, p. H 19.
"There are passions among the partners; there are intense feelings, but they are related with controlled, craftsmanlike dignity." Auchincloss is a "very good" novelist of manners.

B1460   LEHMANN-HAUPT, CHRISTOPHER. "Books of The Times--At the Top of the Heap," New York *Times,* February 14, 1974, p. 45. Also Omaha *World-Herald,* April 21, 1974; Norfolk (Va.) *Ledger-Star,* March 27, 1974; Lincoln (Neb.) *Sunday Journal and Star,* March 17, 1974.
"Granted, [Auchincloss] is no great stylist, no master of sensibilities, no moralist of universal concern. Granted, fewer and fewer of us need to understand the correct

231

A Bibliography of Writings By and About Louis Auchincloss

WORKS ABOUT

(LEHMANN-HAUPT, CHRISTOPHER)
way of displaying wealth. Still, as an entertainer,
Mr. Auchincloss is first rate."

B1461 LE RESCHE, STEVE. "Change and Conflict," Columbia *Missourian*,
March 3, 1974, *Vibrations* Magazine, p. 10.
"The characterization of Beeky Ehninger is the strong
point of this novel." "Only a few" of the other characters
are believable. But the book is "a good character study."

B1462 McCOY, MARTHA. "Cool Tales of Full and Interesting Lives,"
Chattanooga *News-Free Press*, February 10, 1974, p. E3.
"It is a great tribute to [Auchincloss's] style as a
story teller that he can write compelling tales about a
class of people so obviously out of fashion from a literary
point of view."

B1463 McMAHAN, ALLAN. "'Partners' Tricky Novel," Fort Wayne *Journal-
Gazette*, February 24, 1974, p. 5E.
This "is not a perfect novel--whose is--but its minor
blemishes are subdued by really excellent story-telling."

B1464 MALOFF, SAUL. *New Republic*, CLXX (February 23, 1974), 29-30.
"Such unity as the book possesses is conferred by a tone
of voice--and therein lies the problem. For what are we to
make of a tone uneasily situated somewhere between solemni-
ty and irony, respect and ridicule, as its objects seem
ready to collapse beneath satire into slapstick? How can
we possibly take seriously, much less regard sympathetical-
ly, men who are at best pompous bores or sanctimonious buf-
foons?"

B1465 MANNING, MARGARET. "A Man Who Played a Good Hand Well," Boston *Globe*, February 18, 1974, p. 18.
One of Auchincloss's "most agreeable gifts is the ability to find the present meaningful, even enjoyable, perhaps
because he finds the past meaningful as well." This book
is "social comedy of a very high order and an elegant medi-
tation on life near, but not at, the top."

B1466 MELLARD, JAMES M. "The Fictional World of the Law: Shepard,
Putney & Cox," *Chicago Tribune Book World*,
February 24, 1974, p. 3.
The book is "as curiously flawed" as Beeky, "the one
fascinating character in the book." There is "something
bloodless, fleshless, just a bit inverted about it."

A Bibliography of Writings By and About Louis Auchincloss

B1467   MELLORS, JOHN. "Law and Disorder," *The Listener* (London),
         XCII (August 1, 1974), 156-157 [156].
             "Auchincloss writes seriously and with inside knowledge
         of the community, the profession and the place to which he
         belongs. It is too late now, perhaps, to expect a *Middle-
         march* from Auchincloss, but his 23rd book marks solid
         achievement."

B1468   M[OODY], M[INNIE] H[ITE]. "Auchincloss' Folk Urbane As Al-
         ways," Columbus (Ohio) *Dispatch*, February 24, 1974, p. 6D.
             The book is "a satisfying chronicle--some of the epi-
         sodes more readable, or perhaps more amusing than others,
         but all of them deft, and all of them polished to the last
         trick and syllable."

B1469   *New Yorker*, L (February 25, 1974), 126.
             Brief review. None of the characters "step out of their
         elegant molds long enough to do anything very interesting,"
         and "though one appreciates the behind-the-scenes glimpse
         of the complex machinery of a modern law office..., those
         not eager to pass their bar examination will probably find
         more here than they want to know about litigation and
         trust-and-estate law."

B1470   NICHOLS, MARTHA. "Community Critic," Victoria (Texas) *Advo-
         cate*, February 24, 1974, p. 15.
             Auchincloss "weaves his story with words that are too
         rich, too explanatory, too annoyingly precise.... Even
         though he possesses an undoubtedly fine perception of peo-
         ple and the forces that move them, his style lacks the re-
         straint that leaves something to the reader's imagination,
         and his characters are if anything too well drawn."

B1471   O'LEARY, THEODORE M. "Persistence May Create a Murderer or a
         Paragon," Kansas City *Star*, February 24, 1974, p. 3E.
         Descriptive favorable review.

B1472   OLSON, CLARENCE E. "Law As a Way of Loving," St. Louis *Post-
         Dispatch*, February 24, 1974, p. 4D.
             "'The Partners' is almost as complex and diffusive as
         Beeky. It is a book for readers who enjoy light intellec-
         tual entertainment that offers subtlety rather than power."

B1473   PECKHAM, STANTON. "Auchincloss' 'Partners' Just Entertains...
         Is That Bad?" Denver *Post*, March 3, 1974, *Roundup* Maga-
         zine, p. 18.
             "Nobody ever accused Louis Auchincloss of being a darl-
         ing of the literary establishment back East. Very much of

WORKS ABOUT

(PECKHAM, STANTON)
an Easterner himself, he probably finds his most apprecia-
tive audience west of the Hudson, where we are less obsessed with social significance." This is "a most enjoyable" book.

B1474   PENDLETON, WINSTON K. "Book Browsing," *Winter Garden News*
(Windermere, Fla.), June 13, 1974, p. 10A.
Descriptive review.

B1475   PERKINS, BILL. "The Conflicts Are Discreet--'Partners' Struggle For Office Power," *National Observer*, March 30, 1974,
p. 19.
"It is easy to criticize *The Partners*, along with Auchincloss' other works. The characters are generally similar, varying only in quiet shades, and they represent a
small and vanishing breed. Yet Auchincloss offers rewards
that are not easily found in modern fiction--a delicate
narrative and a confident style that perfectly match his
subject matter, a professional's knowledge of one of our
most important institutions, and a shrewd understanding of
the small battles that fill so much of our lives."

B1476   PINE, JOHN C. *Library Journal*, XCVIII (December 15, 1973),
3650.
"Even if these stories are not very memorable, they are
sometimes touching in their depiction of human frailty and
vulnerability, and are invariably interesting to read."

B1477   *Playboy*, XXI (September 1974), 24.
Brief review: "quietly, compellingly authoritative."

B1478   PRYCE-JONES, DAVID. "Fiction," London *Times*, August 1, 1974,
p. 5.
Brief favorable review.

B1479   ROSE, JEANNE. "Life at the Top of Tall Buildings," Baltimore
Sun, February 10, 1974, p. D5.
"The whole book...dazzles with subtleties of language
and thought; Auchincloss is writing at top form."

B1480   RUMLEY, MARJORIE. "A Lawyer Turns Author," Seattle *Times*,
March 17, 1974, Magazine, p. 15.
Descriptive favorable review.

B1481   SANDROF, NANCY. "Some Civilized Leisure," Worcester *Telegram*,
February 17, 1974, p. 6E.
Descriptive favorable review.

B1482   SCHEDL, MARY. "Shades of Morality in a Novel of Manners,"
        San Francisco *Sunday Examiner & Chronicle*,
        February 17, 1974, *This World* Magazine, p. 35.
        Descriptive review.

B1483   SCHOTT, WEBSTER. "A Poured-in-Concrete Realist, But the Best
        Concrete Money Can Buy," *New York Times Book Review*,
        February 24, 1974, p. 2.
        "Auchincloss does a few new things in 'The Partners.'
        He gets closer to sex, which hasn't been one of his larger
        enthusiasms. He wrestles with the possibility that while
        the institutional foundations of our society are changing,
        what men and women may want is changing faster.... But he
        does best what he has always done. He is the gentlest of
        moralists.... Auchincloss is a good man to have writing."

B1484   SCHWELL, JENNIFER. Groton (Conn.) *News*, June 5, 1974, p. 26.
        "We are all equal as we fall subject to the forces of
        our world and Auchincloss is exceptionally adept at rein-
        forcing that universal fact."

B1485   SHEPPARD, R. Z. "Fiduciary Matters," *Time*, CIII
        (February 4, 1974), 76.
        "Despite his rather reserved, fiduciary tone, Auchin-
        closs generates some psychological subtlety and emotional
        range."

B1486   STUMPF, EDNA. "Afternoon of a Stylist," Philadelphia *Inquir-
        er*, February 17, 1974, p. 10-I.
        Auchincloss "is not really at his best in this scattered
        recounting of mundane pain and pleasure--'The Partners'
        doesn't have the intensity of some of his work, or the
        sense of history. But he by no means makes a fool of him-
        self. Novelists share worlds, and Auchincloss knows his
        own world with an objectivity and complaisancy few can
        equal. If we care to make the trip, he can show the way."

B1487   SULLIVAN, SHIRLEY K. "Current Fiction--A Gallery of Portraits
        By Louis Auchincloss," Savannah *News-Press*, April 28, 1974,
        p. 3F.
        Auchincloss "doesn't say anything new in this novel,...
        but he does it beautifully."

B1488   SWEETSER, ALAN. "His Books Are Stylized...But Bloodless,"
        Minneapolis *Tribune*, April 28, 1974, p. 10D.
        "The autobiography is easy, interesting reading, yet it
        is totally without anything gripping or affecting. It is
        all so antiseptic. So are his novels." In *The Partners*,

WORKS ABOUT

(SWEETSER, ALAN)
"the style is easy and fluid, and there is total absence of raw feelings." This is a joint review of *The Partners* and *A Writer's Capital*.

B1489   TASCH, JACKIE. "Law Firm the Frame For 14 Good Stories," Buffalo *Evening News*, February 16, 1974, p. C-12.
"These are people stories and excellent ones. If that's what you like, you won't mind the novel's other shortcomings," such as trying to tie it all together with Beeky instead of a plot.

B1490   THOMAS, PHIL. "'The Partners'--Sparkling Novel By Auchincloss," Dallas *Times Herald*, May 12, 1974, p. 8-D. Also Newport News (Va.) *Daily Press*, March 31, 1974; Asheville (N.C.) *Citizen Times*, March 10, 1974; Allentown (Pa.) *Sunday Call-Chronicle*, March 10, 1974; Monterey (Calif.) *Sunday Peninsula Herald*, March 17, 1974.
"Auchincloss, as he has demonstrated time and again, writes very well and it is because of this talent that some of the stories come off better than they really are." But the book "sparkles" when Auchincloss "gets into the subject of what makes a powerful law firm run."

B1491   TILLOTSON, DOLPH. "All About...Books," Natchez (Miss.) *Democrat*, March 27, 1974, p. 4A.
Although the characters other than Beeky are "really superfluous to what little story exists," Auchincloss "has created some interesting characters here and their individual stories are sometimes highly entertaining."

B1492   TREVOR, WILLIAM. "Critical Health," Manchester (England) *Guardian*, August 1, 1974, p. 14.
"Even in this rather slighter than usual offering," Auchincloss is "an author to admire for his style and his insight."

*B1493   TUTTLETON, JAMES W. "Capital Investment," *Sewanee Review*, LXXXII (Summer 1974), xlviii, l, lii.
Joint review of *The Partners* and *A Writer's Capital*. Both "work out the same theme--the individual's struggle to escape the crippling effect of spurious values absorbed from childhood authority figures and to establish his sense of himself and of his own manhood."

B1494   TYNER, PAUL. "How Rich Folks Live," Chicago *Sun-Times*, March 3, 1974, Sec. 3, p. 19.
Auchincloss "knows whereof he speaks, and it's all very

(TYNER, PAUL)
serious, like a bad afternoon at a bridge table.... The people are faceless but you will remember them."

*B1495　VIDAL, GORE. "Real Class," *New York Review of Books,* XXI (July 18, 1974), 10-15.
"Of all our novelists, Auchincloss is the only one who tells us how our rulers behave in their banks and their boardrooms, their law offices and their clubs. Yet such is the vastness of our society and the remoteness of academics and bookchatters from actual power that those who should be most in this writer's debt have no idea what a useful service he renders us by revealing and, in some ways, by betraying his class." Joint review of *The Partners* and *A Writer's Capital,* which also includes a good deal of Vidal's personal views of Auchincloss as a friend. In *The Partners,* Auchincloss demonstrates that "almost alone among our writers he is able to show in a convincing way men at work." But the book also shows his weaknesses: "Narrative is sometimes forced too rapidly, causing characters to etiolate while the profound literariness of the author keeps leaking into the oddest characters.... Also, there are the stagy bits of writing that recur from book to book...."

B1496　*Virginia Quarterly Review,* LI (Spring 1975), xlix.
"Internal intrigue within an imaginary law firm projected on this level was never more convincingly portrayed than it is here with uncommon adroitness, with taste, quiet humor, absolute conviction."

B1497　WAGENKNECHT, EDWARD. "The New Auchincloss," *News-Tribune* (Waltham, Newton, Weston, Lincoln, Mass.), February 21, 1974, p. 10.
The book shows Auchincloss "at the top of his powers as a writer" and "there is not much about narrative that he does not know."

B1498　WEEKS, EDWARD. "The Peripatetic Reviewer," *The Atlantic,* CCXXXIII (March 1974), 95-96.
Descriptive favorable review. "This blending of legal adventure and private lives is handled with authority and sophistication."

B1499　WELDON, KATHERINE. "Auchincloss' World Becomes Book--'Partners' Depth Skillful," Jackson (Tenn.) *Sun,* April 28, 1974, p. 13-B.
"This knowledgeable group portrait is as skillfully written as it is enjoyable to read."

A Bibliography of Writings By and About Louis Auchincloss

WORKS ABOUT

B1500   WELLEJUS, ED. "Bookshelf," Erie (Pa.) *Times-News,*
         March 24, 1974, Sec. K, p. 18.
             The book "enhances" Auchincloss's reputation "as one of
         the outstanding novelists of our day."

B1501   WILLIAMS, DAVID. "Recent Fiction," London *Daily Telegraph,*
         August 1, 1974, p. 9.
             "It is an urbane and knowledgeable book posing questions
         we are most of us faced with.... The answers are given
         convincingly in human terms, and the tiered, affluent,
         hierarchical business society of East Coast America por-
         trayed in measured, leisured, mandarin prose."

B1502   YARDLEY, JONATHAN. "Memories, Morals, Mush," Washington (D.C.)
         Post, March 3, 1974, *Book World,* p. 3.
             "It has been 10 years since the appearance of *The Rector
         of Justin,* Auchincloss's finest, most ambitious and most
         complex novel. Since then his fiction has been--while al-
         ways intelligent and gentlemanly--more and more predict-
         able. One cannot help wondering whether Auchincloss is
         satisfied with churning out the same product over and over
         again. He is an able and honorable writer, but not a dar-
         ing one."

A Writer's Capital

B1503   BEAM, ALVIN. "'A Writer's Capital,'" Cleveland *Plain Dealer,*
         April 21, 1974, p. 11-H.
             "Auchincloss on Auchincloss is...very good reading.
         The man has wide range in his limited settings and is one
         of our ablest men of letters."

B1504   B[IGELOW], R[OBERT] P. *Law Office Economics and Management,*
         XV (Fall 1974), 455-456.
             Descriptive favorable review.

B1505   BOARDMAN, KATHRYN G. "He Wrote Better When He Had Other Work,"
         St. Paul *Sunday Pioneer Press,* March 24, 1974, *Focus* Maga-
         zine, p. 6.
             Descriptive favorable review.

B1506   DAVIS, PAXTON. "Louis Auchincloss on James, Himself," Roanoke
         Times, August 3, 1975, p. C-4.
             Joint review of *A Writer's Capital* and *Reading Henry
         James.* Auchincloss's autobiography is "a keen and unsenti-
         mentalized view of what has made him and his work what they
         are." The James study is "a modest, brief but to my taste
         extraordinarily perceptive look at James' work."

A Bibliography of Writings By and About Louis Auchincloss

B1507　FRAZER, JAN. "The Lawyer Seen As a Writer," Naples (Fla.)
　　　　　Star, September 13, 1974, Sec. A, p. 15.
　　　　　　Descriptive favorable review.

B1508　GREGG, LOUISE. "Auchincloss Combines Careers," Wichita Falls
　　　　　(Texas) *Times*, June 16, 1974, Magazine, p. 4.
　　　　　　"A quiet, refreshing book about and by one of our fore-
　　　　　most contemporary authors."

B1509　GRUCHOW, PAUL. "Books," *Mpls. Magazine* (Minneapolis),
　　　　　August 1974, pp. 49-50.
　　　　　　The book "makes brief...and pleasant reading, just the
　　　　　thing for a summer's day."

B1510　[JOHNSTON, ALBERT H.] *Publishers' Weekly*, CCV
　　　　　(January 21, 1974), 84.
　　　　　　Brief favorable review: a "modest and engaging memoir"
　　　　　containing "an illuminating succession of insights and
　　　　　candid confessions."

B1511　*Kirkus*, XLII (February 1, 1974), 150.
　　　　　　Descriptive review.

B1512　LEGATE, DAVID M. "With Nothing to Hide," Montreal *Star*,
　　　　　February 1, 1975, p. D-4.
　　　　　　Descriptive favorable review: a "modest and attractive
　　　　　autobiography."

B1513　LEGGETT, JOHN. "What Makes Him Write?" *New York Times Book
　　　　　Review*, May 26, 1974, p. 14.
　　　　　　"If there is a general truth to be drawn from 'A Writ-
　　　　　er's Capital,' it is that the source of any writer's ener-
　　　　　gy is likely to be found in his family relationship and
　　　　　that his writing will reflect some rebellion against his
　　　　　notion of family wrongheadedness and some fulfillment of
　　　　　his concept of family potential."

B1514　MARVIN, JOHN R. *Library Journal*, XCIX (March 15, 1974), 748.
　　　　　　Brief favorable review: a "charmingly wrought memoir."

B1515　MOODY, MINNIE HITE. "Novelist Tells How His Art Developed,"
　　　　　Columbus (Ohio) *Dispatch*, May 26, 1974, p. I-4.
　　　　　　Descriptive favorable review.

B1516　S[TEVENS], J[OHN] H., [JR.] "Auchincloss' Capital," St. Louis
　　　　　Globe-Democrat, August 17-18, 1974, p. 12A.
　　　　　　"Not since Dreiser has there been an American novelist
　　　　　to compare to Auchincloss for his achievement in recording

A Bibliography of Writings By and About Louis Auchincloss

WORKS ABOUT

   (S[TEVENS], J[OHN] H., [JR.])
    how members of America's moneyed power blocs behave in
    their law offices, board rooms and clubs."

SWEETSER, ALAN. "His Books are Stylized...But Bloodless," Minneapolis *Tribune*, April 28, 1974, p. 10D.
    See B1488.

TUTTLETON, JAMES W. "Capital Investment," *Sewanee Review*, LXXII
   (Summer 1974), xlvii, l, lii.
    See B1943.

VIDAL GORE. "Real Class," *New York Review of Books*, XXI (July 18,
   1974), 10-15.
    See B1495.

B1517 WEIR, SISTER EMILY. *Best Sellers*, XXXIV (May 1, 1974), 64.
    "Auchincloss writes about his life with the same care
   and precision with which his novels are written.... He
   does admirably what he sets out to do: explain what it is
   in life that has made him the sort of writer he is. One
   wishes that he had written more extensively because he displays perception and a strong sense of irony which makes
   this book delightful reading."

Reading Henry James

B1518 BRESLIN, JOHN B. "In the Footsteps of the Master," *America*,
   CXXXII (April 19, 1975), 307-309 [309].
    Auchincloss's book is a "lively, informative and highly
   opinionated essay."

B1519 *Choice*, XII (July/August 1975), 678.
    Auchincloss "has written a sensible, fresh, and genuine-
   ly stimulating introduction to the full range of James'
   works."

DAVIS, PAXTON. "Louis Auchincloss on James, Himself," Roanoke *Times*,
   August 3, 1974, p. C-4.
    See B1506.

B1520 HUGHES, JAMES. *Antioch Review*, XXXIII (Summer 1975), 123.
    The book is "less persuasive introduction than illuminat-
   ing commentary, the illumination assuming common familiarity
   and interest."

B1521 [JOHNSTON, ALBERT H.] *Publishers' Weekly*, CCVII
   (March 24, 1975), 44.
    Descriptive favorable review.

B1522   KIRBY, DAVID K. *Library Journal*, C (March 15, 1975), 583.
         "A mature and sensitive reader, Auchincloss has been
         puzzled by things that have puzzled the rest of us...and
         has, where possible, worked out sensible, satisfying an-
         swers. The word for this useful study is *companion*."

B1523   O'CONNELL, SHAUN. "Less Critical Inquiry Than Pious Pilgrim-
         age," Boston *Sunday Globe*, July 6, 1975, p. A8.
         Auchincloss "embellishes and enshrines Henry James in
         this volume in ways which are,...both gratuitous and en-
         dearing."

B1524   ROSENBERG, VICTORIA H. *Dalhousie Review*, LV (Autumn 1975),
         577-581.
         Auchincloss's "analysis is not scholarly, but its ef-
         fect, rather than refreshingly informal, is, instead, ir-
         ritating. For what is so damaging, to James, is that Auch-
         incloss, in trying to make James more readable, drains his
         works of the ambiguity, the subtleties and complexities
         that are their dominant characteristic."

B1525   S., J. H. "On Henry James," St. Louis *Globe-Democrat*,
         July 19-20, 1975, p. 4F.
         "James' shade should be grateful for such an arbiter as
         Louis Auchincloss.... It is in every way a worthy offer-
         ing for that consummate authority on Henry James."

B1526   TERRIE, HENRY L., JR. "The Varieties of Henry James," *Sew-
         anee Review*, LXXXIII (Fall 1975), 695-703 [695-696].
         Auchincloss "should be a refreshing guide to James, but
         he is not. Although his prose is lucid and his sensitivity
         and intelligence are consistently evident, he did not work
         hard enough to produce a study of substance or point."

B1527   TOMPKINS, JANE. "Touring James Country," *Book Forum*, I
         (No. 4, 1975), 537-541.
         "The virtues of *Reading Henry James*--its worldy, supple,
         sympathetic temper--account for what it fails to portray--
         the drama and intensity of James's art. Auchincloss shies
         away from the Medusa-face of the novels and stories, re-
         ducing passion and pain to emotionally manageable terms."
         But Auchincloss "knows more and writes better about James
         than most people. Perhaps the critical lapses occur be-
         cause he is not sure whether there is a literate, curious
         amateur out there to appreciate his insights and make his
         efforts worthwhile."

A Bibliography of Writings By and About Louis Auchincloss

WORKS ABOUT

B1528   WINNER, VIOLA HOPKINS. *American Literature*, XLVII
         (November 1975), 463-464.
             Auchincloss's "expertise as a novelist and devotion as a
         reader give this book its special quality and worth. He
         has the craftsman's insight into the conflicting demands
         of character and design and into what made certain subjects
         richer than others for James. On matters of style...he is
         perceptive. In his appreciation of various novels, espe-
         cially *The Ambassadors*,...he is often eloquent, even wise."

The Winthrop Covenant

B1529   ALLEN, BRUCE. "Puritanism Tracked Through Many Generations,"
         Christian Science Monitor, April 8, 1976, p. 30.
             "As these Winthrops themselves discover, Louis Auchin-
         closs can break free from the thematic 'covenant' which
         binds his book together. Each time he does, he turns up
         fictional situations and characters far more invigorating
         than his book's materials seem to permit."

B1530   BARKHAM, JOHN. "A Family Saga Mirrors a Nation's Transforma-
         tion," San Francisco *Examiner & Chronicle*, March 28, 1976,
         This World Magazine, p. 32. Also Toledo *Blade*,
         March 21, 1976.
             "This book presented a virtuoso challenge to Auchincloss
         which he handsomely surmounts. You might call this his
         Bicentennial book, for in his Winthrops he has mirrored
         the transformation of a nation as well as a family, from
         simple pieties to complex problems."

B1531   BEAM, ALVIN. "Our Durable Puritan Ethic," Cleveland *Sunday
         Plain Dealer*, March 21, 1976, Sec. 5, p. 9.
             "Given the complexity, the difficulty of his theme,
         Auchincloss, that interesting novelist of manners, does an
         often brilliant job here, but occasionally the stories do
         lag and sag. There's a stretching at things--and an un-
         evenness."

B1532   BETSKY, CELIA. *Bookletter*, II (March 15, 1976), 14.
             "As usual, Auchincloss deals only with important people
         and events, with a ruling class, but his protagonists are
         spectators--arbiters of principles and taste rather than
         creators. They stand next to the throne."

B1533   BITKER, MARJORIE M. "Family With a Covenant," Milwaukee *Jour-
         nal*, April 11, 1976, Part 5, p. 4.
             "As every admirer of this practiced novelist would ex-
         pect, the prose is polished, the scenes adroitly staged,

Book Reviews-*The Winthrop Covenant*

(BITKER, MARJORIE M.)
the dialog appropriate to each era and revealing of character. But over all, the stories seemed forced into the
mold of a concept."

B1534   BLOOMINGDALE, TERESA. "Auchincloss' Characters Real and Remarkable," *The Metro* (Omaha, Neb.), April 21, 1976, p. 11.
"What I found most fascinating in the book was the
changing literary style down through the generations....
Auchincloss has, once again, proven his genius."

B1535   Burlington (Vt.) *Free Press*, March 22, 1976, p. 11.
Brief descriptive favorable review.

B1536   CORWIN, PHILLIP. "Wide, Wide World of Books--The Honest Ambiguity of Louis Auchincloss," *National Observer*,
May 15, 1976, p. 21.
Interview-review. Auchincloss talks about the Puritans,
the "mission" of a writer, and his dual career. Auchincloss's "true achievement" is his "very subtle sense of
profundity." To read him "is to walk into a hall of mirrors. It is a very rewarding and revealing experience."

B1537   DUHAMEL, P. ALBERT. "Winthrops, Rockefellers and God," Boston
Sunday Herald Advertiser, April 4, 1976, Sec. 6, p. A26.
Descriptive review: a "very interesting book."

B1538   GLASSMAN, MAXINE. "Puritan Ethic Is the Game," Worcester
Sunday Telegram, April 11, 1976, p. 18E.
Auchincloss, "obviously calling upon his background as
a successful lawyer, presents a sophisticated treatise on
an unusual subject. 'The Winthrop Covenant' may not appeal
to everyone."

B1539   GOLD, EDITH. "Generation By Generation, The Decline of Puritanism," Miami (Fla.) *Herald*, April 4, 1976, p. 7-E.
"Throughout, Auchincloss' subsidiary characters...are
far more interesting and human than his preachy, sanctimonious Winthrops...."

B1540   HAND, JUDSON. "Auchincloss: He Speaks Softly, But Carries
a Big Talent," New York *Sunday News*, March 7, 1976, Leisure
Section, p. 16.
Auchincloss is "a major writer, a formidable social
critic and historian whose place in American letters is all
his own."

B1541   HAUSMANN, ALBERT. *Library. Journal*, CI (February 1, 1976), 546.
Brief favorable review: "the stories are ingeniously
plotted."

A Bibliography of Writings By and About Louis Auchincloss

B1542   HORAN, TOM. Chattanooga *Times*, March 28, 1976, p. B 4.
Descriptive favorable review.

B1543   HUTSHING, ED. "Puritan Ethic Emerges Like Jewel in 'The Winthrop Covenant,'" San Diego *Union*, April 18, 1976, p. E-7.
"The individual tales, like a collection of fine gems,
can stand alone, each a separate jewel. Together, an ex-
quisite necklace, they represent some of the finest writing available this season, noted for some extremely well-
written books."

B1544   KAMMEN, MICHAEL. "In the Shade of the Family Tree," Washington (D.C.) *Post*, March 21, 1976, pp. M1, M4.
Auchincloss's "achievement is considerable because these
individual dramas never become predictable or even formu-
laic, because the historical personages are faithfully
drawn, and because the author has a delicious sense of
irony to offset his sad vision of the tragedy inherent in
disappointed lives."

B1545   KENNEDY, MSGR. JOHN S. "Balancing the Books--Puritans and
Exotics," *Our Sunday Visitor* (Huntington, Ind.), LXIV
(April 25, 1976), 7.
Descriptive review.

B1546   *Kirkus*, XLIV (January 15, 1976), 85.
"There are all the familiar old Auchincloss hangouts
from Back Bay to New York to Washington; there's the per-
sonable, equable tone of voice, never raised; and that
demeanor while if gentlemanly to a fault has an unmistakable virtue--it's vouched for by the wide readership which
obtains."

B1547   LANE, GEORGE. "The Bookshelf--Every Family Has Its Little
Quirks," Quincy (Mass.) *Patriot Ledger*, April 21, 1976,
p. 52.
"'The Winthrop Covenant,' while it casts some appropriate shadows on the family escutcheon, does little to bol-
ster Louis Auchincloss' position among our social histori-
ans, and one whose admiration for his better work goes
back more than twenty years can only regret this."

B1548   LEHMANN-HAUPT, CHRISTOPHER. "Books of The Times--A Clockwork
Auchincloss," New York *Times*, March 22, 1976, p. 23. Also
Omaha *Sunday World-Herald*, April 11, 1976, Magazine, p. 35.
Outside of "two strong stories," "In the Beauty of the
Lilies" and "The Arbiter," the book runs "too much like
clockwork--precise, carefully calibrated and utterly auto-
matic."

B1549   MANNING, MARGARET. "Book of the Day--A Family With a Mission,"
         Boston *Globe*, March 22, 1976, p. 13.
             Auchincloss "is very quiet, very low-key, and doesn't
         get the kind of critical attention he deserves...."

B1550   MOODY, MINNIE HITE. "300 Years of Winthrops and the Puritan
         Ethic," Columbus (Ohio) *Dispatch*, May 2, 1976, p. K-8.
             Auchincloss "offers here far more than a sophisticated
         novel written with his special brand of knowhow and polish.
         Beneath it all lurk social and moral issues with which
         sooner or later most of us must come to grips."

B1551   MURRAY, G. E. "...and Lesser Tribes," Chicago *Sunday Sun-
         Times*, April 4, 1976, *Show* Section, p. 8.
             Descriptive favorable review: "a dazzling experience."

B1552   O'HARA, MARY. "Author Sheds Light on U.S. Past, Present,"
         Pittsburgh *Press*, April 11, 1976, p. H-6.
             This chronicle, "in the hands of one of today's most
         polished writers, albeit not possessed of the depth of a
         Tolstoy or a Flaubert, is a very interesting piece of
         Americana."

B1553   O'LEARY, THEODORE M. "Be Wary of Divine Inspiration," Kansas
         City *Star*, April 25, 1976, p. 14G.
             Basically descriptive review: Auchincloss "refutes the
         Winthrop position not by a dialectic exercise but by show-
         ing with his customary polish and elegance some of the con-
         sequences of their attitudes and behavior."

B1554   PECKHAM, STANTON. "Auchincloss' 'Winthrop Covenant' Traces
         Puritan Ethic," Denver *Sunday Post*, March 7, 1976, *Roundup*
         Magazine, p. 23.
             "'The Winthrop Covenant' is not only a provocative novel
         of changing American manners throughout the past 200 years
         and more. It is, incidentally, fine literary entertain-
         ment."

B1555   *Playboy*, XXIII (April 1976), 24.
             Brief favorable review: "the book is facile and fun--
         and marketable."

B1556   SCHICKEL, RICHARD. "The Ways of the Patriciate," *New York
         Times Book Review*, March 28, 1976, pp. 10, 12.
             The book "is a disappointing performance. It is a
         stiff, correct, rather constipated work."

WORKS ABOUT

B1557   SHEA, JEREMY C.   St. Louis *Post-Dispatch*, April 29, 1976,
         p. 3E.
              "The latest Auchincloss is an impressive novel, yet re-
         ceives only a mediocre ranking on a scale with its prede-
         cessors."

B1558   SMYSER, CRAIG.   "New Auchincloss Novel About Puritans Not His
         Best Effort," Houston *Chronicle*, April 18, 1976, *Zest*
         Magazine, p. 11.
              "As usual, Auchincloss' prose style is fluid and the
         book reads smoothly. However, the book lacks fire. It
         seems Auchincloss wrote *The Winthrop Covenant* with his con-
         siderable craft and mind, but left his passion behind."

B1559   SOLMSSEN, ARTHUR R. G.   "The Rise and Fall of the Puritan Eth-
         ic," Philadelphia *Sunday Bulletin*, April 11, 1976, Sec. 6,
         p. 7.
              Descriptive review.

B1560   THOMAS, PHIL.   "Puritan Rise and Fall," Cincinnati *Enquirer*,
         April 18, 1976, p. H-9. Also Chattanooga *News Free-Press*,
         April 25, 1976.
              Auchincloss "brilliantly displays the thesis that is the
         backbone of this book as well as superbly capturing the es-
         sence of the period his various Winthrops happen to be liv-
         ing in. 'The Winthrop Covenant' truly is a remarkable fic-
         tional feat.

B1561   _____.   San Francisco *Examiner*, May 1, 1976, p. 6.
              Very brief review. Auchincloss writes "with the glassy
         smoothness that fits the aristocratic coolness of his char-
         acters."

B1562   TODD, RICHARD.   "The Rich Get Rich, But They Also Get Chil-
         dren," *The Atlantic*, CCXXXVII (April 1976), 112.
              Auchincloss's novels "suffer from artificiality of plot
         and manner. I suspect, though, that unlike most writers,
         he's probably more embarrassing at the moment than he will
         be in the future." These stories "are uneven; some of
         them suffer from being more nearly outlines for novels.
         And there is the difficulty of Auchincloss' rarefied dic-
         tion. His seventeenth-century figures often sound more
         contemporary than his contemporaries."

B1563   WAGENKNECHT, EDWARD.   "The Book Parade--Three Master Tale
         Tellers," *News-Tribune* (Waltham, Newton, Weston, Lincoln,
         Mass.), March 26, 1976, p. 7.
              Auchincloss's "skill as a purveyor of tightly-wrought,
         sometimes multi-leveled fiction is seen at its best through-
         out, and the level of interest remains remarkably and uni-
         formly high."

PLAY REVIEWS

"The Club Bedroom" (Theatre de Lys, New York)

B1564   LEWIS, EMORY. "The Theatre--A.P.A. is a Synonym for Joy,"
         Cue, XXXVI (December 16, 1967).
              "Mr. Auchincloss has a gift for Manhattan upper-class
         dialogue and a remarkable insight into the complexities
         of wasted lives. He must be encouraged to write a full-
         length play for Broadway."

B1565   SULLIVAN, DAN. "Theater: Generation Gap--Auchincloss Offers
         His Ironic View in 'Club,'" New York *Times*,
         December 6, 1967, p. 41.
              "It is an interesting and likable little play. For con-
         temporary taste, it has two drawbacks. The dialogue is
         often too grammatical to suggest genuine conversation...
         and the ending is a little too patly ironic."

Author and Subject Index to
Writings about Louis Auchincloss

The index which follows is keyed only to
entries in the second (or B) section of the
bibliography. Works by Louis Auchincloss as
subjects are listed below in capital letters.

Beckwith, Ruth A., B253
Bell, Eleanor, B111
Bell, Lisle, B112
Bellasis, M., B254
Bellow, Saul (subject), B47,
   B901, B979
Benedictus, David, B1320
Bennett, Alice Kizer, B1260
Bergamo, Ralph, B1073
Bernkopf, Elizabeth, B808
Berthelsen, John, B1261
Betjeman, John, B187
Betsky, Celia, B1532
Bienen, Leigh Buchanan, B809
Bigelow, Robert P., B1504
Biggs, Barton M., B1150
"BILLY AND THE GARGOYLES," B380
Bischoff, Barbara M., B308, B550
Bitker, Marjorie M., B1321, B1427,
   B1533
Blake, Fran, B370
Blakeston, Oswell, B437, B592
Blicksilver, Edith, B1151
Blinder, Rabbi Robert J., B810
Bliven, Bruce, Jr., B438
Bloomingdale, Teresa, B1428,
   B1534
Blythe, Olive, B309
Blythe, Ronald, B1429
Boardman, Kathryn G., B811, B1430,
   B1505
Boeschenstein, C. K., B1074
Boger, Mary Snead, B812, B1322
Bohner, Charles H., B930
Bond, Alice Dixon, B669, B813
Bonner, Ruth, B740
Booth, Sonya, B1323
Boroff, David, B593
Boston, Richard, B1262
Bowen, Elizabeth, B372, B439
Boyden, William C., B741
Bradbury, Anne, B670
Bradbury, Malcolm, B594
Bradley, John, B373
Bradley, Van Allen, B188
Brady, Charles A., B671, B1324
Brady, Sister Mary William, B1263
Brandeis, Adele, B310
Breslin, John B., B1325, B1518
Brewer, Norman, B1326
Bright, Yvonne Younger, B116
Broaddus, Marian Howe, B117, B311

Brooks, John, B440, B815
Brooks, Rae, B551
Brophy, Brigid, B742, B816
Brothers, S. C., B631
Brown, Earle, B552
Brown, Ivor, B1224
Brown, J. Adger, B1152
Brown, John Mason, B817, B970
Brown, Louise Fielding, B441,
   B553
Browning, Robert (subject), B1030
Brudney, Victor, B442
Brundige, Lenore, B971
Brunk, Charlotte, B1264
Brunsdale, Mitzi M., B1327
Bryan, C. D. B. (subject), B58
Bryant, Jack, B506
Bryden, Ronald, B443, B554
Bryer, Jackson R., B1298
Buchan, Bliss S., B672
Buckley, Thomas, B19
Buckner, Sally, B743
Bugbee, Emma, B20
Bullough, Geoffrey, B312
Burgess, Anthony, B673
Burgess, Charles E., B632, B674
Burick, Rae, B118
Burke, Ted, B21
Burnett, Whit, B191
Burnette, Frances, B555
Burnham, Scott, B1328
Burns, John A., B507
Burns, Warren, B744
Burton, Hal, B1329
Bush, M., B1153
Butcher, Fanny, B675, B931, B972,
   B1265
Cable, Mary, B973
Cain, Lillian Pike, B676
Calder-Marshall, Arthur, B818
Caldwell, David S., B819
Callison, Lee H., B120
Campbell, Ken, B374
Campbell, Priscilla T., B556
Canfield, Cass, B74
Cantrell, Bill H., B1330, B1432
Carbon, Carmen, B974
Carman, Bernard R., B975
Carnahan, Ken, B192
Carney, Robert, B1401
Carrere, Thomas A., B257
Carter, Peter, B821

Read, David W., B1041
READING HENRY JAMES, Reviews:
    B1506, B1518-B1528
THE RECTOR OF JUSTIN, Reviews:
    B798-B923; B3, B5, B12, B17,
    B24, B46, B47, B50, B51,
    B67, B74, B82, B83, B95,
    B981, B991, B1000, B1007,
    B1025, B1041, B1067, B1150,
    B1170, B1187, B1193, B1205
    B1208, B1268, B1392, B1502
Redman, Ben Ray, B623
Rees, Goronwy, B535
Reeves, Campbell, B1282, B1378
REFLECTIONS OF A JACOBITE, Re-
    views: B631-B658; B30
Reid, Margaret W., B722, B1042,
    B1199
Reynolds, J. F., B650
Reynolds, Jerry, B536
Rhodes, Anthony, B351
Rhodes, Richard, B1200
Rhodes, Royal W., B893
Richardson, John, B232
Richardson, Maurice, B485, B578,
    B723
RICHELIEU, Reviews: B1398-B1422;
    B29
Richelieu, Cardinal Armand Jean
    du Plessis de (subject), B29,
    B1398-B1422
Richmond, Sylvia B., B161
Ricketson, Anna, B162
Ries, Bernard, B780
Riordan, Helen, B724
Roberts, F. M., B163
Robertshaw, James, B352
Robins, Michael, B537
Robinson, Maude, B164
Robinson, Olive C., B413, B486,
    B781, B894
Rockwell, Kenneth, B233, B287
Rodgers, Richard, B166
Rodriguez, Mary, B1201
Rogers, W. G., B487, B579, B782,
    B1043, B1202, B1379
Rolo, Charles J., B86, B353,
    B414, B488, B580, B651
THE ROMANTIC EGOISTS, Reviews:
    B367-B434; B99
Rose, Jeanne, B1380, B1479
Rosenberg, Victoria H., B1524

"Rosmersholm" (Henrik Ibsen),
    B1151
Rosofsky, H. L., B1120
Ross, Mary, B288
Rouse, Blair, B959
Routley, Erik, B489, B538
Rowe, Percy, B895
Rowland, Stanley J., Jr., B783
Rowley, Peter, B1381
Roy, Gregor, B896
Royce, James, B167
Ruffin, Carolyn F., B1283
Rumley, Marjorie, B1480
Russell, H. K., B660, B925
"SABINA AND THE HERD," B1141
Sachs, Martha, B1203
"THE SACRIFICE," B1269, B1271
Sandrof, Nancy, B1481
Savino, Guy, B784
Sayre, Nora, B1123
Scardino, Katherine M., B898
Scardino, Kay, B415
Schedl, Mary, B1482
Scherman, Bernardine, B1383
Schickel, Richard, B1556
Schlesinger, Tom, B785, B1204
Schlueter, Paul, B1044
Schmidt, Sandra, B1045
Schott, Webster, B2, B1124, B1483
Schulberg, Budd (subject), B1161
Schwartz, Joseph, B1046
Schwell, Jennifer, B1484
Scott, J. D., B289, B582
Scott, Winfield P., B1248
Scribner, Charles, Jr., B74
Scrutton, Mary, B416
Sears, William P., B960
SECOND CHANCE, Reviews: B1255-
    B1295; B22, B91, B99
A Separate Peace (John Knowles),
    B839
Seymour-Smith, Martin, B1249
Seymour, Whitney North, Jr.,
    B1125
Shackelford, Arn, B1384
Shaffer, Peter, B490
Shakespeare, William (subject),
    B905, B1220-B1254
Shannon, Opal, B1126
Sharp, Sallie, B1284
Shaw, Russell, B1047
Shea, Jeremy C., B1557

INDEX

Wilson, Angus, B432
Wilson, Dorothy D., B246
Wilson, Helena Perin, B1215
Wilson, Sloan, B503, B589
Wilson, W. Emerson, B1067, B1216, B1393
Wilson, William E., B922
Winebaum, B. V., B180
Winn, Elizabeth Smith, B247
Winner, Viola Hopkins, B1528
THE WINTHROP COVENANT, Reviews: B1529-B1563
Wise, Marvin, B547
Woessner, Bob, B1394
Wolfe, Tom, B100
Woodberry, Carol A., B735, B797
Woodbury, Dr. George, B1395
Woolsey, Bill, B433
Wordsworth, Christopher, B1217

A WORLD OF PROFIT, Reviews: B1146-B1219; B55, B58
Wright, John A., B248
A WRITER'S CAPITAL, Reviews: B1488, B1493, B1495, B1503-B1517
Wyndham, Francis, B630
Yaeger, Susan M., B1068
Yaffe, James, B304
Yardley, Jonathan, B1295, B1396, B1397, B1502
Yoder, Edwin M., Jr., B923, B1218, B1253
Yount, J. B., III, B102
Yu, Anthony, B1254
Zinnes, Harriet, B249
Zolotow, Sam, B103